Multicultural and Ethnic Children's Literature in the United States

Donna L. Gilton

THE SCARECROW PRESS, INC.
Lanham, Maryland • Toronto • Plymouth, UK
2007

KH

SCARECROW PRESS, INC.

Published in the United States of America
by Scarecrow Press, Inc.
A wholly owned subsidiary of
The Rowman & Littlefield Publishing Group, Inc.
4501 Forbes Boulevard, Suite 200, Lanham, Maryland 20706
www.scarecrowpress.com

Estover Road
Plymouth PL6 7PY
United Kingdom

British Library Cataloguing in Publication Information Available

Library of Congress Cataloging-in-Publication Data
Gilton, Donna L.
　Multicultural and ethnic children's literature in the United States / Donna L. Gilton.
　　p. cm.
　Includes bibliographical references and index.
　ISBN-13: 978-0-8108-5672-1 (pbk. : alk. paper)
　ISBN-10: 0-8108-5672-7 (pbk. : alk. paper)
　1. Children of minorities—Books and reading—United States. 2. Minority
teenagers—Books and reading—United States. 3. Multiculturalism—United States—
History. 4. Multicultural education—United States—History. 5. Children's literature,
American—History and criticism. 6. American literature—Minority authors—History
and criticism. 7. Ethnic groups in literature. I. Title.
Z1039.M56G55 2007
810'.93529—dc22　　　　　　　　　　　　　　　　　2007006391

7/29/08

To the memory of my father,
Reverend Charles W. Gilton Sr. (1916–1959).

This book is dedicated, as well,
to my still-vibrant mother, Hattie Franklin Gilton.

Contents

Acknowledgments

I would like to thank the following for their help, support, and assistance as I prepared this work: the Children's Room staff at the Chinatown Branch of the San Francisco Public Library; the library staff at the Newberry Library in Chicago; Rose Mitchell of the Black Resource Center of the County of Los Angeles Public Library; John D. Berry of the Native American Studies Collection at the Ethnic Studies Library of the University of California, Berkeley; and Kathleen Horning of the Cooperative Children's Book Center at the University of Wisconsin in Madison. Special thanks go to two librarians who gave me important leads and information for this project: Jane Courant, the children's librarian at the Asian Branch of the Oakland (California) Public Library; and Gabriella Kay, the children's librarian at the Mashantucket Pequot Museum and Research Center in Connecticut. Special thanks also go to Dr. Norman Horrocks of Dalhousie University; Lyn Miller-Lachmann, editor of the *MultiCultural Review*, for extensive help, guidance, and encouragement; and my editors, Martin Dillon and Kellie Hagan, for bringing this book through the entire editorial process.

1

Multicultural Children's Literature: An Introduction

I, too, sing America
I am the darker brother
They send me to eat in the kitchen
When company comes,
But I laugh,
And eat well,
And grow strong.[1]

THE PURPOSE OF THIS WORK

It is the purpose of this work to describe the many initiatives taken by people committed to multiculturalism in the field of U.S. children's literature, with an emphasis on people of color. It will consider the history of this field; general trends; multicultural initiatives and responses from the mainstream; specific initiatives from people of African descent, Latinos/as, Native Americans, Asian Americans, and their supporters; and information about emerging groups, possible directions for research, and other conclusions. This chapter will consider the many ways that people pass on their cultures to the next generation, and it will relate these phenomena to each other and to the field of children's literature. It will also discuss characteristics of ethnic groups in general, and end with a discussion of four ways to consider race relations.

TERMS AND DEFINITIONS

Early Writing on Assimilation and Cultural Diversity

One of the first popular works on assimilation was *The Melting Pot*, "a play by Israel Zangwill, an English writer of Russian-Jewish descent."[2] It debuted in Washington, D.C., in 1908. This play was about a young New York composer of similar descent writing a symphony on the theme of the harmonious integration of races in America. It was very popular with both President Theodore Roosevelt and the general public and would long be very influential. However, the "races" referred to were only from Europe—German, French, Irish, English, Jewish, and Russian. Unfortunately, people of color were not mentioned in this context at all. Other early writers on this topic also focused on the assimilation of people originally from Europe.[3]

Several critics of "the melting pot" or assimilation advocated cultural diversity in the early twentieth century,[4] including John Dewey and Horace Kallen,[5] but again they focused mostly on people of European descent. Kallen was not optimistic about the future of African Americans. People of color have not always been considered to be possible subjects of either assimilation or cultural pluralism. It would take the fight against Nazism in World War II and the civil rights movement and other struggles of the 1950s and 1960s before this position was seriously reconsidered.

Definitions of Multicultural Children's Literature throughout Time

Both *minority* and *multiculturalism* are modern terms originating in the mid-twentieth century. At this time, *multicultural* was almost synonymous with *minority*, but both terms have changed in meaning over the years. The term *minority* was not used until 1932 when Donald Young published *American Minority Peoples: A Study in Racial and Cultural Conflicts in the United States*. In 1992, William Safire noted that the term *multicultural* was first used in a 1941 *Herald Tribune* book review, describing "a fervent sermon against nationalism, national prejudice and behavior in favor of a 'multicultural' way of life." Safire also noted that by the 1980s, *multicultural* was defined as "not dominated by whites."[6]

Controversies over the Term

The meaning of the term *multicultural* has generated much controversy because of the ongoing debate over who is included under the umbrella part of the term, *multi*. Mingshui Cai cites this quote from Fishman[7] as he analyzes three schools of thought on this subject:

> The first view holds that multiple + cultures = multiculturalism. Therefore, multicultural literature should include as many cultures as possible with no distinction between the dominant and the dominated. The second view focuses on racial and ethnic issues in multicultural literature. The third view maintains

that every human being is multicultural (e.g., an Asian American who is female, middle-class, Buddhist, and disabled) and all literature is multicultural.

How Terms Will Be Defined in This Book

I believe that the term *multiculturalism* can encompass people from all ethnic groups and nationalities, and I will discuss some characteristics and activities of ethnic people from all continents. However, the main focus of this work will be on people of African descent, Latinos/as, Native Americans, and Asian Americans, as well as, to some extent, their respective diasporas. Even though each of these groups encompasses multiple ethnic groups that differ from each other, it has been necessary for people within these different groups (such as those from various Native American or Asian nations) to work together, so this will be reflected in this book. Some differences between the specific ethnic groups will also be briefly mentioned as appropriate. The terms *multicultural* and *ethnic* will be almost—but not quite—synonymous. *Multicultural* refers to the movement as a general concept and to organizations, people, and work devoted to more than one of the major groups emphasized here. *Ethnic* refers to organizations, people, and projects focusing on one group (e.g., African Americans or Native Americans only).

The major ethnic groups are referred to in this book as African American, Latino/a, Native American, and Asian American. The term *pan-African* will be used to refer to the African diaspora. Latino/a is spelled as such to incorporate the masculine and feminine versions. I will try to avoid using the word *Indian* as much as possible because it is too confusing. Indigenous people in the Americas are referred to as *Native Americans, indigenous people,* or by specific tribal names. People from the area of India, Pakistan, Bangladesh, and Sri Lanka are referred to as *South Asians.* I will use the spelling *Muslim* rather than *Moslem* to describe followers of Islam, and the spelling *Qur'an* (rather than *Koran*) to refer to their holy book. These seem to be the spellings preferred by Muslims. *Children's literature* refers to works written specifically for children or adolescents, even though I will also discuss works for adults that have been assigned as readings in high schools and books for the general public that are of interest to young people.

HOW PEOPLE PASS ON THEIR CULTURES

People from all ethnic groups pass on their cultures to their children in a number of ways, including the following:

- informal education
- official formal education
- separate full-time day schools
- part-time language and ethnic schools
- the development of sacred and secular institutions, organizations, and media
- the publication of literature for adults, much of which may be of interest to the young
- the publication of literature specifically for children and young people

Informal Methods

All groups use informal methods to pass on their cultures, including modeling and apprenticeships, oral traditions, stories, proverbs, and rituals and ceremonies, especially coming-of-age rites. Stories from the oral tradition are often the first things to be published as a more formal, written children's literature is created or as information on previously neglected groups is published by the mainstream.

Official Formal Education

Official formal education has existed in most developed countries since the nineteenth century and in other countries since the twentieth. Most of the time, formal schooling promotes the culture and the interests of the dominant group(s) in a society. In the United States, some groups of people have been systematically segregated, excluded, or given inferior education, and others have been taught to assimilate to the predominant culture. This will be further discussed in chapter 2. However, in recent years, educators committed to multiculturalism have tried to incorporate cultural information from a variety of groups into the curriculum. Some have also studied learning styles of diverse students and have learned how to teach to these styles. Schools, school media centers, and public libraries have a major impact on what children read and are important potential consumers of multicultural and ethnic children's literature.

The development, promotion, and use of supplementary curricular materials in public schools is an important development in multicultural education. Educators and professionals, some of whom come from the most maligned, misunderstood, and stereotyped groups in our society, have developed much of these materials to fight these misconceptions. For example, Carter G. Woodson developed books and other materials on African American history in the 1920s, 1930s, and 1940s. Later, during and right after the civil rights movement in the 1960s, African American educators developed materials in black history and biography that teachers could use in the classroom. More recently, Native American and Muslim American professionals have been engaged in similar activities. (Some of these initiatives will be described in chapters 2, 4, and 5.) I believe that this development may also indicate groups potentially on the verge of creating and developing children's literature of quality.

Alternative Day Schools

Since the nineteenth century, people from almost all groups in the United States have used public schools to educate their children. However, it is interesting to note the groups that decided to create their own schools, and why and when. In the nineteenth century, for instance, Catholics created their own system of parochial day schools rather than send their children to public schools that were either secular or oriented to Protestants.[8] In the late twentieth century, fundamentalist Christians have done the same for many of the same reasons. These schools exist to promote values of the group, but those maintaining them must also pay enough attention to accreditation and other external concerns to enable their students to work or to continue their education elsewhere. The curriculum in these alternative schools is geared to meet both sets of goals. Colleges and universities created for specific groups of people and, in many respects, ethnic studies programs represent two more approaches to passing on cultures and cultural values.

Language, Ethnic, and Cultural Schools

Immigrants from some European, Middle Eastern, and Asian groups have developed language, ethnic, and cultural schools that meet in the evenings, on the weekends, and occasionally in the summer.[9] These schools were designed not to replace the public school curriculum but to supplement it. One of the first studies to specifically investigate such programs was *Ethnic Heritage and Language Schools in America*,[10] which was published by the Library of Congress in 1987. This work describes thirteen programs created by people from a wide variety of ethnic groups around the United States. It was intended to be a snapshot of some programs existing at that time. However, the researchers also commented on changes that had occurred over the years in older programs. They found that language and ethnic schools were often organized by a fairly united group of immigrants who had been in the United States for approximately a decade. The original purpose of most of these programs was to pass on the language of the home country to the children of immigrants. However, over time, the study of language would be emphasized less relative to the study of other cultural information. Support for some programs would wane as immigrants and their descendants assimilated at different rates and in different ways, and as they moved to other neighborhoods. The needs of first- and second-generation people would often differ from those of third- and fourth-generation descendants. Programs that have lasted a long time have tended to shift in their goals and emphasis. As more assimilated families moved to suburban and other scattered communities, daily programs would turn into less-intensive weekly ones.

Public schools and ethnic programs have influenced each other. Even though the most knowledgeable people often staffed ethnic schools from the beginning, these programs were eventually influenced by U.S. public schools in their governance, curriculum, and teaching methods. For example, the schools began to have school boards, PTAs, and professional associations for teachers. They also used graded classes, evaluative grades, textbooks, and tests. As ethnic schools emphasized language less and other cultural studies more, teachers used music, drama, crafts, recitations, and other methods to teach about their cultures.

As a rule, ethnic schools shifted from intensive language study to less-intensive language study and then to cultural study before eventually disbanding. However, a fresh wave of immigration has sometimes led either to the renewal or revival of old programs or to the creation of new ones. There is evidence of this with some Polish,[11] Portuguese,[12] and Chinese[13] schools. Schools tied to religious practices, such as those for Greek Americans and Jewish Americans, also tend to last.

Mainstream educational systems have also been affected by ethnic schools that have maintained strong language programs. Some ethnic language schools have been working with public schools and other agencies to make sure that their students get credit for knowing a foreign language. In the 1980s, Polish schools in Chicago sought recognition from the Illinois State Board of Education for this purpose.[14] In 1986, high school students from New York State taking Chinese and those enrolled in Chinese language schools for three years could take the Regents examination, which could also lead to foreign language credit as they went on to the university. Chinese schools have made similar arrangements with Maryland's Montgomery County, as well as with several school systems in California. In some cases, school systems worked with qualified Chinese educators to establish programs in high schools. In addition, the Task Force on Asian Languages successfully urged the College Board to offer proficiency tests in Asian languages.[15]

The ways languages were taught, even for the same ethnic group, varied over time. Jewish schools are either secular or religious, and the religious may be Orthodox, Conservative, or Reform. They have offered courses in Hebrew, Yiddish, and English, and have emphasized a wide variety of subjects in their curricula.[16] Depending upon the times and other circumstances, Chinese language schools have taught courses in Cantonese or Mandarin, and have emphasized the use of either the traditional *zhuyin fuhao* script, still used in Taiwan, or the simplified *Hanyu pinyin* script adopted by China in the 1950s.[17]

Both ethnic schools and children's literature exist to pass cultural information about a group to the next generation. Ethnic schools focus on factual information and use textbooks, while children's literature focuses more on fiction and other literary works. However, ethnic, religious, and other cultural schools can promote the use of traditional stories and literature through their cultural activities, and children's literature includes nonfiction.

In the case of Jewish Americans, religious schools were a major impetus to the development of modern Jewish children's literature. In 1922, the Reform movement commissioned several authors to write texts about the Bible, worship, ceremonies, holidays, and traditional stories for Hebrew schools. This led to a graded body of children's literature illustrated by artists. In addition, as new suburban Jewish synagogues were built after World War II, Jewish libraries were established there and in Jewish community centers to collect both popular and traditional fiction and nonfiction. All of this encouraged the production of Jewish children's literature.[18]

Since the publication of *Ethnic Heritage and Language Schools in America*, a number of dissertations and other studies have been written about these programs. While some attention has been paid to schools run by Greek Americans and Jewish Americans, almost all documentation and research has focused on the many programs created by Asian Americans, especially Chinese Americans and Japanese Americans.

Other Organizations, Institutions, and Media

People from all ethnic groups have formed their own sacred and secular institutions and organizations, and almost all have created their own specialized media, including periodicals, newspapers, books, television and radio programs and stations, and more recently, websites.[19] Recent immigrants to the United States are often eager to learn English, but they usually want to stay in touch with their home countries as well. However, as a group remains in the United States, community members develop media reflecting their experiences in the new country, in addition to any interest in the home country. The medium may be only in the group's original language at first, then sometimes bilingual, but eventually it usually is published or conveyed in English only.

The first ethnic literature produced for people of all ages is usually published by ethnic presses and reviewed by ethnic media. For some groups, this is the major or only source of their literature.

Ethnic Literature

Most of the initiatives described above have been by group members for group members, and are not always well known to people outside the group. They have not been documented as well as they could be, especially in the general society. This tendency continues to some extent with ethnic literature for adults and children. However, some of this literature is now published by mainstream presses and is more available to the general public.

People from many ethnic groups have published fiction and nonfiction materials about their groups for adults. Much of these have also been of interest to young adults and children. There is a fairly extensive amount of Jewish literature for children that has been well documented and is described in chapter 5. Some of this literature has been published by specialized presses and can be found in specialized Judaica collections. However, most Jewish children's literature is published by mainstream presses and is available to public libraries.[20]

Traditional stories and other oral literature may be the first materials published. In addition to any specialized children's and young adult literature, some literature for adults, especially literary works and some genre literature, may also be used by the young. Some teenagers read assigned high school readings relevant to their group. In some cases, the first young adult (YA) and sometimes children's literature is written by authors who had started out writing for adults. Childhood accounts and bildungsromans or "coming of age" biographies and novels are popular with people of all ages, and this can also be a bridge to the development of a more specialized literature for young people.

WHY THIS MATTERS

All of these activities reflect the many ways that ethnic groups from all continents have passed on their cultural heritage. These initiatives can be connected in a number of ways.

Maintaining informal traditions, alternative or supplementary education, sacred and secular institutions and organizations, and ethnic literature for young and old served as intermediate steps for some European immigrants who were slow to assimilate. All of these activities have also been vital to people of color who have not been able to completely assimilate into this society. Ethnic writers, especially those of color, have found it necessary to educate both their own children and their neighbors' children (from other groups). These activities are also important because they indicate groups that view themselves as culturally distinct, that need to be able to create literature and other resources not already in the mainstream, and that could create some excellent new literature in the future.

ISSUES AFFECTING ETHNIC GROUPS FROM ALL CONTINENTS

People from most ethnic groups grapple with the issues of identity, language, diaspora, and worldview, as well as generational issues. However, there are also major differences both between and within groups.

Identity, Language, and Diaspora

Identity is a major issue for any nondominant group in a society. Many ethnic people, particularly people of color, juggle with two (if not more) cultures, and they express the situation in various ways. If the West is "the universe," many people find themselves "at two with the universe," to quote a quip from Woody Allen. One hundred years ago, W. E. B. DuBois expressed this as the "double consciousness" African Americans feel as they consider their African past and their American present:

> After the Egyptian and Indian, the Greek and Roman, the Teuton and Mongolian, the Negro is a sort of seventh son, born with a veil, and gifted with second-sight in this American world—a world which yields him no self-consciousness, but only lets him see himself through the revelation of the other world. It is a peculiar sensation, this double-consciousness, this sense of always looking at one's self through the eyes of others, of measuring one's soul by the tape of a world that looks on in amused contempt and pity. One ever feels his two-ness—an American, a Negro; two souls, two thoughts, two unreconciled strivings, two warring ideas in one dark body, whose dogged strength alone keeps it from being torn asunder.
>
> The history of the American Negro is the history of this strife—this longing to attain self-conscious manhood, to merge his double self into a better and truer self. *In the merging, he wishes neither of the older selves to be lost.*[21] (emphasis added)

Chicano/as and other Latino/as use the theme of borders in their literature,[22] referring to those they navigate between countries, languages, and cultures. People of mixed race use this concept as well in order to discuss borders that they see between all of the races that affect them.[23] Some Asian American theologians[24] and other scholars from different groups discuss the related concept of *marginality*. This sense of ambiguity is also expressed in reference to generational differences by many Asian Americans and some ethnic European Americans. The issue of generational conflict will be explored more in the next section. This perspective can be both alienating and creative for all, depending on how it is handled.

The importance of language cannot be overemphasized. All languages reveal much about the cultures that they describe and represent, and they are connected to people's root cultures. Languages are also tied to ways that people think and perceive the world, or to their worldviews. No language can be completely translated into another, and when a language is lost, so is much of the thinking and values behind the language.

Some European, Middle Eastern, and Asian immigrants have tried to maintain their languages through language schools. This works fairly well as long as there are parents and grandparents at home who still speak the language. Successful language-intensive programs tend to last two to three generations. Other groups, such as a number of Native American tribes, have been attempting to maintain or restore languages that are dormant or have recently died. Since Gaelic and Hebrew have both been resuscitated elsewhere, this may be quite possible.

A major controversy in the United States is whether immigrants should maintain their languages of origin, use them as a bridge to learn English, or learn English strictly by immersion.[25] This controversy is also a major issue in ethnic children's literature. Experts debate and discuss, for instance, whether, when, and how to use Spanish in bilingual or predominantly English books—and which version(s) of Spanish to use. Even when group members, such as African Americans, speak English, the question of whether to ever use Ebonics or Black English, a form of Caribbean Creole, or any other dialect—and if so, in what ways—is still an issue.

The diaspora is an issue to people from a number of ethnic groups as they answer Countee Cullen's question, "What is Africa (or home) to me?" This concept first emerged in discussing Jewish people who are scattered around the world.[26] There are also African, Chinese, Greek, Irish, Italian, Muslim, and other diasporas. The concept entails remembering roots and history, interacting with people from the country or countries of origin, looking for surviving cultural traits, and studying and relating to people with similar roots who live in other parts of the world. Interest in diasporas is expressed in scholarly conferences, publications, organizations—and sometimes children's literature! A small modern English-language literature on and by South Asians for adults and for the young has emerged from the United States, Canada, and England.[27] This literature is diasporan in nature.

It is an international literature read by fans around the world. Latino/a literature from the United States and Latin American literature are somewhat diasporan, and it can be difficult to tell where one begins and the other ends. African, Caribbean, and African American children's literature have all developed separately, but authors writing from one country can affect writers from others. An example is Negritude,[28] an early black consciousness movement that originated in the French-speaking countries in West Africa in the mid-twentieth century and that influenced Caribbean and African American writers. African American writers have historically written books about Africa, and writers from Africa and the Caribbean publish in Europe, Canada, and the United States. People from related countries can influence each other. Many of these trends will be described in chapter 4.

People do not have to leave home to experience a diaspora. Indigenous people from all over the world have been meeting and visiting each other to share ideas and encourage each other. Examples of these activities include the World Christian Gathering of Indigenous People,[29] the International Indigenous Librarians' Forum[30]; and the World Indigenous Nations Higher Education Consortium,[31] for leaders of the world's tribal colleges. On her website, If I Can Read, I Can Do Anything,[32] Loriene Roy has a page entitled A Gathering of Readers, where children from indigenous schools around the world can communicate with each other.

Worldview

Worldview is also very important. Worldview is the way people perceive themselves, other people, and the world in general and why they feel this way. All groups have worldviews, but nondominant groups are seldom able to share theirs with the world outside their group. Worldview reflects the preponderance of opinions of people from a specific group. It is as old as Columbus and as recent as Hurricane Katrina. It comes from people's original cultures, their histories, and their present realities. Worldviews of people from ethnic groups can be found in their literature, scholarly work, and popular work by ethnic writers, and in ethnic journals, periodicals, newspapers, and websites. Differences in worldview emerge as people from different groups are asked about their reactions to particular issues. A pattern of statistically significant responses may indicate divergent worldviews. It can also be expressed by comedians of different backgrounds, such as Jay Leno and Paul Mooney, making different comments on the same event, such as the O. J. Simpson trials.

Different worldviews are also reflected in books on race relations published over the years by writers such as Lena Williams,[33] Studs Terkel,[34] David K Shipler,[35] Farai Chideya,[36] and the correspondents of the *New York*

Times.[37] These popular titles show differences of opinion both between and within racial groups. Research on racial development theories by authors such as William E. Cross,[38] Beverly Daniel Tatum,[39] Gary R. Howard,[40] Ilan Katz,[41] Charmaine L. Wijeyesinghe, and Bailey W. Jackson III[42] describes how people from different groups view themselves, as well as people from other ethnic groups, over time. This research explains very well the various reactions of people from all groups to racial incidents or situations.

Themes that are consistent over time and how these themes are handled represent the worldview of a community. There are many examples of people's perspectives differing from group to group. One example—whether Columbus Day should be a day of celebration or a day of mourning—depends upon whom one asks. For another, white people of British descent living in Great Britain, Canada, and the United States use different terminology in describing Americans loyal to King George III during the American Revolution. Most Americans call these individuals Tories, while people in Britain and Canada call them Loyalists. This reflects a slight difference in worldview. Another example is the way that white northerners and southerners view the major conflict occurring in the United States in the years 1861 to 1865. Most northerners call this conflict the Civil War. Many white southerners call this same conflict "the War Between the States." This also reflects a difference in worldviews. One can also see some differences in how the mainstream presses and the African American, Latino/a, and Native American presses covered Hurricane Katrina in 2005. For instance, Native American publications focused on how Native American tribes in Mississippi, Louisiana, Alabama, and Texas survived the storms, a subject not seen very much in other media.

However, while worldviews can reflect a preponderance of opinion within any group, people vary widely in how they view life, and there are always those who disagree with the dominant thought of their community. People do not walk in lockstep. Understanding differences in worldviews is essential to understanding many of the major controversies in the field of multiculturalism. The issue of worldview will be considered in discussions about the "Insider/Outsider" debate over cultural authenticity in chapter 3, issues in Native American literature in chapter 4, and cultural issues faced by Arab Americans, Muslim Americans, and people of mixed race in chapter 5. Readers should remember that people from all groups have something valuable to bring to the table that others may not have thought about. Cultural worldviews often start with one set of cultural or historical roots (usually the old country or the original culture). As time goes on, group members may go into several directions, answering Martin Luther King's question, "Where do we go from here?"

Changes through Time: Ethnic Generations

Assimilation of recent immigrants may occur slowly or relatively quickly. Isolated families or well-educated immigrants who are already fluent in English can assimilate in a generation or two. Poorly educated immigrants not fluent in English who live in larger ethnic enclaves may take about four generations. The average seems to be two to three generations or twenty-five to fifty years. This pattern was clear with European immigrants who came to U.S. cities in the Northeast or Midwest from 1880 to1924. The first generation (adult immigrants) was often working class, started out in ethnic neighborhoods, and spoke little or no English, or spoke with accents, even if otherwise fluent. The second generation (their children) was more likely to be bilingual, bicultural, and conflicted. This generation was under both external and internal pressure to assimilate. The third generation would often be assimilated and was monolingual in English. Members of this generation have difficulty learning the original language, when they choose to try. Third-generation members of ethnic groups are sometime curious about their grandparents and their generation, and in some cases want to reconnect with their roots.

By the mid-1940s, the European immigrants of 1880 to 1924 and their families were beginning to assimilate by moving up the socioeconomic ladder. They were moving out of old neighborhoods and into scattered communities where they were now in the minority. They were also inter-marrying with people from other groups with some ties in common (for example, Italian Catholics marrying German, Irish, or Polish Catholics). Loss of the old language would also be a part of this process. Concerns of these immigrants and their children can be found in some social science research,[43] publications of professionals working with these groups,[44] au-tobiographies,[45] and bildungsromans or works of fiction by immigrants or their children.[46]

Some Asian Americans also describe their situations in generational terms. Japanese Americans refer to the Issei (original immigrants), Nisei (children of immigrants), Sansei (grandchildren of immigrants), and Yonsei (great-grand-children) in their research and writing.[47] The more recent Korean American immigrants talk about Generation 1.0 (the *ilse*, or immigrants), Generation 2.0 (the *ise*, or children born in the United States), and the *ilchom ose*, or Generation 1.5, for children who remember Korea but grow up here![48]

Differences between Groups: Who Can Assimilate?

In spite of many of these similarities, immigrants from different continents differ from each other in major ways. European immigrants in many cases were able to temporarily and privately hold on to many aspects of their cultures, despite being urged to assimilate. A few ethnic or cultural European groups, such as the Greeks, Armenians, and Jews, have maintained some cultural education through their churches or synagogues. African Americans, on the other hand, were separated from both their lands and their original cultures through slavery, Jim Crow, and lynching; and boarding schools, reservations, and sometimes genocide separated Native Americans from their lands and cultures. The society demanded, yet forbade, their assimilation, leaving people from these groups in a serious quandary and double bind!

Like the Europeans of a century ago, some Latino/as and Asian Americans have gone through the generational changes common to most immigrants and have been able to hold on to aspects of their cultures. All of these groups have stressed the importance of language, either through pressing for bilingual programs in schools or through starting and maintaining their own language schools. However, like Native Americans and African Americans, Latino/as and Asian Americans are viewed as people of color, and are unable to fully assimilate into the United States because of racism. In spite of the fact that some Latino/as have been here longer than anyone besides Native Americans, Latino/as and Asian Americans are not always viewed as being "from here," no matter how long their families have been in the country. This tendency is expressed in the work of Ronald Takaki[49] and other scholars. People of color are seldom viewed as "all-American," "from the heartland," or the boy or girl "next door."

Arthur Schlesinger Jr.[50] and Nathan Glazer,[51] both critics of many aspects of multiculturalism, view African Americans as being unable to assimilate because of racism in our society. Schlesinger asks the majority to accept African Americans and to allow them to integrate into U.S. society. He briefly mentions serious cultural issues faced by Native Americans, but does not go into more detail on this subject.[52] Glazer reluctantly supports multiculturalism because he sees a need for African Americans to practice cultural pluralism. He views multiculturalism as a black issue. Glazer believes that Latino/as, Native Americans, and Asian Americans are now assimilating, based on their residential patterns and rate of intermarriage.[53] He argues that Asians, who are doing well in school, were more concerned in the 1980s with discrimination at the college level than with a Eurocentric curriculum, and that the demand for more Asian content in the curriculum may be coming from relatively assimilated and native-born spokespeople. Glazer also believes that Mexican Americans will eventually assimilate, as earlier European immigrants did in the long run, but that this assimilation could be delayed by continuous Mexican immigration, the closeness of Mexico to the United States, and the establishment of both bilingual education and Spanish-language assistance in voting. He also states that Puerto Rican leaders' call for more bilingual education and more Puerto Rican content in U.S. school curricula is a result of the frequent movement of Puerto Ricans between the U.S. mainland and Puerto Rico. He does not believe that Puerto Ricans are as militant in their educational demands as African Americans. According to Glazer, Cuban Americans want a mixture of sound education and some culturally distinct content, and Latin American immigrants from other countries are very similar to earlier European immigrants in their educational goals.[54]

Glazer views Native Americans as small, relatively self-contained groups largely in special schools and colleges on reservations, though in fact many Native American students are now urban. He believes that they can be accommodated with little strain on traditional curricula.[55] However, Native Americans and their supporters raise some of the most crucial and provocative questions about their portrayal in children's literature, and their scholarly and educational literature also reflects worldviews not seen elsewhere. Indigenous peoples differ from everybody else. They have been in the Americas far longer than anybody else, and many do not consider themselves to be "ethnic." Native American tribes recognized by the U.S. government are still legally sovereign nations with their own laws. However, indigenous peoples have histories and issues that are extremely relevant here and are part of the multicultural mosaic. These issues will be described in more detail in chapter 4.

I agree with Glazer that multiculturalism is a black issue,[56] but do not agree that it can be limited to that. Assimilation is more complicated than Glazer indicates. Some indications of assimilation that Glazer does not mention in this context include graduating from top schools, moving into good jobs, and successfully running for political office. Some African Americans have been doing these things for years. On the other hand, one can be a minority-group member living in a predominantly white area and not feel or be assimilated at all. Intermarriage with white people also does not guarantee assimilation, either for the couples or for their children. Issues faced by mixed-race families will be described in chapter 5.

A Banquet Table in a Room Called America

Western civilization and the Western canon is a banquet table with a variety of foods on it. Most of the food is European, with side dishes from elsewhere. Some of it is delicious and nutritious for everybody. Some of it is delicious junk food. Some of the food (such as dairy products) is all right for some people but not others. There is also some poison on that table that nobody should touch. There is less of that than there used to be, but some is still there.

White Anglo Saxon Protestants are seated in the middle of the table. They have been there the longest and eaten the most. On both sides of them are

European immigrants and their children, who joined the table (and assimilated) later.

Serving the banquet table are African Americans, who were brought to
the room in chains. Their job has been to set up the table, serve it, and clean
it up afterward. They have never been invited to join the table. I agree with
both Schlesinger and Glazer that African Americans have not been allowed
to assimilate.

I disagree with Glazer on the roles of other people of color in the room.
The Native Americans own the room and were the first ones there, but they
have been pushed to the corner. This is also true for some Mexican Americans.
Other Latino/as (such as Puerto Ricans) have experienced colonization in their
own countries. While Glazer believes that Latino/as and Asian Americans are
being seated at the table, I would state that they are also working the room,
although on a more voluntary basis than the African Americans. Whether
people from these groups are being invited to or seated at the table of Western
civilization is a subject of debate. Another issue is the price of the ticket to
the banquet. Must one "pass" philosophically, psychologically, culturally, and
sometimes physically to be seated? The issue of how ethnic scholars, professionals, and writers are sometimes treated by the mainstream will be discussed
in chapter 3. Their contributions will be further mentioned in chapter 4.

The people working the banquet room, who have not been invited to
dine at the table, have been living off a combination of scraps from the
Western table, crumbs that they sweep up from under the table, and the
cedar chests of their own cultures. Like the food on the banquet table, the
items from the cedar chests also vary in quality, including things that are
necessary and excellent for everyone, items all right for some but not all,
and items that nobody should touch. People of color are just beginning to
unpack their cedar chests. African Americans and Native Americans, who
have been separated from their original cultures, do not know everything
that is in their chests, and are in the process of discovery and rediscovery.
The guests at the banquet table are reluctant to deal with anything from any
of the cedar chests. They are using the worst of the materials as an excuse
not to deal with this issue at all. The controversy over Afrocentrism will be
discussed in chapter 3.

FOUR WAYS TO LOOK AT RACE RELATIONS

In his book *Beyond Racial Gridlock*,[57] George Yancey describes four approaches to race relations, each with its advantages and disadvantages. He
concludes that none of these approaches can solve racial problems by itself,

but that all can be helpful at times. The four approaches that he describes are color blindness, Anglo conformity, white responsibility, and multiculturalism.

Color Blindness

Proponents of color blindness[58] maintain that we will have racial reconciliation once we ignore race and forget past discrimination. They also maintain that we can overcome racism by concentrating on advances already made and by acting in a color-blind manner. Proponents write that race should not be used as a reason for doing (or not doing) anything. The concept of color blindness was instrumental both in the passing of anti-discrimination civil rights legislation and in the repeal of laws against interracial marriage.

The goal of color blindness and a race-neutral society, with the belief that no positive or negative values should be assigned to any group, is a laudable one. There are also several serious flaws to the concept of color blindness. It is an incomplete approach to race relations, ignoring both past and present racism. It assumes that the civil rights movement solved all racial issues and that the problem of ethnocentrism no longer exists, at a time when the gains of the civil rights movement are being dismantled piece by piece. In addition, not all advocates of color blindness really want an equal society. At its worst, color blindness can render people of color and their concerns invisible. It also depends very much on individualistic solutions to racial problems.

Anglo Conformity

Advocates of Anglo conformity[59] encourage racial minorities to adopt European American values in order to move up the economic and social ladders. They maintain that once minorities gain economic equality with majority-group members, racism will disappear. Proponents of Anglo conformity are as historic as Booker T. Washington and as current as Jack Kemp or Lou Dobbs. Some advocates of this approach emphasize class differences over racial differences. I maintain that cultural literacy is an educational and cultural version of Anglo conformity. Promoters of cultural literacy argue that if all are literate in Western culture, all can also assimilate. (Cultural literacy will be described in more detail in chapter 3.) Like color blindness, Anglo conformity is an individualized approach to race relations favored mostly by Europeans, more conservative African Americans, and some members of other racial minorities.

Anglo conformity and cultural literacy are wonderful philosophies—as far as they go. Both can be used to enable all people to make a good living in this economy and to learn the Western canon. Both philosophies are helpful and practical in helping all people with the opportunity to overcome economic disadvantages and to function in society, and they both encourage self-help and initiative.

However, being culturally literate and trying to assimilate do not ensure that people of color will be welcomed to the banquet table. Minority group members are sometimes urged to give up their own cultures in order to pursue the sometimes elusive goal of assimilation. The goals of both Anglo conformity and cultural literacy are good, but they are not quite enough to solve all problems. Like color blindness, neither Anglo conformity nor cultural literacy takes structural and institutional racism into account. They also do not consider that people with non-Western roots may have some useful ideas of their own for everybody.

White Responsibility

The white responsibility school[60] locates racial problems within majority cultures and individuals. Advocates of this model maintain that since current racism began in the West, it is up to Westerners to end it. In other words, "you broke it, you fix it." The white responsibility school focuses on institutional and structural racism and the official responsibilities of groups of people. Proponents from all backgrounds demand that white people share much of their power with people neglected and victimized in the past. The movements for reparations for African Americans to atone for slavery and for Japanese Americans to atone for World War II concentration camps are two examples of this philosophy.

Several academic schools have emerged to study the history and phenomenon of white racism, including historical studies of racism, studies of "white privilege," white studies, and critical race theory. Studies of cultural stereotyping are also part of this school of thought. In addition there are more popular books about race relations describing the reactions of a variety of people to racial issues, as well as books on racial identity development, which have been mentioned above.

The earliest studies related to the history of systematic white racism were largely by white scholars, such as C. Vann Woodward,[61] Kenneth Stampp,[62] and Winthrop Jordan.[63] Studies of "white privilege" include those by scholars such as Paula S. Rothenberg,[64] Frances E. Kendall,[65] Michelle Fine,[66] Robert Jensen,[67] Gary R. Howard,[68] Lani Guinier, and Gerald Torres.[69] These studies focus not only on the phenomenon of "white privilege," but also on what white people can do about racism.

Research in the areas of white studies and critical race theory seem to be interrelated. White studies can be compared to men's studies, a sympathetic scholarly male reaction to the women's liberation movement and to women's studies. The field of white studies is intended to do the same for race relations. Critical race theory grew out of law schools, and some scholars in ethnic studies and the social sciences are also conducting this line of research. Scholars in both fields include Kimberlé Crenshaw,[70] Derrick Bell,[71] Richard Delgado,[72] and Angela Harris.[73]

Some scholars have studied the stereotyping of various groups in all aspects of culture—the media in general, advertising, movies, television, and literature for adults and children. Much of this focus has been on the stereotyping of African Americans and Native Americans. Some of these works will be described in chapters 2 and 4 of this work.

The greatest strength of the white responsibility model is its ability to portray white racism as a phenomenon that goes far beyond individuals, such as Archie Bunker, or organized groups, such as the Ku Klux Klan. Institutions, organizations, and systems can be constructed to consistently favor some groups over others, and this is not always intentional. The white responsibility model also shows that people do not rise or fall completely on their own, and it refutes the color-blind theory. Insights from this model will be extensively applied in chapter 2, with descriptions of educational discrimination and cultural stereotypes. Chapter 3 will discuss diversity in publishing and related fields, as well as schools designed for white, middle-class children. Both chapters will also mention the intricate relationships between publishing, education, library science, and the media, and how racial issues in any one of these fields affect them all. Systems designed for one group of people do not always work as well for everybody unless they are redesigned to more truly incorporate all.

However, the white responsibility model also has some glaring weaknesses. Some advocates believe that only white people can be racist, and blame all problems on the majority. It does not make sufficient room for either the responsibility or the initiative of ethnic people to address their own issues. It also ignores the fact that all people can be right at times, as well as wrong.

Multiculturalism

Multiculturalism[74] emphasizes the value and worth of all cultures, particularly minority ones. Multiculturalists take a more structured and group-oriented approach to race and ethnic relations than do advocates of color blindness or Anglo conformity. They come from a wide variety of backgrounds, but quite a few are bicultural people of color promoting their own (and other people's) cultures to others, especially the mainstream. Some multiculturalists also come from applied fields, such as business, education, social work, and aspects of the Christian ministry.

Multiculturalism is applied cultural diversity. At its best, it enables all to participate in general U.S. public culture and to maintain their own cultural base. It enables bicultural people who cannot completely assimilate to live very creatively. If done well, it also encourages people to be interested not only in themselves but in their neighbors as well.

There are many strengths of multiculturalism. In the past, most mirrors in this society (books, media, educational materials, and so forth) were created by people in the majority, and perpetuated many stereotypes of people in the minority. People of color and some other ethnic people have always needed to be bicultural in order to survive and to thrive. Most white Americans, especially of western European descent, have been able to be relatively monocultural until recently. However, considering the rise of several countries in East Asia and major population shifts in both Europe and the United States, Europeans and Euro-Americans may not be able to afford this luxury much longer. Multiculturalism is for everybody. It allows people in the majority to see themselves as others see them, and it helps people in minority groups to learn, know, celebrate, and promote their own cultures.

In addition, some of the findings of multicultural research have been very useful in the business world, in education, and in other fields as professionals work with diverse staffs and clientele, both in the United States and abroad. Research of this type includes books on diversity in the business world by John Fernandez[75] and the work of James Banks,[76] a founder of multicultural education. This information is meant to be practical "hands-on" information that can be applied to the "real world." However, for all of this to work, groups must have mutual respect. There is room for criticism on all sides, and conflict negotiation between groups is a major issue, but mutual respect is paramount.

Multiculturalism has its weaknesses as well.[77] If applied poorly, it can promote a more divisive society. Several of the weaknesses of this movement may be caused by overcompensation for the past. This includes the possibly rigid use of multiple standards for cultural authenticity in textbooks and the failure to be critical enough of some materials, such as the worst of Afrocentric research. I do not agree that multiculturalists are too critical of the West, however. As harsh as this may be, such criticism is very necessary, especially at this time. Multiculturalists may also need to discuss more positive features from the West, and how all can better work together on this issue.

In my opinion, the multicultural movement combines aspects of both the white responsibility and the Anglo conformity schools. Multiculturalists tend to see Western culture as the root of many of their problems. However, multicultural and ethnic producers of children's literature borrow from the conservative Anglo conformity and cultural literacy approaches in two respects. First, many are trying to use Western means to preserve the best aspects of their own culture, and some are trying to combine the best of two worlds. Quite a few are attempting to share their own materials both with their own children and with a wider audience. Second, multicultural and ethnic producers are not relying completely on the mainstream to help them. People in the field have been writing their own books; creating their own publishing houses, distribution centers, and critical reviews; and building their own library collections. They are taking initiatives of their own. Many of these activities will be further described in chapters 4 and 5.

Taking a more neutral and nonjudgmental look at some cultures deemed inferior or primitive in the past is a real necessity at this time. However, there are additional philosophical questions that multiculturalists and other professionals will have to deal with over the long run. They include the following: [78]

- Are there universal social norms and laws recognizable to all societies?
- How does one deal with authentic but negative cultural phenomena, particularly those that apply specifically to women?
- Does multiculturalism stress relativism over a more absolute and universal morality? Does it stress harmony and cooperation over truth and justice?
- How does one either prevent or resolve the inevitable conflict that arises between groups of people?

Multiculturalists and other professionals will need to consider these questions now and in the future. A few are just beginning to raise these issues.

I do believe that this literature is still in an early stage. Just getting items published and distributed and documenting this process has been very intensive. I am sure that as time goes on and more materials are published, professionals will also take a more critical look at those materials. For instance, the earliest bibliographies of books about black children only listed and described those books.[79] Later, similar bibliographies have focused more specifically on African American writers.[80] Others take a more critical look at the materials.[81] In addition, the *MultiCultural Review* takes a critical look at this literature and analyzes it in various ways. All of these approaches can be observed in the work of a single major bibliographer, Isabel Schon, who has extensively documented children's books on the Latino/a and Latin American experience. Her work is further described in chapter 4.

I also see the stringent application of criteria for cultural authenticity (at least in textbooks) and the strong criticism of the West decrease as more ethnic and multicultural materials are published and promoted. As time goes on, professionals from all aspects of this field will be able to take a more nuanced look both at multicultural and Western literature.

REFERENCES

1. Langston Hughes, "I, Too, Sing America" in *American Negro Poetry*, ed. Arna Bontemps (New York: Hill and Wang, 1983).

2. Arthur Schlesinger Jr., *The Disuniting of America* (New York: Norton and Company, 1998), 38–39.

3. Nathan Glazer, *We Are All Multiculturalists Now* (Cambridge, Mass.: Harvard University Press, 1997), 96–110.

4. Glazer, *We Are All Multiculturalists Now*, 110–13.

5. Horace Kallen, *Culture and Democracy in the United States* (New York: Boni and Liveright, 1924), 127, 165.

6. Karen Patricia Smith, "The Multicultural Ethic and Connections to Literature for Children and Young Adults," *Library Trends* 41, no. 3 (Winter 1993): 340–41; Mingshui Cai, "Multiple Definitions of Multicultural Literature: Is the Debate Really Just 'Ivory Tower' Bickering?" *The New Advocate* 11, no. 4 (Fall 1998): 312. Revised and updated in *Stories Matter: The Complexity of Cultural Authenticity in Children's Literature*, ed. Dana L. Fox and Kathy G. Short (Urbana, Ill.: National Council of Teachers of English, 2003), 116–34.

7. A. R. Fishman, "Finding Ways In: Redefining Multicultural Literature," *English Journal* 84, no. 6 (October 1995): 73–79.

8. Diane Ravitch, *The Great School Wars: New York City, 1805–1973* (New York: W. W. Norton, 1973).

9. Diane Ravitch, "Minority Group Education in the United States," in *The Schools We Deserve: Reflections on the Educational Crises of Our Times* (New York: Basic Books, 1985), 190–192; Glazer, *We Are All Multiculturalists Now*, 85.

10. Elena Bradunas, developer, and Brett Topping, comp. and ed., *Ethnic Heritage and Language Schools in America* (Washington, D.C.: Library of Congress, The American Folklife Center, 1988).

11. Margy McClain, "Polish Saturday Schools," in *Ethnic Heritage and Language Schools in America*, 138–55.

12. Marsha Penti, "Escola Officializada Portuguesa do Taunton Sports Club," in *Ethnic Heritage and Language Schools in America*, 68–93.

13. Him Mark Lai, "Retention of the Chinese Heritage, Part II: Chinese Schools in America, World War II to Present," *Chinese America: History and Perspectives* (2001): 8–10.

14. McClain, "Polish Saturday Schools," 153.

15. Lai, "Retention of the Chinese Heritage," 3–7.

16. Nathan Glazer, "American Pluralism: Voluntarism or State Action?" in *Ethnic Dilemmas: 1964–1982* (Cambridge, Mass.: Harvard University Press, 1983), 140.

17. Lai, "Retention of the Chinese Heritage," 6–8.

18. Marcia W. Posner, "Jewish Children's Literature," in *Jewish-American History and Culture: An Encyclopedia*, ed. Jack Fischel and Sanford Pinsker (New York: Garland, 1992), 294.

19. Ravitch, "Minority Group Education in the United States," in *The Schools We Deserve*, 189; Glazer, *We Are All Multiculturalists Now*, 118.

20. Posner, "Jewish Children's Literature," 294.

21. W. E. B. DuBois, *The Souls of Black Folk* (Greenwich, Conn.: Fawcett, 1961), 16–17.

22. Carmen L. Medina and Patricia Enciso, "'Some Words Are Messengers/Hay Palabras Mensajeras': Interpreting Sociopolitical Themes in Latino/a Children's Literature," *The New Advocate* 15, no. 1 (Winter 2002), 35–47.

23. Maria P. P. Root, "Issues and Experiences of Racially Mixed People," in *Multicultural Child Resource Book*, ed. Maria P. P. Root and Matt Kelley (Seattle, Wash.: MAVIN Foundation, 2003), 19–25.

24. Peter C. Phan and Jung Young Lee, eds., *Journeys at the Margin: Towards an Autobiographical Theology in American-Asian Perspectives* (Collegeville, Minn.: Liturgical Press, 1995); Jung Young Lee, *Marginality: The Key to Multicultural Theology* (Minneapolis, Minn.: Augsberg Fortress, 1995).

25. Glazer, "American Pluralism," 126–44; Glazer, "Bilingualism: Will It Work?" in *Ethnic Dilemmas, 1964–1982* (Cambridge, Mass.: Harvard University Press, 1983), 145–56; Rosalie Pedalino Porter, *Forked Tongue: The Politics of Bilingual Education* (New Brunswick, N.J.: Transaction Publishers, 1996); Frances Willard von Maltitz, *Living and Learning in Two Languages: Bilingual-Bicultural Education in the United States* (New York: McGraw-Hill, 1975); Colman Brez Stein Jr., *Sink or Swim: The Politics of Bilingual Education* (New York: Praeger, 1986); Tom Stritikus, *Immigrant Children and the Politics of English-Only: Views from the Classroom* (New York: LFB Scholarly Publishers, 2002).

26. "Diaspora," in *The Dictionary of Global Culture*, eds. Kwame Anthony Appiah and Henry Louis Gates Jr. (New York: Knopf, 1997).

27. Meena G. Khorana, "Break Your Silence: A Call to Asian Indian Children's Writers," *Library Trends* 40, no. 3 (Winter 1993): 393–413; Uma Krishnaswami, "On the Seashore of Worlds: Selected South Asian Voices from North America and the United Kingdom," *Bookbird* 42, no. 2 (April 2004): 23–37; Krishnaswami, "South Asia in Children's Literature," http://www.umakrishnaswami.com/southasia.html (26 June 2006).

28. Kwame Anthony Appiah and Henry Louis Gates Jr., eds., *The Dictionary of Global Culture* (New York: Knopf, 1997), 480; William Andrews, Frances Smith Foster, and Trudier Harris, eds., *The Oxford Companion to African American Literature* (New York: Oxford University Press, 1997), 531–32.

29. Don Maples, prod., *The Inaugural World Christian Gathering on Indigenous People* (video) (The Whole World Network, 1997).

30. "The International Indigenous Librarians' Forum," http://www.5iilf.org/ (26 June 2006).

31. "World Indigenous Nations Higher Education Consortium," http://www.win-hec.org/ (26 June 2006).

32. Loriene Roy, "A Gathering of Readers," on If I Can Read, I Can Do Anything, http://www.ischool.utexas.edu/~gathread/ (26 June 2006).

33. Lena Williams, *It's the Little Things: Everyday Interactions That Anger, Annoy and Divide the Races* (New York: Harcourt, 2000).

34. Studs Terkel, *Division Street: America* (New York: Pantheon, 1967); Terkel, *Race: How Blacks and Whites Think and Feel about the American Obsession* (New York: New Press, 2005).

35. David K. Shipler, *A Country of Strangers: Blacks and Whites in America* (New York: Knopf, 1997).

36. Farai Chideya, *The Color of Our Future* (New York: Morrow, 1999).

37. Correspondents of the *New York Times*, *How Race Is Lived in America: Pulling Together, Pulling Apart* (New York: Henry Holt, 2003).

38. William E. Cross, *Shades of Black: Diversity in African American Identity* (Philadelphia: Temple University Press, 1991).

39. Beverly Daniel Tatum, *"Why Are All the Black Kids Sitting Together in the Cafeteria?" And Other Conversations about Race* (New York: Basic Books, 1997).

40. Gary R. Howard, *We Can't Teach What We Don't Know: White Teachers, Multiracial Schools*, second edition (New York: Teachers College Press, 2006).

41. Ilan Katz, *The Construction of Racial Identity in Children of Mixed Parentage: Mixed Metaphors* (London: Jessica Kingsley Publishers, 1996).

42. Charmaine L. Wijeyesinghe and Bailey W. Jackson III, eds., *New Perspectives on Racial Identity Development* (New York: New York University Press, 2001).

43. Alejandro Portes and Rubén G. Rumbaut, *Legacies: The Story of the Immigrant Second Generation* (Berkeley, Calif.: University of California Press, 2001); Alejandro Portes, ed., *The New Second Generation* (New York: The Russell Sage Foundation, 1996); Rubén G. Rumbaut and Alejandro Portes, *Ethnicities: Children of Immigrants in America* (Berkeley, Calif.: University of California Press, 2001); Carola Suarez-Orozco and Marcelo M. Suarez-Orozco, *Children of Immigration: The Developing Child* (Cambridge, Mass.: Harvard University Press, 2001).

44. Xue Lan Rang and Judith Preissle, *Educating Immigrant Children: What We Need to Know to Meet the Challenges* (Thousand Oaks, Calif.: Corwin Press, 1997); Joti Bhatnagar, *Educating Immigrants* (New York: St Martin's Press, 1981); Kathleen W. Craver, "Bridging the Gap: Library Services for Immigrant Populations—Newly Arrived, Second and Third Generations, Guest Workers and Refugees," *Journal of Youth Services in Libraries* 4 (Winter 1991): 123–30; Kevin Scanlon and Lisa Young-blood, "Living in the Salad Bowl: Serving Immigrant Teens," *Young Adult Library Services* 2, no. 1 (Fall 2003): 15.

45. Jade Snow Wong, *Fifth Chinese Daughter* (Seattle, Wash.: University of Washington Press, 1989); Piri Thomas, *Down These Mean Streets* (New York: Vintage, 1997); Esmeralda Santiago, *When I Was Puerto Rican* (New York: Vintage, 1993); M. Elaine Mar, *Paper Daughter* (New York: Harper Perennial, 2000); Daniel D. Challener, *Stories of Resilience in Childhood: The Narratives of Maya Angelou,*

Maxine Hong Kingston, Richard Rodriguez, John Edgar Wideman, and Tobias Wolff (New York: Garland, 1997).

46. Henry Roth, *Call It Sleep* (New York: Farrar, Straus and Giroux, 1991); Julia Alvarez, *How the Garcia Girls Lost Their Accents* (New York: Penguin, 1992); Cristina Garcia, *Dreaming in Cuban* (New York: Ballantine Books, 1993); Amy Tan, *The Joy Luck Club* (New York: Putnam, 1989); Paule Marshall, *Brown Girl, Brownstones* (New York: The Feminist Press at City University of New York, 2006); Edwidge Danticat, *Breath, Eyes, Memory* (New York: Vintage, 1998); Mitali Perkins, "The Fire Escape: Books by and about Young Immigrants," http://www.mitaliperkins.com (26 June 2006).

47. Ronald Takaki, *Strangers from a Different Shore: A History of Asian Americans* (New York: Penguin, 1987), 212–29.

48. Takaki, *Strangers from a Different Shore*, 286–93; Win Moo Hurh, *The Korean Americans* (Westport, Conn.: Greenwood, 1998), 164–65.

49. Takaki, *Strangers from a Different Shore*, 212–29, 186–293.

50. Schlesinger, *The Disuniting of America*, 23–24, 65.

51. Glazer, *We Are All Multiculturalists Now*, 12–121, 147–61.

52. Schlesinger, *The Disuniting of America*, 95–96.

53. Glazer, *We Are All Multiculturalists Now*, 120–21.

54. Glazer, *We Are All Multiculturalists Now*, 91–93.

55. Glazer, *We Are All Multiculturalists Now*, 93–94.

56. Glazer, *We Are All Multiculturalists Now*, 120–21.

57. George Yancey, *Beyond Racial Gridlock: Embracing Mutual Responsibility* (Downers Grove, Ill.: Intervarsity Press, 2006).

58. Yancey, *Beyond Racial Gridlock*, 29–40.

59. Yancey, *Beyond Racial Gridlock*, 41–52.

60. Yancey, *Beyond Racial Gridlock*, 64–74.

61. C. Vann Woodward, *The Strange Career of Jim Crow* (Oxford: Oxford University Press, 2001).

62. Kenneth Stampp, *The Peculiar Institution: Slavery in the Ante-Bellum South* (New York: Vintage, 1989).

63. Winthrop Jordan, *The White Man's Burden: Historical Origins of Racism in the United States* (Chapel Hill, N.C.: University of North Carolina Press, 1995); Jordan, *White Over Black: American Attitudes Towards the Negro, 1550–1812* (Chapel Hill, N.C.: University of North Carolina Press, 1995).

64. Paula S. Rothenberg, *White Privilege: Essential Readings on the Other Side of Racism* (New York: Worth Publishers, 2004).

65. Frances E. Kendall, *Understanding White Privilege: Creating Pathways to Authentic Relationships across Race* (New York: Routledge, 2002).

66. Michelle Fine, *Off White: Readings in Power, Privilege, and Resistance* (New York: Routledge, 2004).

67. Robert Jensen, *The Heart of Whiteness: Confronting Race, Racism, and White Privilege* (San Francisco: City Lights Publisher, 2005).

68. Howard, *We Can't Teach What We Don't Know*.

69. Lani Guinier and Gerald Torres, *The Miner's Canary: Enlisting Race, Resisting Power* (Cambridge, Mass.: Harvard University Press, 2002).

70. Kimberlé Crenshaw, Neil Gotanda, Gary Peller, and Kendall Thomas, eds., *Critical Race Theory: The Key Writings That Formed the Movement* (New York: New Press, 1996).

71. Derrick Bell, *Faces at the Bottom of the Well: The Permanence of Racism* (New York: Basic Books, 1989); Bell, *And We Are Not Saved: The Elusive Quest for Racial Justice* (New York: Basic Books, 1992).

72. Richard Delgado, *Critical Race Theory: The Cutting Edge* (Philadelphia: Temple University Press, 1999); Delgado, *Critical White Studies: Looking behind the Mirror* (Philadelphia: Temple University Press, 1997).

73. Angela Harris, *Critical Race Theory: An Introduction* (New York: New York University Press, 2001).

74. Yancey, *Beyond Racial Gridlock*, 53–63.

75. John Fernandez, *The Diversity Advantage: How American Business Can Outperform Japanese and European Companies in the Global Marketplace* (New York: Lexington, 1993); Fernandez, *Managing a Diverse Work Force: Regaining the Competitive Edge* (Lexington, Mass.: Lexington Books, 1971); Fernandez, *Race, Gender and Rhetoric: The True State of Race and Gender Relations in Corporate America* (New York: McGraw-Hill, 1999).

76. James Banks, *Multicultural Education: Issues and Perspectives* (New York: Wiley, 2002); Banks, *Cultural Diversity and Education: Foundations, Curriculum, and Teaching* (Boston: Allyn and Bacon, 2005).

77. Yancey, *Beyond Racial Conflict*, 57–59, 61–63.

78. Weimin Mo and Wenju Shen, "Accuracy Is Not Enough: The Role of Cultural Values in the Authenticity of Picture Books," in *Stories Matter: The Complexity of Cultural Authenticity in Children's Literature*, eds. Dana L. Fox and Kathy G. Short (Urbana, Ill.: National Council for the Teaching of English, 2003), 202–3.

79. Charlemae Rollins, et. al., *We Build Together: A Reader's Guide to Negro Life and Literature for Elementary and High School Use* (Champaign, Ill.: National Council of Teachers of English, 1941, 1954, 1967); Augusta Baker, *Books about Negro Life for Children* (New York: New York Public Library, 1963).

80. Deborah Kutenplon and Ellen Olmstead, *Young Adult Fiction by African American Writers, 1968–1993* (New York: Garland, 1996); Barbara Thrash Murphy, *Black Authors and Illustrators of Books for Children and Young Adults: A Biographical Dictionary* (New York: Garland, 1999); Donna Rand, Toni Trent Parker, and Sheila Foster, *Black Books Galore! Guide to Great African American Children's Books* (Stamford, Conn.: Wiley, 1998).

81. Karen Patricia Smith, *African American Voices in Young Adult Literature: Tradition, Transition, Transformation* (Metuchen, N.J.: Scarecrow, 1994); Rudine Sims Bishop, *Shadow and Substance: Afro-American Experience in Contemporary Children's Fiction* (Urbana, Ill.: National Council of Teachers of English, 1982); Dianne Johnson, *Telling Tales: The Pedagogy and Promise of African American Literature for Youth* (New York: Greenwood, 1990).

2

A History of U.S. Multicultural Children's Literature

MULTICULTURAL AND ETHNIC CHILDREN'S LITERATURE: ANOTHER ROSE FROM CONCRETE?

The late rap artist Tupac Shakur wrote a poem entitled "The Rose That Grew from Concrete."[1] This title may very well describe the best of rap and hip-hop music, which emerged in the 1980s after Proposition 13 in California and similar initiatives around the country caused cuts in school funding, which led to the end of arts education in many urban schools. Young people without access to music education learned to play instruments by ear if they were especially talented. Otherwise, they took their own speech and poetry, some LPs and a turntable, and made music anyhow! Thus were rap and hip-hop music born.

Multicultural and ethnic literature in the United States also emerged out of a difficult climate. The history of this literature cannot be divorced either from the general and educational histories of diverse peoples or from cultural stereotypes existing in books, texts, and all aspects of culture and the media. Developments before and during the nineteenth century are still affecting us in the twenty-first!

The general world of children's literature can be viewed as a tree with many roots and branches. The trunk is an integrated one encompassing children's, young adult, and adult literature; formal education; libraries; and all aspects of publishing, media, and culture. The roots include Western philosophical and religious traditions, Western folklore and legends, and some non-Western roots influencing the West, such as the Bible. Unfortunately, they also include personal and structural racism and the stereotyping of people.

The tree of children's literature has many branches. Some of these branches, such as the focus on stereotypes, cultural authenticity, socially conscious literature, and the qualifications of writers and illustrators, are reactions to the past as well as to the present. Other branches are reactions to the reactions, and they include criticism of the excesses of multiculturalism as well as the promotion of core curricula and cultural literacy. Chapter 3 will discuss current issues directly related to historical developments in the early nineteenth and twentieth centuries, including educational discrimination and cultural stereotyping, phenomena that reinforced each other. This chapter will further define and describe these two issues before portraying the history of this literature.

Other vestiges of the nineteenth and early twentieth centuries include an ongoing tension between American ideals and realities, and issues of self-perception and the perception of others—all related to the issues of self-esteem and stereotyping. There has always been a contradiction between the democratic ideals of the United States and its treatment of ethnic peoples, especially people of color. A few leaders, such as Martin Luther King Jr. and César Chávez, were able to draw on these ideals to advocate better treatment of all people, with some degree of success. The U.S. educational system has been in a similar dilemma. Do schools exist to promote democracy and upward mobility, or are they to preserve the status quo?

In spite of this tension, multicultural and ethnic children's literature has definitely emerged, especially during the last forty years. The creators and promoters of this literature have always had several goals—to tell their own stories, to share their cultures and histories with a variety of young people, and more indirectly, to address and counteract cultural stereotypes. Conveying accurate and authentic portrayals of cultures has always been important to these individuals.

TALES IN AND OUT OF SCHOOL:
EDUCATIONAL HISTORIES

Diane Ravitch states that the United States has always had a wide variety of racial, ethnic, and religious minorities. Members of these groups have been extremely diverse, and specific groups were treated differently over time and in different places. In addition, not all groups attended public schools.[2]

This is all true. However, there were still consistent patterns in the treatment of particular groups. Like a theme in several movements of a symphony, certain occurrences repeat over and over. Our educational system was designed for white children, especially native-born children of western European and Protestant descent. Other European immigrants were encouraged to assimilate and were allowed to privately maintain their own cultures, but at their own expense.

Descendents of non-Europeans, on the other hand, were originally barred from schools altogether, even when they paid taxes. Private schools for northern black children in the early nineteenth century and similar southern schools established during Reconstruction were sometimes attacked by mobs. Legislation in San Francisco from 1871 to 1885 kept Chinese children out of public schools altogether.

Before 1954, when children of color did attend school, they would often be segregated, either in separate schools or in separate classes in integrated buildings. There was limited integration in some isolated northern and western towns with relatively few children, but this was rare.

The schools were separate, but hardly equal. Students of color attending segregated schools had inferior facilities, secondhand textbooks, poor funding (or misappropriation of funds in some cases), and less-qualified teachers. Some students, particularly in the rural South, also had shorter school years because they were expected to work in the cotton fields. Educators used "advising" and a variety of tests to either eliminate students or discourage them from academic courses or from college. Students of color were often tracked into vocational courses at the high school and college level.

These students' cultures and languages were also dismissed, downplayed, and discouraged in a variety of ways. Until the mid-twentieth century, their cultures were either ignored in texts or described as inferior. Native American children were separated from their original cultures as much as possible through the use of missions in Spanish colonial areas, "praying villages" in colonial New England and upstate New York, and, most of all, U.S.-sponsored boarding schools at the turn of the twentieth century. African Americans at first did not attend formal schools, but were separated from their original cultures through practices occurring during the Middle Passage and slavery.

For the most part, there were few educators from racial minority groups. One exception to this tendency was the large number of black educators teaching in southern segregated schools. Once these schools were integrated, many of these professionals were either downgraded or dismissed. In addition, parents and community leaders of color had little say in how their children were educated. Their views were ignored, for the most part.

People of color resisted all of these trends. When totally excluded from public education, they would use their own often meager funds to educate their own children. They accepted separate schools where there were no alternatives. Where the exclusion was legal or de jure, they went to court and sued. People of color would agitate for common schools for *everybody* in the North before the Civil War, and in the South and other parts of the country afterward.[3] This section will briefly describe educational experiences of white, Native American, African American, Latino/a, and some Asian American children from colonial times to the Supreme Court decision *Brown v. Board of Education* in 1954.

General Developments before the Twentieth Century

English and other colonists who settled the original thirteen colonies of the United States were influenced by both Renaissance classical humanism and Protestant teachings and traditions from the Reformation (except for those in Maryland, a Catholic colony). They brought two kinds of schools from Europe that were on totally different tracks—vernacular schools for common people and Latin grammar schools and colleges to train elite males for secondary schools and college. The vernacular schools emphasized reading, writing, arithmetic, and basic religious doctrine. The Latin schools combined classical European studies with religious training.[4]

By the time of the American Revolution, several systems of education had emerged in these colonies. New Englanders had a consensus about what knowledge should be passed on to their children, and they stressed organized education. The Middle Atlantic colonies were settled by people of different religions and ethnicities, so, while people established schools locally, there was no network of town or district schools. The southern states had plantation economies with sparse and scattered populations, and this discouraged the establishment of formal schools. The dominant social class (the planters) saw education as a private matter only. It was something mostly for the white, male elite. This would have major implications for later developments. As Anglo Americans moved westward, vernacular schools that did not lead to higher education were replaced by common schools that could and did. These schools were designed to educate all children in a community and to lead them to secondary and eventually university education, if desired.[5]

Common schools developed in the United States between 1820 and 1860. They were locally controlled, tax-supported elementary schools that were supposed to be open to all children living in a district, and they offered a common curriculum. They were especially prominent in New England and other northern states. Middle Atlantic states worked more with private and parochial schools, and southern states did not start common schools until after the Civil War.[6] Common schools served a dual role. They were "conduits of upward social and economic mobility," and they served as a means of social control by stressing and imposing the language and ideological outlook of the dominant group.[7]

There were several forms of secondary schools in the nineteenth century. The first were grammar schools established to prepare elite boys for college. Students would attend these after learning to read and write in English, and the curriculum was based on the Greek and Latin languages. Grammar schools were replaced by the academy, which emphasized instruction in English as well as practical and scientific subjects. They were profit-making organizations offering subjects demanded by the public[8] and could be compared to contemporary proprietary postsecondary trade schools.

Modern high schools emerged in the United States after the Civil War and replaced the academy. Like modern libraries, they were the result of industrialization and urbanization, and reflected the need for better-educated workers. High schools became the links between common schools and public universities, and their curricula would later combine academic with vocational courses.[9]

Native Americans and Education

The general and educational history of Native Americans is especially complex. Most indigenous peoples were driven west of the Mississippi River, and by the twentieth century, they were largely confined to reservations. Yet they were expected to assimilate into U.S. society and forget their own cultures.

Before Europeans came to the western hemisphere, young indigenous people informally learned their "tribal language, customs, values, traditions and ethics" by observing and imitating their elders. The Europeans introduced several forms of education to Native Americans, such as mission schools and federal schools, which included the notorious boarding schools of the late nineteenth and early twentieth centuries. A few colleges that were established to educate others, such as Dartmouth College and Hampton University, included the education of Native Americans as part of their early missions. The purpose of much of this education was to separate indigenous people from their own cultures. Boarding schools away from home were especially devastating. Some graduates of these programs were unable to fit in either in Western society or in their own original cultures. An important difference between Native education and U.S. education in general at this time was how they were managed. Most formal education for indigenous people during this time was centrally controlled by the federal government with little input encouraged from indigenous adults and elders. This contrasts sharply with the U.S. educational system, under local control with little input from the federal government. All of these things would change in the mid-twentieth century.[10]

African Americans and Education

Before the Western slave trade, African youth informally learned about their cultures from their elders, including griots, who recited the history of the village. The effects of the Middle Passage and of Western slavery would be devastating. When captured, Africans were mixed with people of other tribes and forbidden to do any drumming, making it extremely difficult for them to communicate. Once they were slaves in the West, their literacy was not only discouraged, but legally forbidden in most U.S. slave states.[11] In addition, slave families could be separated at any time by the selling of spouses, children, and parents.

While slavery was a national system, most black people in the North were gradually freed after the American Revolution. However, even as free people they were often banned from common schools. They had to start their own schools, attend public segregated schools, tutor children privately, or do without.[12] African American parents and leaders went to court during this period to sue for integrated schools. This prefigured similar battles that would take place nationally a century later.

There were no common schools for anybody in the South until after the Civil War. African Americans serving as delegates to state constitutional conventions during Reconstruction advocated for compulsory common schools for everybody.[13] During this time, the federal Freedman's Bureau, Congregational missionaries (mostly from New England), and northern black churches and denominations moved south to start schools. Newly independent southern black churches also worked with other groups to start schools, and a number of these schools became private colleges. Many of the early colleges stressed a curriculum in the liberal arts.

However, the end of Reconstruction in 1876 marked the beginning of a very difficult period for southern African Americans, leading to civil rights reversals and legal segregation. As public schools developed in this region, they were segregated and far from equal. Hampton Institute and, later, Tuskegee Institute were established as vocational institutions, and black land-grant institutions in the southern states would develop a similar mission. Booker T. Washington and W. E. B. DuBois debated whether a vocational or a liberal arts education would be best for black students, and most northern philanthropists and southern whites were more supportive of the former. Public schools in the South and some other areas would be legally segregated until the *Brown v. Board of Education* decision of 1954.[14] De facto segregation continued to exist in the North and West. As neighborhoods were segregated, so were schools. In some places, there was segregation of classes within integrated buildings. Again, this was not equal.

Latino/as and Education

While England and France colonized most of North America north of Mexico, Spain colonized most of South America, Central America, Mexico, and some Caribbean islands, as well as the present-day U.S. states of California, Arizona, New Mexico, Texas, Florida, Nevada, Utah, California, and parts of Colorado and Wyoming. The Spanish had a racial hierarchy consisting of Europeans from Spain at the top, followed by criollos, or Europeans born in the "New World"; Native Americans; people of African descent; and mestizos—people of Spanish and indigenous descent. In spite of their varied, ambiguous, and "nebulous legal and political status" during the Spanish colonial period, mestizos would eventually become the major population in Latin America. The Spanish designed three kinds of education—settlers' schools, missions, and nonformal education.[15]

The settlers' schools were established to provide formal education for cultural transfer. They were originally only for children of Spanish leaders, but eventually they included criollos and some mestizos. Their curriculum was a combination of classical and Roman Catholic learning. They were strikingly similar to Latin grammar schools in the English colonies.[16]

The most prevalent form of education consisted of missions and mission schools. This form of education was for indigenous people and their children *only*. Missions were designed to replace Native American cultures with the Spanish language, Roman Catholic faith, and European customs, and they emphasized vocational education.[17] Missions can be compared to the praying villages established by some New England and New York colonists, and to boarding schools established by the U.S. government at the turn of the twentieth century. Nonformal education was also very popular in New Spain, especially in isolated areas. People would read books on their own and sometimes share information.[18]

Most formal education in the Spanish colonies was closely tied to the church. This would change as countries became independent. For example, schools in most of Mexico secularized after independence in 1821.[19] Mexican independence also marked the end of state-sponsored religious missions and brought a limited rise in public education. The closing of missions impeded the development of a strong public school system, however. Constitutional guarantees were in place, but not funding.[20] This was especially problematic in the northern frontier states of California, Texas, and New Mexico, which at that time included present-day Arizona.[21]

In the years 1821–1848, students living in U.S. states that were then northern Mexico were educated mostly at home, at a neighbor's house, or in private or public schools. Children from elite families continued their education in the United States, England, France, and the Sandwich Islands. In Texas, San Antonio created and funded public schools, and Lancaster Plan schools were established for other major cities and towns in that province. In these schools, advanced students were trained to "monitor" younger students. California had a "patchwork system" of schools in the early 1820s. By 1833, the state legally required all towns to establish primary schools. Initiatives for public education in that state came from the top. Nonformal education was used much more in rural New Mexico, even though there was some concern about the qualifications and performance of teachers.[22]

After 1848, as a result of the Mexican-American War, Mexican Americans were suddenly immigrants in a new land—without leaving home! They were basically a conquered people. The results included land loss; a major, if gradual, loss of power; more racialization; and educational discrimination. As a country, Mexico lost half of its land to the United States, and as individuals, most Mexicans in the United States also lost their lands. They were "racialized" in the sense that only Mexicans who were considered white could be eligible to vote. Nonwhites were barred from practicing law, becoming naturalized citizens, marrying Anglos, and attending integrated schools. Existing laws such as the Treaty of Guadalupe Hidalgo were ignored.[23]

The first English-only laws were passed in Texas in 1856, but German immigrants and Tejanos (Mexican Americans from Texas) were allowed to continue to use their respective languages until the 1880s. The presence of the Spanish language and the use of Tejano teachers continued throughout the nineteenth century, especially in rural areas.[24] Catholic and Protestant parochial schools and other private schools played important and positive roles in the education of Tejano children, and the line between public and private schools was sometimes blurred. By the twentieth century, separate Mexican American public schools were also being created.

Tejanos and Californios (Mexican Americans from California) wanted both to maintain Spanish and to learn English. In the early years, Californios still wielded considerable influence in the community. However, the state passed English-only legislation for public schools in 1855. Anglo parents refused to send their children to schools that included the Spanish language. In response, some Mexican American parents enrolled their children in parochial schools that did include Spanish. Some of these schools had been supplied with public funds from the state, but this also stopped in 1855. Latino/a children in California were also racialized in this period. Legislation mandating the segregation of "Negros, Mongolians, and Indians" affected Californios as well.[25]

Hispanos in New Mexico were able to preserve both the Spanish language and blended private and public schools longer than their counterparts in Texas or California. Arizona was part of New Mexico until 1864, and Hispanics and Native Americans greatly outnumbered Anglos until the late 1880s. Public schools did not really form there until the 1870s.

When Arizona first created its education laws as a separate territory, Mexican Americans were part of the power structure, and the state was relatively liberal about bilingualism until the late nineteenth century. By the twentieth century, tension arose between racial groups, and public schools were segregated. The Mexican American community maintained Spanish-language newspapers and their own organizations.[26]

Although Arizona schools secularized by the mid-1870s, New Mexico's public schools maintained ties with both the Spanish language and the Catholic Church for a long time. Catholic influences in public schools and the question of whether school governance should be centralized (as promoted by Anglos) or localized (as promoted by Hispanos) were sources of major tensions between Hispanos and Anglos in New Mexico. Hispanos dominated school leadership for a long time, which enabled schools to provide instruction in Spanish or in both English and Spanish longer than elsewhere.[27]

After 1900, new linguistic and cultural policies increasingly segregated Mexican American children in much of the Southwest and deprived them of equal opportunity. This was usually in the form of de facto not de jure segregation. Excuses used to justify segregation include Latino/a students' poor English language scores or low scores on other tests. Compulsory school attendance was also not enforced for Mexican American children. Where segregation occurred, most resources went to white schools.[28] Some students also faced classroom harassment and other forms of blatant racism.[29]

As a result of the Spanish-American War of 1898, the United States colonized Puerto Rico and governed Cuba as a protectorate. These and other countries were transferred from one colonial power to another. U.S. government officials believed that promoting public schools in these countries and teaching students the English language would "convince Puerto Ricans and Cubans of the superiority of American culture and democracy."[30]

Americanization of both teachers and students was heavily promoted in Puerto Rico. From 1915 to 1928, Spanish was the language of instruction in the first four grades, and English was taught as a separate subject in the middle grades. In 1926, experts from Columbia University recommended continuing this approach for the first eight grades and then teaching *in* English in high schools. However, educators followed the advice of the Brookings Institution instead and implemented intensive English from the earliest grades. This instruction harmed rather than helped most students, who learned very poor English. Their Spanish was not promoted or maintained.[31]

The University of Puerto Rico was created during this time and had an emphasis on teacher training and agricultural and mechanical arts. It was very similar to state and vocational colleges for African Americans. A few students were also sent from Puerto Rico to U.S. colleges—usually Hampton or Tuskegee.[32]

In the case of Cuba, Americans decided to focus on Americanizing the teachers, not necessarily the students (at least not directly). Approximately twenty-five hundred Cuban teachers traveled to the United States for exposure to U.S. ideas and customs. Most came from elite families. White Cubans were sent to Harvard, New York State Normal School at New Paltz, and similar schools. Afro-Cubans and Cubans of mixed race had more difficulty getting scholarships, and when they did, they were sent to schools such as Hampton and Tuskegee, where they were also more welcomed.[33]

Some Puerto Ricans had lived on the U.S. mainland since the nineteenth century, but others started emigrating there en masse after World War II. Most settled in the New York City area and in other parts of the Northeast. When Puerto Rican children first attended schools in large numbers in New York City, they were "viewed as defective, in need of remedial education, and of less intelligence than their white counterparts." A few Puerto Rican substitute auxiliary teachers (SATs) helped students in the 1940s and 1950s by introducing alternative methods of teaching English as a second language.[34]

Asian Americans and Education: Japanese Americans and Chinese Americans in California

Among the first Asian Americans to come to the continental United States were Chinese and Japanese immigrants who settled in California and in other western states. Chinese men came to California in the 1850s and 1860s to take advantage of the gold rush and other economic opportunities. They were hoping to make enough money to eventually return to China as wealthy men, and to support their families in the meantime. They were welcomed at first, but the public turned against them quickly with a series of hostile legislative acts. This included the Foreign Miner's Tax in 1852, an 1854 California court decision forbidding non-whites from testifying against white people in court, a series of anti-Chinese and anti-Asian laws between 1855 and 1862, and the Chinese Exclusion Act in 1882, 1892, and 1902. A national immigration law was passed in 1924 forbidding the entry of aliens ineligible for citizenship, automatically excluding most people of color. Chinese immigrants were also gradually driven into a limited number of dead-end jobs.[35]

Most of the early Chinese immigrants were either bachelors or married men who left their families in China. Some of them eventually returned to their families, but most were unable to do this. For the most part, they were also unable to bring their wives, send for them later, or marry women from the United States. Most lived and died as bachelors. Chinatowns did not have large numbers of children or families until the 1920s.[36]

Japanese immigrants (the Issei) came to California in the 1890s. Unlike the Chinese, many of them either brought wives with them or sent for them later. Most early Japanese Americans also tried a variety of occupations and were driven from most of them by hostile whites. In the early twentieth century, Issei were becoming successful as store owners and farmers. Like the Chinese Americans before them, they would also face discriminatory legislation. In 1907 the California legislature proposed laws that would deny landownership to Japanese immigrants. It passed a series of increasingly stringent landownership legislation between 1913 and 1923. Meanwhile, the Issei were encouraging their children, the Nisei, to be well educated about both the West and Japan. They hoped that the Nisei, as English-speaking citizens, would have opportunities denied their Issei parents.[37] Chinese Americans also had similar goals for their children.[38]

A series of laws were also passed in California (and elsewhere) to restrict educational opportunities of Asian American children. In 1859, the San Francisco Board of Education closed a public school for Chinese children, in spite of the fact that their parents were paying taxes. A state law was passed in 1860 to exclude Asians, Native Americans, and African Americans from white public schools in California. Between 1871 and 1885, Chinese children were the only group to be totally denied a state-supported education in California. In 1884, Joseph and Mary Tape successfully sued the San Francisco Board of Education. After this court case, the school board lobbied for a separate school system for Chinese children.[39]

Once *Plessy v. Ferguson* was decided by the Supreme Court in 1896, racially segregated schools were legal all over the country.[40] In 1906, the San Francisco Board of Education directed all principals to send Chinese, Japanese, and Korean students to a separate "Oriental School." When parents protested, President Theodore Roosevelt mediated this dispute with the mayor of San Francisco and members of the Board of Education. As a result, the Japanese Americans were exempted from this ordinance, but President Roosevelt used the dispute as an opportunity to strongly restrict all immigration from Japan.[41] Outside of California, the treatment of Asian American students varied. Some attended mostly white schools and were tolerated as long as there was no objection in the community, but Asian American students could be expelled—for excelling![42]

In the years before World War II, many Chinese Americans and Japanese Americans went to predominantly white colleges, but most had difficulty finding jobs in their fields and outside their ethnic communities upon gradua-tion.[43] This situation would not begin to change until after the war.

European Immigrants and Americanization

Many European immigrants came to the United States in the years 1880–1924, and most of them were from eastern and southern Europe. They and their children were the intended audience for Americanization programs designed to teach the English language, citizenship information, U.S. history, literacy, and other information useful in adjusting to America. Americaniza-tion activities were led by public schools and libraries, as well as by im-migrants themselves and their media and organizations. In fact, immigrants started night schools to become literate in English.[44]

This form of outreach was quite benign at first, but became more hos-tile and coercive during and right after World War I. Contributing factors included a fear that immigrants might be subversive, the existence of English-only and anti-foreign legislation, and some anti-German feeling. The worst aspects of Americanization included not only a requirement that immigrants learn English, but an insistence on the use of English only; ignoring or dismissing immigrants' own cultures; the use of intimidating slogans; and the suppression of ethnic media. At its best, Americaniza-tion could be welcoming and helpful, and at its worst, it could be crude and chauvinistic.[45]

LOOKING IN THE FUNHOUSE MIRROR:
CULTURAL STEREOTYPES

Until the 1960s, most books, texts, plays, and media about people of color were written and produced by white people for a white audience, and most of these materials presented derogatory stereotypes and misinformation about other ethnic groups. Relatively few writers of color were being published, and there was little opportunity to counter stereotypes in these materials.

Stereotyping of non-Europeans and Europeans from southern and eastern Europe has been occurring for centuries. It can be seen in William Shake-speare's treatment of Prospero and Caliban in his play *The Tempest* and his treatment of Shylock, a Jew, in *The Merchant of Venice*. Thomas Jefferson and George Washington were both slave-owning founding fathers caught between their beliefs in liberty and their treatment of people of color. They both were representative and indicative of ways that future Americans would deal with race.

Jefferson represents America at both its best and its worst. He was a multitalented genius who contributed to his young nation in many ways—by writing the Declaration of Independence, helping to create the Constitution, founding the University of Virginia, serving as an early ambassador to France, donating his personal library to be the foundation of the new Library of Congress, and serving as president of the United States. As president, he doubled the size of the United States through the Louisiana Purchase, and he was an early opponent of slavery.

However, Jefferson was also a committed racist who genuinely believed many stereotypes about African Americans, which he described in his work *Notes on the State of Virginia*.[46] Not only was he a slave owner, but he had African American relatives whom he could not openly acknowledge.[47] Last, Jefferson dismissed any possible intellectual achievements of African Americans. He refused to comment on the poetry of Phillis Wheatley, and did not believe that Benjamin Banneker had compiled an almanac on his own.[48] These are characteristic of attitudes that would continue through the nineteenth and twentieth century in American society, and vestiges of them still exist.

George Washington, on the other hand, may offer a more hopeful vision of the future. Originally, he was more committed to slavery than Jefferson. However, he came to respect black troops who fought in the American Revolution, and he freed a number of slaves upon his death.

By the nineteenth century, the United States was developing an integrated world of Western popular and literary culture, represented in trade and textbooks, school curricula, newspapers and magazines, church activities, and plays and other entertainment.[49] Trends in one area also appeared in others. Authors of children's books were former teachers such as William T. Adams, Lydia Maria Child, Harriet B. Stowe, and John T. Trowbridge; writers for children's magazines, such as Adams, Mark Twain, Joel Chandler Harris, Thomas Nelson Page, and Martha Finley, and former reporters like Twain and George A. Henty.[50] Teachers and librarians in the late nineteenth century were creating a canon of "classic books" through reading lists, and many of these titles reflected the racism of their time.[51] Donnarae MacCann documents these developments in her book *White Supremacy in Children's Literature: Characterizations of African Americans, 1830–1900*.[52]

She also describes in detail the writings of white defenders of slavery and abolitionists before the Civil War,[53] Northerners and Southerners throughout the nineteenth century,[54] imperialists and anti-imperialists at the turn of the twentieth century,[55] and people sympathetic to African Americans and those who were not. Before the Civil War, white authors were divided over the question of the abolition of slavery, and much later on, there was some division over colonialism and imperialism. However, almost all of the authors from this period believed in cultural stereotypes and presented them in their literature.

The late nineteenth and early twentieth centuries represent a Gilded Age, when "scientific racism" and Social Darwinism were at their peak. Wounded Knee in 1890 had marked the end of organized Native American resistance to white western expansion, and with the Supreme Court decision of *Plessy v. Ferguson* in 1896, racial segregation could now be the law of the land, and lynchings were widely tolerated. Legislation to restrict Asian immigration was in place, and more would follow. Mexico was conquered and divided in two, and the former Spanish colonies of Puerto Rico, Cuba, Guam, and the Philippines were transferred to the United States as a result of the Spanish-American War of 1898. Historian Rayford Logan later referred to this period as "The Nadir": western European and Anglo American civilizations were viewed as the best of all civilizations. Southern and eastern Europeans, and especially people of color, were viewed as having little or no culture or history, and their intellectual achievements were dismissed.

MacCann[56] shows that self-esteem was a major issue in children's literature a century ago. The self-esteem of Euro-American children, especially those from western Europe, was raised at the expense of everybody else. Internationally, this was also the case with literature defending the European colonization of the world. In the United States, after Reconstruction, both northern and southern white writers stressed the reunification of the North and South and they did so at the expense of African Americans.[57] People of color who were able to publish before the mid-twentieth century were very rare, so alternative points of view were seldom presented. Too many people of all backgrounds believed the stereotypes presented in the media, and white people used these as an excuse to discriminate against others, particularly in education. After all, it was reasoned that inferior people did not need superior education. By being deprived of good education, many people lived up (or down) to stereotypes. The two trends reinforced each other.

Other research has been conducted on stereotypes in all aspects of our cultures, especially those referring to African Americans and Native Americans. Important studies of historical stereotypes include *White Over Black: American Attitudes Towards the Negro* by Winthrop Jordan,[58] *The Black Image in the White Mind* by George M. Frederickson,[59] *Toms, Coons, Mulattoes, Mammies, and Bucks: An Interpretive History of Blacks in American Films* by Donald Bogle,[60] *They Called Them Greasers: Anglo Attitudes Towards Mexi-*

cans in Texas, 1821–1900 by Arnoldo De Leon,[61] *Native Americans as Shown on the Stage* by Eugene H. Jones,[62] and *Shadows of the Indian: Stereotypes in American Culture* by Raymond William Stedman.[63]

The Council on Interracial Books for Children did extensive studies of stereotypes of a wide variety of groups in children's literature in the 1960s and 1970s. They published several special issues of their newsletter and several books and research guides on this topic. This organization conducted the earliest studies on some groups. There have also been a number of books and articles specifically on the image of Native Americans in children's books from the 1970s on. Other early works on stereotyping in children's literature are *The Black American in Books for Children*[64] and *Cultural Conformity in Books For Children,* both by MacCann and Gloria Woodard.[65] The second book is about the stereotyping of a variety of groups.

Some research has also been conducted on cultural stereotyping and the lack of diversity in the modern media in general, including plays, movies, television programs, advertising, and the press. A historical study of developments up to 1980s is *Minorities and Media: Diversity and the End of Mass Communication* by Clint C. Wilson II and Félix Gutiérrez.[66] A more recent text of essays and news reports on this subject is *Facing Difference: Race, Gender, and Mass Media* edited by Shirley Biagi and Marilyn Kern-Foxworth.[67]

The issues of cultural stereotyping and the self-esteem of children and their elders are major concerns that still affect everybody in the fields of youth literature and education. When people of color and their supporters complain of stereotypes in children's literature or textbooks, they are reacting to current literature, to what they have experienced in their own pasts, and to the history described above. The controversial issues to be discussed in the next chapter—stereotypes, criteria for cultural authenticity, "socially conscious" and "melting-pot" books, and the question of who is qualified to write on whom—are all connected to this past. So are the mainstream reactions that are critical of multiculturalism and committed to cultural literacy. Criticism of multiculturalism is especially pointed on the issues of the self-esteem of children of color, as well as the importance of role models for all children. Few people of any background, opinion, or political persuasion seem to realize how all of these contemporary issues are tied to the past.

Intellectuals of color have not been fully recognized or acknowledged by their critics. This also has roots in the past, as exemplified by Thomas Jefferson's dismissal of the works of Wheatley and Banneker two centuries ago. One hundred years ago, most ethnic people were presented as intellectually and morally deficient. Today, too many scholars still underestimate the work of black intellectuals, and no one seems to be aware of the work of other scholars of color. All of these issues will be further discussed in chapters 3 and 4.

However, these problems and issues do not take away from the considerable progress made in this field, especially during the last forty years. The rest of this chapter will describe the history of multicultural and ethnic literature from the late nineteenth century to the present. Some attention will also be paid to the recent history of multiculturalism in school curricula.

PIONEERS, PRECURSORS, AND PROPHETS IN THE WILDERNESS: ETHNIC CHILDREN'S LITERATURE BEFORE 1940

The earliest materials for children by authors of color were produced by independent Native Americans and African Americans in the late nineteenth and early twentieth centuries. A number of Native American authors wrote directly for young people. Examples include Charles Eastman, Francis La Flesche, Luther Standing Bear, Arthur Caswell Parker, and later D'Arcy McNickle. These authors were among the most successful early graduates of mission schools and boarding schools, and they also had a grounding in their original cultures. All of these people lived in two worlds and wrote to pass on their cultures to their own children, as well as to explain their cultures to a more general audience.

They represented roughly three generations. Eastman, La Flesche, and Standing Bear were all born in the 1850s and 1860s, and they all died during the 1930s. Parker lived from 1881 to 1955. The youngest of these authors, D'Arcy McNickle, was a contemporary of several other people who will be described in this chapter—Pura Belpré, Langston Hughes, Arna Bontemps, Charlemae Rollins, and Lorenz Graham. McNickle lived from 1904 to 1977 and observed and participated in many positive developments during this time.

Charles Alexander Eastman, also known as Ohiyesa, was a Santee Sioux doctor who treated wounded Native Americans at Wounded Knee in 1890, immediately after the massacre. He lived a traditional indigenous lifestyle until he was fifteen years old. That year, Eastman and his father converted to Christianity, and Eastman agreed to go to a mission school that was away from his tribe. After graduating from this school, he attended and graduated from Dartmouth College and the medical school at Boston University. Over the years, he was involved in many activities, both to help his own people and to promote his culture to others.[68]

His books centered on several themes. A major one was his own traditional boyhood. He wrote several books about this, including *Indian Boyhood*, *Old Indian Days*, and *From the Deep Woods to Civilization: Chapters in the Au-*

tobiography of an Indian. Eastman's other works were on Native American folklore (*Wigwam Evenings: Sioux Folk Tales Retold*), philosophy (*Soul of the Indian*), culture (*Indian Scout Craft and Lore*), and history (*Indian Heroes and Great Chieftains*). Many of these themes were repeated in works by other indigenous writers then and later.

Francis La Flesche (who was Omaha) is best known as an anthropologist and linguist active in the late nineteenth century who wrote scholarly works for adults, such as *Dictionary of the Osage Language.* He wrote several books for the young, but it appears that most of those were not published until after his death. They include *Ke-Ma-Ha: The Omaha Stories of Francis La Flesche*, *The Omaha Tribe*, and *The Middle Five*, the story of five Native American children at a mission school.

Luther Standing Bear, a Lakota Sioux, adopted his name after entering the Carlisle Indian School in Pennsylvania. He eventually became the chief of his tribe. His works, published in the 1920s and 1930s, include *Stories of the Sioux*, *Land of the Spotted Eagle* (a history of the Sioux), *My People the Sioux*, and *My Indian Boyhood*, which was written especially for the young. It captures the routine everyday life of Sioux people during that time.

Arthur Parker, who was Iroquois-Seneca, was from the state of New York. He has been viewed as both an advocate for Native Americans and an assimilationist. His books, which were mostly first published in the 1920s, include *Sunny Wunny: Seneca Indian Tales*, *Seneca Myths and Folktales*, *Red Jacket, Seneca Chief*, and *The Indian How Book*, which explained how and why Native Americans did a variety of activities.

D'Arcy McNickle, an enrolled member of the Montana Flathead tribe, started his career during this time, and would be very active until the mid-1970s. He was a respected anthropologist who worked closely with John Collier, who helped to create the "Indian New Deal" in the 1930s. As an early "pan-Indianist," he was a founding member of the National Congress of American Indians, and in 1971, he became the first director of the Newberry Library's Center for the History of the American Indian. The D'Arcy Mc-Nickle Center for American Indian History at this library is now named after him. McNickle published a novel approximately every twenty years—*The Surrounded* in 1936, *Runner in the Sun* in 1954, and *Wind from an Enemy Sky* in 1978. He also published biographies and histories for young people, as well as more scholarly works for adults.

African Americans also had a number of initiatives during this time. In the period between 1880 and 1894, Mrs. A. E. Johnson published *The Joy*, the first periodical for black children. She also published two novels about white children, *Clarence and Corinne, or God's Way* and *The Hazleby Family*. During the 1890s, the National Baptist Publishing Board and the African

Methodist Episcopal Church produced the first Sunday school literature for black children. In 1905, Silas X. Floyd published *Floyd's Flowers or Duty and Beauty for Colored Children*.[69]

W. E. B. DuBois and Carter G. Woodson established black publishing houses in the 1920s and 1930s, respectively. DuBois and Augustus G. Dill started the company DuBois and Dill, which produced *The Brownies Book*, the second periodical for black children, and several titles on African American history. *The Brownies Book* did not last long, but it would prove to be very influential. The teenage Langston Hughes would publish some of his first pieces in this periodical, and Arna Bontemps was also a devoted reader.[70] Fauset, Hughes, and Bontemps were later very active in the Harlem Renaissance.

Carter G. Woodson, who is considered to be the father of black history, started the Association for the Study of Negro (now African American) Life and History, established Negro History Week (now Black History Month), and founded Associated Publishers, which to this day publishes *The Journal of African American History* and the *Black History Bulletin*. In the early days, Woodson wrote and published a number of books on poetry, history, folklore, and music reflecting the pan-African experience. One memorable work is *African Heroes and Heroines*. His books were used in black schools and churches, especially in the South.[71]

The first African American writers to be published by mainstream publishers were Arna Bontemps and Langston Hughes. The lifelong friends wrote and published together *Popo and Fifina*, a book about Haitian children, in 1932. Bontemps, who has been referred to as the father of modern black children's literature, continued to create a variety of books for children until his death in 1973.[72] He also wrote for adults and directed the Fisk University Library for many years.

Pura Belpré, who was originally from Puerto Rico, was the first Latina librarian to work for the New York Public Library (NYPL), and the first Latina in the United States to publish and write for children. She began her career at NYPL in the 1920s and was there until she married in 1944. During this time, she pioneered in the field of multicultural librarianship by building collections of Spanish-language books, working with community agencies and organizations, and giving bilingual story hours and other programs. She was also known as a puppeteer. During the 1920s, she started to write down stories that she told, and published her first book, *Pérez and Martina*, in 1932.[73]

During her marriage, from 1944 to 1960, Belpré produced many other books of folklore with an emphasis on tales from Puerto Rico. From 1960 to 1968, after her husband died, she returned to the NYPL as the Spanish children's specialist, and after she retired in 1968, she worked with the South

Bronx Library Project, helped establish the Archivo Documentacion Puertor-riqueña, and developed children's programs at the Museo del Barrio. The Pura Belpré Award and a school are named after her.[74]

Another librarian with a long and varied career was Augusta Baker, who started her career at NYPL in 1937 and retired from there in 1974. In the early years (1937–1954), she established and built the James Weldon Johnson Memorial Collection of Children's Books at the 135th Street Branch (later the Countee Cullen Branch). This collection of books that accurately portray black children still exists. She would later initiate a series of bibliographies based on this collection.

Baker also perfected her storytelling skills, which would strongly affect the rest of her career and life. From 1954 to 1961, she served as assistant coordinator of Children's Services for the NYPL system, becoming the first administrator of color in the system, and served as coordinator of Children's Services from 1961 to 1974. During this time and afterward, Baker wrote several collections of folklore, as well as the textbook *Storytelling: Art and Technique* with Ellin Green. Later in life (1980–1994), Baker served as the storyteller-in-residence at the University of South Carolina. A(ugusta) Bak-er's Dozen: An Annual Celebration of Stories and a collection of children's books, which are both at the University of South Carolina, have been named for her.[75]

In the 1920s and 1930s, a reform movement affected Native American schools. During the 1920s, the Brookings Institution, under the direction of Dr. Lewis Meriam, produced a report, *The Problem of Indian Administration*, that highlighted the problems of the Bureau of Indian Affairs, with board-ing schools receiving the most criticism. The report criticized the schools' curricula, their emphasis on vocational training for obsolete jobs, and their emphasis on assimilation. In the 1930s, John Collier, director of the Bureau of Indian Affairs, instituted several reforms, including the use of some bi-lingual books, the promotion of bilingual education, the establishment of community day schools, and the closing of some boarding schools. However, true and more thorough reforms did not take place until the 1960s, 1970s, and 1980s.[76]

It was during this time that reading series and other books were pro-duced by Ann Nolan Clark and other white writers and editors who had either taught in Native American schools or who worked as linguists on Native American reservations. Community leaders were consulted, and young Native American artists illustrated the books. Some of these young people later became famous major artists in their own right. In some cases, Native American students themselves wrote booklets. White teach-ers and linguists also wrote down stories told by students and community members. Some of the stories were traditional, and some attempted to portray the daily lives of contemporary Native American children. Teams of writers and illustrators who were supervised by Clark created three series of readers for the Diné (Navajo), the Lakota and Dakota Sioux, and the Pueblo nations.[77]

This literature has not been without controversy, however. It was intended both to confirm aspects of Native American cultures and to promote the assimilation of indigenous peoples into mainstream society, and some see the second goal as a form of colonialism. Written traditional stories have also been viewed as a shorthand, not a substitute, for the oral versions, and some indigenous professionals and scholars have been concerned that writing these stories down could affect oral traditions in negative ways. Today, some Native American tribes produce their own materials, but this is done in order to actively preserve their languages and cultures, not necessarily to promote assimilation.[78]

By 1940, Native Americans and African Americans had written and published a few books themselves. By this time, Eastman, La Flesche, and Standing Bear had written, if not published, all of their works, and McNickle, Bontemps, Hughes, and Belpré were just beginning their writing careers. Early librarians of color such as Belpré and Baker (who were now joined by Charlemae Rollins at the Chicago Public Library) were beginning to make some inroads. Otherwise, this period was very bleak. The next period, 1940–1965, would show minor changes at first and eventually lead to much more revolutionary ones.

SOME LIGHT ON THE SUBJECT: 1940–1965

This period marked four major trends—the appearance of some positive books and a few more writers of color in the 1940s and 1950s; some critical attention paid to literature by and about people of color; a strong emphasis in U.S. culture on integration and assimilation, including a stress on intercultural education; and many historic events in the 1950s and early 1960s, which would usher in the next era. World War II was definitely the most important event affecting the United States and the world during the early forties. Men went to war, and women temporarily did riveting and other work formerly reserved for men. Japanese Americans were sent to concentration camps during this time. Before the end of the decade, Yoshiko Uchida, a young woman who graduated from the University of California, Berkeley, in absentia because she was sent to such a camp, would become one of the first Asian American authors to write for children.

A few books with positive portrayals of modern children of color were published by mainstream presses. One example is *My Dog Rinty*, by African American writer Ellen Tarry, the first book ever published about modern, urban African American children. During this period, a few Anglo writers also wrote books about Mexican American children,[79] and some mainstream publishers produced a few books of Native American traditional stories.[80] D'Arcy McNickle published his second novel, *Runner in the Sun*, in 1954, which included one of the first appearances in print of the illustrator, Allan C. Houser, who would go on to become a world-renowned sculptor and a major figure in the Native American art world. Aside from Dhan Gopal Mukerji, who had won a Newberry Award in 1928, the first Asian Americans to write for children, Yoshiko Uchida, Jade Snow Wong, and Taro Yashima, also started to publish during this period.

During the 1940s and 1950s, the more established writers, Hughes, Bontemps, Belpré, and McNickle, were also joined by several more African American writers—Jesse Jackson (not the civil rights leader) and the brother and sister Lorenz and Shirley Graham. The Grahams had quite separate writing careers. Lorenz wrote several novels about contemporary issues in the United States, north and south, and in Liberia. He also published several bible stories in a Liberian dialect. His sister, Shirley, wrote mainly biographies and other nonfiction. Later in life, she would marry W. E. B. DuBois. As the children of African Methodist Episcopal missionaries to Liberia, both Grahams, as well as Hughes and Woodson, were among the first African American authors to write on African-related themes. In addition, several African American writers known for their literature for adults, such as Gwendolyn Brooks and Ann Petry, also started to write for children.[81]

Outside the United States, third world countries were emerging from colonialism during the 1940s, 1950s, and 1960s. In the United States, the 1950s were the time of the Supreme Court's *Brown v. Board of Education* decision, which declared segregated schools to be unconstitutional. That decade also saw the beginning of the civil rights movement. There was a general drive in U.S. society toward integration and assimilation. A number of "message movies" were produced in the 1950s and early 1960s showing African Americans as dignified people trying to assimilate into the society. All of the works of Jackson and the U.S.-oriented works of Lorenz Graham reflected these themes. In the meantime, Native Americans were encouraged to move to urban areas, and quite a few did, affecting everybody in many ways.

Intercultural education, which was created largely by Jewish Americans and promoted in the 1940s and 1950s, was a direct response to Nazism, World War II, and the Holocaust. It would be the United States' response to Hitler's promotion of hatred. This movement emphasized two themes—pride in one's own heritage and toleration of racial, religious, and cultural differences.

Students were taught to be tolerant of others and to avoid prejudice and discrimination. Intercultural education also emphasized national loyalty over traditions of specific groups, and promoted assimilation. Organizations devoted to this included the Center for Intergroup Education in Cooperating Schools within the American Council of Education, the Service Bureau of Intercultural Education, and the Common Council for American Unity. A newsletter related to this movement was *The Intercultural Education News*.[82] The publication that most closely relates to the goals of intercultural education is *Teaching Tolerance*,[83] which emerged much later, not directly from this movement but as an outgrowth of the civil rights movement.

During this entire time period, pioneering librarians and their supporters were beginning to pay serious attention to literature about people of color. Baker,[84] Eva Knox Evans,[85] and Helen Trager[86] published several major articles specifically about African American literature for children. In 1941, Charlemae Rollins published *We Build Together: A Reader's Guide to Negro Life and Literature for Elementary and High School Use*, an early bibliography on juvenile literature about African Americans.[87] In some ways, this prefigured *Kaleidoscope*, a more multicultural bibliography published by Rudine Sims Bishop in the 1990s and 2000s for the same organization, the National Council of Teachers of English. By the late 1940s, Baker would publish *Books about Negro Life for Children* based on the James Weldon Johnson Collection that she had built at the Countee Cullen Branch of the NYPL.[88] This would later be published as *The Black Experience in Children's Books*,[89] a bibliography eventually taken over by Barbara Rollock, Baker's successor.[90]

Furthermore, by the mid-1960s, many events were happening that would lead to the next era, including the following:

- The civil rights movement of the 1960s
- The successful publication of *A Snowy Day* by Ezra Jack Keats, the first book about a non-stereotypical child of color to be awarded a Caldecott Medal for the best U.S. picture book of the year
- The Library and School Construction Act
- The War on Poverty

These events impacted one another. *A Snowy Day* won the Caldecott as the civil rights movement was in full swing. The popularity of the title showed that it was possible to publish books with non-stereotypical ethnic main characters and market them to the general public. The Library and School Construction Act led to massive funding of school and public libraries, especially in poor areas, giving these libraries substantial money to spend for materials. Head Start and other programs of President Lyndon Johnson's War on Poverty helped to spark demand for much more material on children of color. Political activism in all ethnic and in other communities also brought about a cultural awakening that encouraged new writers of color as well as other authors to write.

However, instead of recruiting more writers of color, most mainstream publishers encouraged white writers to write on people of color—with decidedly mixed results. On the one hand, there was more information on more diverse groups of people. All children could benefit from seeing such a world reflected in these new titles. Some white writers, including Rose Blue, Milton Meltzer, Harold Courlander, Joan Lexau, Dorothy Sterling, Arnold Adoff, Lee Bennett Hopkins, William Loren Katz, Charlotte Zolotow, and Eve Bunting, produced some fairly good materials about African Americans. The best of this material was historical or biographical, in the form of poetry or folklore collections, or relatively generic picture books that were not culturally specific. In the 1980s, Rudine Sims[91] would refer to these picture books as "melting-pot books."

However, publishers were criticized for paying more attention to quantity than to quality. The new materials dropped some of the worst stereotypes from the past, but continued others, and they sometimes created new ones! The worst of the melting-pot picture books and readers either colored in formerly white characters or drew all nonwhite characters alike.[92] Sims[93] also later discussed books on "socially conscious" themes published by mainstream publishers and authors for white children; these attempted to explain people of color to this audience. Many of these books were about people of color (usually African Americans) trying to fit into a white world, and in many cases, the main character was a white (usually male) one who saved or at least helped the black character. A popular theme was black children integrating a school or a neighborhood, and the main focus would be on the reaction of a white classmate or neighbor. In many ways, these books were similar in theme to the movie *Guess Who's Coming to Dinner?* They meant well, but were often condescending, and they sometimes promoted new, subtle stereotypes.[94] Two major responses to all of these trends occurred in 1965: a report entitled "The All-White World of Children's Books" and the formation of the Council of Interracial Books for Children. These led to many more changes, to be described in the next section.

THE FIRST FLOWERING: 1965–1980

The late 1960s and early 1970s were turbulent years in U.S. history marked by protests over the Vietnam War and many other events. The civil rights movement morphed into the separate but related political black power and cultural black arts movements. There were also political and cultural movements happening among Latino/as, especially Chicanos, and among Native Americans, Asian Americans, and people from other groups, such as ethnic European Americans and people with disabilities. Two very pivotal events in 1965 would have a huge and permanent impact on the development of multicultural and ethnic children's literature of the future. These events were the publication of "The All-White World of Children's Books" in the *Saturday Review* by Nancy Larrick, a white author and founder of the International Reading Association,[95] and the formation of the Council on Interracial Books for Children.[96]

Larrick affirmed many trends earlier noted by Baker and Rollins, and mentioned some others. First, she noted the extremely low number and percentage of books published about people of color in the United States in the years 1962–1964. She found that only 6.7 percent of books published by sixty-three mainstream publishers had black characters. As Baker did earlier, Larrick noted that African Americans during this period were usually portrayed as slaves, sharecroppers, and manual laborers. In addition to the trends and events of the early 1960s that are mentioned above, Larrick's article shamed mainstream publishers into looking at this issue. Several publishing houses hired African Americans to recruit writers of color, and the proportion of books with African American characters doubled by the mid-1970s.[97]

The Council on Interracial Books for Children (CIBC)

The Council on Interracial Books for Children (CIBC) was organized in 1965 as a direct result of the civil rights movement in general and Mississippi Summer in particular. Civil rights workers teaching in Freedom Schools noted the lack of appropriate materials for African American children. After some investigation, the founders of CIBC also noted the lack of textbooks and trade books on many groups, and stereotypical and derogatory treatment of diverse people where materials did appear.[98]

The impact of the CIBC on the field of multicultural and ethnic children's literature has been substantial. Before CIBC and the Larrick article, the number of authors of color writing for children was miniscule, portrayals of diverse children were rare, and most of these portrayals were still stereotypical and inaccurate. The CIBC did several major things to change that. They offered prizes to unpublished writers, analyzed and criticized existing materials on diverse people, and strongly encouraged people from the mainstream to work with authors, producers, and leaders of color.

By awarding prizes to new writers of color, CIBC launched the careers of several notable authors, including Walter Dean Myers, Mildred Taylor,

Sharon Bell Mathis, Virginia Driving Hawk Sneve, and Cruz Martel.[99] Later other organizations were encouraged to develop similar prizes for new and established authors from different groups. By compiling book lists and establishing prizes, professionals of color and their supporters were doing what their white counterparts had done earlier with their book lists and Newbery and Caldecott medals—establishing a canon of the best of their literature. The CIBC started this process for most ethnic peoples and their supporters concerned with children's literature. It was also important that this organization encouraged all publishers to work with ethnic authors, producers, and professionals.

As long as the CIBC was additive in their approach and not more critical, they were relatively noncontroversial. This changed when members criticized mainstream materials for racism, sexism, and many other issues. Two things were happening here—stridency from the CIBC, and opposition from a mainstream not used to being questioned or criticized, especially in this way.

The CIBC was viewed by some as too strident because of the number and the stringency of their criteria for racism, sexism, classism, ageism, and other "isms," especially as the criteria were reflected in the publication *Human and Anti-Human Values in Children's Books*.[100] CIBC was strongly criticized for urging librarians and later ALA to avoid or weed books deemed racist, and it was viewed as a heavy-handed pressure group. Some critics called organization members "censors from the left," and were especially disturbed to see classics from the past and prize-winning books from the present being criticized in this way. Observers had mixed opinions on whether only minorities should write about their group, but most critics were not pleased with this philosophy. However, some of these critics were criticized in turn for not admitting that there have been serious biases in children's books.[101]

The CIBC will hold an important place in the history of children's literature because it set the first standards for the depiction of formerly neglected groups. CIBC members took discrimination in the children's book field very seriously.[102] The special issues of their bulletin were often the first publications to investigate the portrayal of a group. Their filmstrips *Unlearning Indian Stereotypes*[103] and *Unlearning Asian Stereotypes*[104] were very useful tools for teachers and librarians, and their study *Stereotypes, Distortions and Omissions in U.S. History Textbooks*[105] was very thoughtfully done. Their "10 Quick Ways to Analyze Children's Books for Racism and Sexism"[106] are still very influential and cited in many articles on general criteria to use. Just as some authors who won CIBC prizes have become very prominent writers, some of the CIBC's early critics and reviewers such as Doris Seale and Sonia Nieto are still very active in this field.

The CIBC was active until roughly 1990, and its bulletin is still the most important source of information on this topic from 1965 to 1990. Since 1992, the *MultiCultural Review* has replaced the bulletin. While it criticizes materials for cultural authenticity, it pursues a much more additive approach to this literature by describing what exists and analyzing it in a variety of ways.

Emerging Writers from Emerging Communities

At least two excellent series of nonfiction books were developed in this period. One was the Zenith Books, a series of African American history books created by Doubleday. Another was the multicultural Crowell biography series. African American writers participated in both series. Later publishers of multicultural nonfiction include Chelsea House and the Lerner Publishing Group. The 1960s and 1970s was also a time when African American educators developed curricular materials to encourage public schoolteachers to teach black history in the classroom. This material emphasized major events in black history and biographical information.

All of these developments sparked "The First Flowering" of writing by authors of color. A small but strong cadre of African American writers, such as Virginia Hamilton, Walter Dean Myers, Mildred Taylor, Sharon Bell Mathis, Eloise Greenfield, Lucille Clifton, Tom Feelings, and John Steptoe, produced a body of outstanding work. The first two Newbery Awards to go to African American writers went to Hamilton and Taylor during this time. The establishment of the Coretta Scott King Award in 1969 and the launching of *Ebony, Jr.*, in 1975 may have also encouraged more people of color to write. *Ebony, Jr.*, published by the Johnson Publishing Company, a black firm, was the third magazine to be produced for black children.

When African Americans were able to write more about their own culture, they wrote what Sims refers to as "culturally conscious" books from black points of view.[107] African Americans were now the main characters, and black children the implied primary (but definitely not the only) audience. Themes reflecting black culture and history could begin to emerge from the literature.

This would also be true of writers from other groups who were just beginning to be published by mainstream publishers. Latino/a writers were coming from several streams. One consisted of Chicano and Mexican American educators involved in school bilingual programs who wrote folktales and other stories for bilingual readers. Some critics[108] are now calling for the republication of the best works from these readers. Other Chicano writers were inspired to write by La Raza, "los movimientos of the sixties," a grassroots anti-assimilationist political and cultural movement that affirmed their culture. Much of today's Latino/a literature for children is viewed as a continuation of the activism and vision of the 1960s.[109] During this time, Nicholasa Mohr and Cruz Martel were among the first Puerto Rican writers on the mainland since Belpré to write specifically for young people. Classic books for children and teenagers were also beginning to be published in some numbers on the island of Puerto Rico in the 1960s and 1970s.[110] Books for adult readers published in the 1960s, 1970s, and 1980s, including *And the Earth Did Not Move* by Tomás Rivera, *Down These Mean Streets* by Piri Thomas, *Bless Me, Ultima* by Rudolfo Anaya, and *House on Mango Street* by Sandra Cisneros, became assigned reading in some high schools.[111] More Latino/a writers would contribute in the 1980s and beyond. Some of them would be established adult writers, such as Gary Soto or Francisco Alarcón, who would also decide to write for the young.[112] Keeping track of all of this and more was Isabel Schon, who started publishing bibliographies on Spanish-language and related books for children during the late 1970s.

Latino/as and Asian Americans were especially affected by the Immigration Act of 1965.[113] This major legislation, which revoked the National Origin Act of 1924 and parts of the McCarran-Walter Act of 1952, was another outgrowth of the civil rights movement. The earlier acts established a quota system for immigrants coming to the United States that greatly favored Europeans. Asian, Latin American, and African immigration was greatly discouraged. The Immigration Act of 1965 welcomed immigrants based on their skills or professions, not their ethnic or national background. It also made provisions for refugees. This act impacted both the Latino/a and the Asian American communities, with the result that significantly more people came to live in the United States from many more countries.

This had a particularly major impact on the Asian American community. Both the success of the civil rights movement and the result of the Immigration Act of 1965 encouraged U.S. pan-Asian activism in the 1970s. For the first time, Asian Americans and Pacific Islanders from different ethnic groups and nationalities were establishing united organizations. In 1976, a committee of Asian American book reviewers identified and evaluated U.S. books on Asia and Asian Americans for the CIBC. The committee found the sixty-six books evaluated to be "racist, sexist, elitist, and grossly misleading."[114] There was also a slight increase in the number of Asian American writers at this time. Wong, Uchida, and Yashima were now joined by Laurence Yep, Frank Chin, Allen Say, and Ed Young. Uchida had earlier written children's books on Japanese and Japanese American culture, but during this time she began to address her own experience in a U.S. concentration camp during World War II.

By the early 1970s, Mary G. Byler[115] had published a bibliography on Native American children's authors. Virginia Driving Hawk Sneve and other writers representing a new generation were beginning to emerge during this time, and the children's periodical *The Weewish Tree* was also published. In addition, many events were happening to Native Americans both on and off the reservation that would encourage more to write and publish, including the following:

Major changes in education. Several studies and pieces of legislation in the 1960s, 1970s, and 1980s led to Native Americans assuming more control of their children's education. Native American teachers, some of whom were trained in programs like the American Indian Leadership Program at Pennsylvania State University, were also beginning to have an impact. Some schools were incorporating their own indigenous cultures into the educational process and the curriculum. Reforms postponed from the 1920s and 1930s also were implemented during this time.[116]

The establishment of public libraries on reservations with funding from the federal government. This was the first time that this had been done in many places, and it was a direct outgrowth of the War on Poverty.

Western Native Americans established *tribal colleges on reservations*, starting with the Navajo Community College (now Diné College) in 1968. These colleges started as two-year community colleges, but some have now grown to four-year programs and beyond. Some have also developed libraries that serve their communities.

The publication of controversial and provocative works, such as *Custer Died for Your Sins* and *God is Red* by Vine Deloria.

The publication of Native American writers by mainstream presses and the emergence of authors such as Deloria, N. Scott Momaday, and others.

During the 1960s and 1970s, Native Americans created several schools and programs, and published their own publications that supported these programs. The Navajo Curriculum Center of the Rough Rock Demonstration School in Arizona developed a series of books on Navajo history. The Red School House, an alternative school for Ojibway children in St. Paul, Minnesota, created a coloring book series, and the Akwesasne Mohawks of New York put "teaching tales" into picture book format.[117]

However, the true emergence of Latino/a, Native American, and Asian American literature, especially for the young, did not occur until the 1980s and beyond. A publisher who would encourage this trend emerged during the 1970s. Harriet Rohmer established The Children's Book Press in 1975 as a direct result of her son's participation in Head Start. She started by successfully writing a grant and by collecting folktales, finding local artists from the cultures represented to do the illustrations, and publishing bilingual editions of many of her books for schools, preschools, and day care centers. The Children's Book Press is now one of the major publishers of multicultural children's materials in the United States.[118]

More Tales out of School

Before the 1960s, African Americans appeared in history textbooks mainly as slaves, and slavery was portrayed as a benign institution for them. Interactions between European Americans and Native Americans were described as foreordained clashes between cultures. The domination of the West over everybody else was portrayed as inevitable. Most traditional historians emphasized political and to some extent economic history. At the end of the 1960s, the field of history changed dramatically at the college level with the rise of social history and a new focus on African, African American, Native American, and women's history. A new generation of diverse scholars built on the foundation established by their seniors and added insights of their own.[119]

However, there was a lag in the adjustment of portrayals of various groups in school textbooks during this time. Schools began to present the United States as a multicultural society not because of changes in scholarship, but because of the pressure of school boards in cities with large ethnic and minority populations. Textbooks still had some Eurocentric biases, they were inconsistent, and they de-emphasized economic life, inequality, violence, and conflict.[120]

According to Gary Nash, schools were slow to change because most social studies teachers had few history courses in their education, and most were trained at state schools that were not hiring many young, new scholars at that time. Textbook companies were also very cautious about introducing changes.[121]

In 1966, the State Board of Education in California issued guidelines on the treatment of ethnic and cultural minorities in textbooks, and then called for a new history textbook for Grade 8. John Caughey of the University of California, Los Angeles, invited Ernest May of Harvard University and John Hope Franklin, a prominent African American historian then at the University of Chicago, to join him in writing this textbook. Their text, *Land of the Free*, was published by Franklin Publications and approved by the State Board of Education and the Textbook Commission. After the book was published, a copy was placed in every public library in the state to enable parents and citizens to read it and comment on it.[122]

Right-wing groups in the state strenuously opposed this text. Opponents published a pamphlet and filmstrip, sent a motor caravan from Southern

California to Sacramento, and put women on picket lines at state buildings in Sacramento and Los Angeles. *Land of the Free* was also cited in 1968 by *Time* magazine on a list of books that should be banned.

On the other hand, the three historians received support from a Mexican American member of the Los Angeles Board of Education, and the text was positively reviewed in *The Grade Teacher*. It was officially adopted in some school systems, such as Philadelphia, and unofficially used in others, such as Baltimore. This text was used at least throughout the 1970s.[123]

INTO THE DESERT: 1980–1985

The year 1980 marked the election of Ronald Reagan as president and the beginning of a long conservative period in U.S. civil rights. Affirmative action, the War on Poverty, and all other initiatives from the 1960s were seriously questioned, and multicultural literature for children was viewed as a fad that had passed.[124] The number and percentage of books by and about people of color dropped dramatically in the early 1980s. In 1985, Ginny Moore Kruse and Kathleen T. Horning of the Cooperative Children's Book Center[125] found that only eighteen books published in the United States that year had black authors or illustrators, and the numbers were lower for all other groups. At that time, the author Walter Dean Myers[126] also observed that new writers of color were having trouble getting published, and even established writers had publishing dry spells that lasted for years. Award-winning books also went out of print. By 1987, the number of books published by black authors rose to thirty, but the overall number of books published that year also rose.[127]

In spite of these setbacks, there were two important events that took place in the early 1980s. One was the publication of Rudine Sims (Bishop)'s book *Shadow and Substance: Afro-American Experience in Contemporary Children's Fiction*.[128] Sims analyzed books written about African Americans and concluded that they could be divided into three groups—the melting-pot books, which ignore cultural differences; the socially conscious books, usually written about people of color from outsiders' perspectives; and culturally conscious books that attempt to portray ethnic cultures from the point of view of people in the culture described. Her analysis has been cited many times and used to evaluate books written about many cultures. The other event was the premier in 1983 of *Reading Rainbow*, a public television show for children. It promoted multicultural children's literature and published a handbook, *The Reading Rainbow Guide to Children's Books* in 1995.

However, after Kruse, Horning, and the Cooperative Children's Book Center started to keep statistics, the status of multicultural and ethnic children's literature changed once again. After 1985 the age of institution building in this field would begin.

A TIME TO BUILD: 1985–

Multicultural Issues in School Curricula

By the 1980s and early 1990s, there were many changes both in the academic field of history and in the way that it was taught in schools. School texts began to reflect more developments from the universities. However, resistance to these changes had gathered both in academia and in school settings. Historians were divided over "whose history to teach." Social history was viewed by opponents as chaotic and lacking overarching themes and grand syntheses. Historians were uncomfortable over the loss of old paradigms.[129] Similar developments occurred among educators in other fields, both in universities and in the schools. Ethnic studies programs in colleges and universities and multicultural education in schools were resisted through core requirements, core curricula, and cultural literacy, which were all designed to stress traditional European curricula, with or without other ethnic or multicultural influences. Nash states that history based on alternative experiences was pointing to a serious need for new story lines, themes, and paradigms.[130] This would be true in other subjects, as well.

Major conflicts in the late 1980s and 1990s over multicultural guidelines and textbooks in the social sciences surfaced in California and New York State, as well as nationally, revealing divisions not only between communities but within them. These conflicts highlighted a number of issues that are yet to be resolved.[131]

In 1988, a committee chaired by Charlotte Crabtree, which also included Diane Ravitch, created *History–Social Sciences Framework for California Public Schools for the California State Board of Education*.[132] These guidelines greatly increased the roles of women and minorities in school texts while also stressing the creation of good narrative history and the roles of religion in U.S. life. The guidelines were approved with little controversy, but were criticized by some liberal and minority scholars for emphasizing immigrants to California over racial minorities, for pursuing an additive rather than a transformative approach to multiculturalism, and for ignoring racial and cultural hierarchies in the state and in the nation. Houghton Mifflin developed social science textbooks in response to this framework, and it was then up to local school districts to either accept or reject the books. In an eerie echo of what happened to the text *Land of the Free* in the 1960s, there was more opposition to textbooks at the school district level, this time from the left.[133]

There were intense battles over the development of preliminary guides for social studies curricula in the state of New York starting in 1989. Thomas Sobol, the new state commissioner of education, appointed a curriculum committee composed of African American and Latino/a educators to consider issues affecting black and Latino/a education. Leonard Jeffries, a very intense Afrocentrist scholar, was employed as a consultant to this committee, which issued a report, *A Curriculum of Inclusion*,[134] that highlighted the negative educational histories of children of color and the effects of these on their self-esteem. It recommended distinct curricula for each group and lumped all people of European descent together. This report was promptly condemned by Diane Ravitch, Arthur Schlesinger, other leading U.S. historians, and major newspapers in the state.[135]

A second, more balanced committee was then appointed, which was evenly divided between academics, teachers, and administrators from a wide variety of ethnic groups. Members included Arthur Schlesinger; Kenneth Jackson of Columbia University; Asa Hilliard, an Afrocentric scholar not active on this committee; Ali Mazrui, an African political scholar; and Nathan Glazer. This committee issued a much more moderate report, *One Nation, Many Peoples: A Declaration of Cultural Interdependence*,[136] which was also attacked by academics, Governor Cuomo, and the media. Schlesinger and Jackson dissented from this report. After this, the state of New York had more committees and reports. Educators in the state continued to use standards from 1991, and teachers continued to use and test multicultural materials on their own.[137]

Several of the creators of the California social studies standards were also involved in creating national standards in this field. These standards were intended to be models to be adopted on a voluntary basis by states and school systems. Funds were provided to Charlotte Crabtree, the head of UCLA's National Center for History in the Schools, who had chaired the committee that created the California standards, as well as Gary Nash, who wrote a textbook based on those standards. Funds came from Lynne Cheney, who then headed the National Endowment for the Humanities, and from Diane Ravitch, who was then head of the Office of Educational Research and Innovation in the Department of Education. The National Council of History Standards, which consisted of scholars with widely varying views toward multiculturalism, oversaw this process, and a multitude of scholarly and professional groups from both the mainstream and diverse communities also participated. The result of this effort was *Lessons from History: Essential Understandings and Historical Perspectives Students Should Acquire*,[138] a three-volume set of historical standards published in 1994, which was harshly criticized by Cheney in the *Wall Street Journal* and condemned by the entire U.S. Senate.[139]

In reaction, the conservative Council for Basic Education (CBE) assembled a panel to create more moderate standards. Panelists included Diane Ravitch and Stephen Thernstrom. The CBE panel set standards that eliminated the controversial "teaching examples" of the previous group. Cheney also denounced the CBE standards because of their coverage of the Great Depression of the 1930s and of European and Western colonization in the nineteenth century.[140]

A number of issues emerging from the work of the two national panels are still unresolved. How many perspectives can and should be presented in history textbooks? Which should be taught or emphasized—the political history of democracy in the United States, or the convergence of people from several continents? Are these topics mutually exclusive? If not, how can they be combined? How detailed and specialized should non-Western histories be? How should ancient non-Western civilizations be treated? What should be the overall framework of our history?[141] All of these questions and more are issues of vital concern to all of us. It will take time and much thought from people from all cultures and political persuasions to sort this out.

Growth of Multicultural Children's Literature

The status of multicultural and ethnic children's literature started to improve in the mid-1980s for several reasons. One may be the increasing number and proportion of people of color in the United States, particularly in the younger generation, leading to the availability of more authors.[142] A second reason may be the fact that Kruse, Horning, and the Cooperative Children's Book Center were keeping records on the number of books published about each ethnic group, as well as the number of books published by African American authors. (They added authors from other groups in the early 2000s.) Since the mid-1980s, the number and percentage of children's books on and by people of color have increased from the low figures of 1985 and have been consistent across the years. New writers from all groups have emerged, and Latino/a, Native American, and Asian American children's literature is just beginning to take off. A few examples of new writers include Patricia McKissack, Angela Shelf Medaris, Gary Soto, Francisco Alarcón, Lulu Delacre, Pat Mora, Cynthia Leitich Smith, Shonto Begay, Louise Erdich, Marie G. Lee, Ken Mochizuki, Lensey Namioka, Paul Yee of Canada, and the Newbery Award winners An Na and Christopher Paul

Curtis. A number of authors who originally wrote for adults, such as Soto and Erdich, are now also publishing for children. Some families, such as the Pinckneys and the Bruchacs, and sons of authors such as Walter Dean Myers, John Steptoe, June Jordan, Virginia Hamilton, and Arnold Adoff are also writing, illustrating, or both. There have been parent-children writing teams such as Lessie Little and Eloise Greenfield (mother/daughter) and Toni and Slade Morrison (mother/son).

Two contradictory trends have also been observed since 1985. One is the publishing of more socially conscious and melting-pot books by white authors from mainstream publishers. The other is the publication of very culturally specific books by writers of color, many by alternative presses.[143]

The last twenty years have marked the establishment of new ethnic and multicultural publishers, periodicals, prizes, and institutions, as well as other activities. Such presses include the multicultural Lee and Low and the more culturally specific Just Us Books, Black Butterfly Press, and Arte Publico/Piñata Books. *The Council on Interracial Books for Children Bulletin* is no longer being published, but periodicals such as *MultiCultural Review*, *Teaching Tolerance*, and, for a number of years, *New Advocate*, also emerged, as well as more specialized ethnic review media, such as *Black Issues Book Review* and *Criticas*. The Tomás Rivera Award, the Americas Award, and the Pura Belpré Award were all created in the 1990s to encourage Latino/a and other writers. Two Asian American library groups, the Chinese American Librarians' Association (CALA) and the Asian Pacific American Librarians' Association (APALA) have also jointly established a prize, the Asian Pacific American Award For Literature. The Skipping Stones Award for multicultural materials and other prizes were also started during the 1990s.

In 1989, the Barahona Center for the Study of Books in Spanish for Children and Adolescents/Centro Barahona para el Estudio de Libros Infantiles y Juveniles en Español [144] was established at California State University at San Marcos, with Isabel Schon as the director. More recently, the Center for Multicultural Literature for Children and Young Adults[145] has been established as part of the Department of International and Multicultural Education at the University of San Francisco. The director is Alma Flor Ada, an educator and children's author. The center offers courses in children's literature with an emphasis on multicultural and international education.

Since 1990 two important collections of texts about multicultural and ethnic children's literature have been published, and there have been conferences and activities by other groups. The collections, both edited by Violet J. Harris, are *Teaching Multicultural Literature in Grades K–8*[146] and *Using Multiethnic Literature in the K–8 Classroom*.[147] For a time, the Multicultural

Publishers' Exchange, based at the Highsmith Press, was encouraging writers of color. Along with the Cooperative Children's Book Center at the University of Wisconsin, Madison, they sponsored a conference in the early 1990s that led to the publication of *The Multicolored Mirror*.[148] They also matched authors with publishers.

The last twenty years have been a period of more consistent, if not increasing, publishing of materials and of institution building related to multicultural and ethnic children's literature. The rest of this book will describe these and many more initiatives in more detail.

PEOPLE IMPORTANT TO MULTICULTURAL CHILDREN'S LITERATURE

People listed here come from many different backgrounds and have played an important part in the field of multicultural children's literature, have been involved in general multicultural issues as well as those affecting one group of people, or have written works or done projects affecting at least two groups of people. A few pioneers will also be listed. Contributors to more specific ethnic children's literature will be mentioned in chapter 4.

Alma Flor Ada. Author and educator. Ada has written and published several children's books, including *Gathering the Sun: An Alphabet in Spanish and English* and *Under the Royal Palms: A Childhood in Cuba*. She is now professor and director of the Center of Multicultural Literature for Children and Young Adults at the University of San Francisco.

Augusta Baker. Pioneering librarian who collected, documented, and criticized materials on African American children. She also wrote several collections of folktales for children, published a text on storytelling, and was later storyteller-in-residence at the University of South Carolina. Her career lasted from the late 1930s until the mid-1990s.

Beryl Banfield. An active official of the Council on Interracial Books for Children.

Pura Belpré. Pioneering Latina librarian and children's book author who developed and implemented a variety of library and community programs, still emulated today by practitioners of multicultural librarianship. Her career was from the 1920s to the early 1980s.

Rudine Sims Bishop. Author of the landmark text *Shadow and Substance: Afro-American Experience in Contemporary Children's Fiction*. She has also compiled several editions of *Kaleidoscope: A Multicultural Booklist for Grades K–8* and has written columns on multiculturalism for *The Horn Book Magazine*.

Naomi Caldwell. An important critic in the area of Native American children's literature. She teaches Multiculturalism in Libraries and Multicultural Resources for Youth at the University of Rhode Island.

Bradford Chambers. A founder of and pivotal spokesman for the Council on Interracial Books for Children.

Frances Ann Day. Author of *Multicultural Voices in Contemporary Literature: A Resource for Teachers*, *Latina and Latino Voices in Literature: Lives and Works Updated and Expanded*, and *Ethnic Book Awards: A Directory of Multicultural Literature for Young Readers*.

Violet J. Harris. Editor of two important collections of readings on multicultural and ethnic children's literature, *Teaching Multicultural Literature in Grades K–8* and *Using Multiethnic Literature in the K–8 Classroom*. She was also the editor of *The New Advocate*.

Kathleen Horning. Cowriter, along with Ginny Moore Kruse and Megan Schliesman, of *Multicultural Literature for Children and Young Adults: A Selected List of Books, 1980–1990, by and about People of Color*. She has also kept track of publishers of color by writing an article, "The Contribution of Alternative Press Publishers to Multicultural Literature for Children," and the book *Alternative Press Publishers of Children's Books: A Directory*.

Ginny Moore Kruse. Serving on a committee for the Coretta Scott King Award led her to collect children's materials on and by people of color at the Cooperative Children's Book Center of the University of Wisconsin, Madison. Along with Kathleen Horning, she has kept annual statistics on the number of books published, and Kruse, Horning, and Megan Schliesman published a bibliography on this topic entitled *Multicultural Literature for Children and Young Adults: A Selected Listing of Books, 1980–1990, by and about People of Color*.

Philip Lee. A founder of Lee and Low, a major publisher of multicultural children's books.

Donnarae MacCann. Author or editor of *Social Responsibility in Librarianship: Essays on Equality*; *White Supremacy in Children's Literature*; *The Black American in Books for Children* and *Cultural Conformity in Books for Children* (both with Gloria Woodard); *Apartheid and Racism in South African Children's Literature, 1985–1995* and *African Images in Juvenile Literature: Commentaries on Neocolonialist Fiction* (both with Yulisa Amadu Maddy). MacCann has also written several evaluative articles over the years on the treatment of different groups in children's literature.

D'Arcy McNickle. Anthropologist, author, and first director of the Newberry Library's Center for the History of the American Indian.

Lyn Miller-Lachmann. Author of *Our Family, Our Friends, Our World: An Annotated Guide to Significant Multicultural Books for Children and*

Young Teenagers; *Global Voices, Global Visions: A Core Collection of Multicultural Books*; and *Schools for All: Educating Children in a Diverse Society*, and the current editor of the *MultiCultural Review.*

Brenda Mitchell-Powell. Founding editor of the *MultiCultural Review*, which replaced the *Council on Interracial Books for Children Bulletin.*

Daphne Muse. Compiler and editor of *The New Press Guide to Multicultural Resources for Young Readers* and author of articles on African American children's literature.

Harriet Rohmer. Founder and president of the Children's Book Press in San Francisco, California, a major publisher of multicultural children's books.

Charlemae Rollins. A pioneer librarian from the Chicago Public Library who was a contemporary of Augusta Baker and Pura Belpré. She compiled one of the first bibliographies on literature about black children, entitled *We Build Together*, in the early 1940s. She was also an early multicultural children's writer, publishing an anthology of Christmas literature and several collections of biographical essays.

Isabel Schon. *The* major bibliographer of all aspects of Spanish-language, Latin American, and U.S.-based Latino/a children's literature. She is the director of the Barahona Center for the Study of Books in Spanish for Children and Adolescents/Centro Barahona para el Estudio de Libros Infantiles y Juveniles en Español.

Rudine Sims. See Rudine Sims Bishop.

Cynthia Leitich Smith. She has a website that discusses many aspects of children's literature, providing bibliographies and commentaries on literature for Native Americans, Asian Americans, and children from bi- and multicultural families. She has also published several novels featuring contemporary Native American children.

Gloria Woodard. Compiled two early studies, *The Black American in Books for Children* and *Cultural Conformity in Children's Books* with Donnarae MacCann.

REFERENCES

1. Tupac Shakur, *The Rose That Grew from Concrete* (New York: Pocket Books, 1999).

2. Diane Ravitch, "Minority Group Education in the United States," in *The Schools We Deserve: Reflections on the Educational Crises of Our Time* (New York: Basic Books, 1985), 184.

3. Meyer Weinberg, *A Chance to Learn: The History of Race and Education in the United States* (New York: Cambridge University Press, 1977).

4. Gerald L. Gutek, *Education in the United States: An Historical Perspective* (Englewood Cliffs, N.J.: Prentice-Hall, 1986), 1–2.

5. Gutek, *Education in the United States*, 3–4.

6. Gutek, *Education in the United States*, 82–83.

7. Gutek, *Education in the United States*, 87.

8. Gutek, *Education in the United States*, 111–13.

9. Gutek, *Education in the United States*, 114–15.

10. Duane Champagne, ed., "Education," in *The Native North American Almanac*, second edition (Detroit: Gale, 2001), 991–97.

11. Ravitch, "Minority Group Education in the United States," 198.

12. Ravitch, "Minority Group Education in the United States," 199.

13. Ravitch, "Minority Group Education in the United States," 199–210.

14. Ravitch, "Minority Group Education in the United States," 199–201.

15. Victoria-Maria MacDonald, ed., *Latino Education in the United States: A Narrated History from 1513–2000* (New York: Palgrave Macmillan, 2004), 7–9.

16. MacDonald, *Latino Education in the United States*, 9–14.

17. MacDonald, *Latino Education in the United States*, 14–16.

18. MacDonald, *Latino Education in the United States*, 9.

19. MacDonald, *Latino Education in the United States*, 17.

20. MacDonald, *Latino Education in the United States*, 31–32.

21. MacDonald, *Latino Education in the United States*, 38.

22. MacDonald, *Latino Education in the United States*, 39–44.

23. MacDonald, *Latino Education in the United States*, 56.

24. MacDonald, *Latino Education in the United States*, 59–60.

25. MacDonald, *Latino Education in the United States*, 63–65.

26. MacDonald, *Latino Education in the United States*, 67–68.

27. MacDonald, *Latino Education in the United States*, 68–69.

28. MacDonald, *Latino Education in the United States*, 118–19.

29. MacDonald, *Latino Education in the United States*, 120.

30. MacDonald, *Latino Education in the United States*, 93–94.

31. MacDonald, *Latino Education in the United States*, 99–100.

32. MacDonald, *Latino Education in the United States*, 97–98.

33. MacDonald, *Latino Education in the United States*, 94–96.

34. MacDonald, *Latino Education in the United States*, 122–23.

35. Ronald Takaki, *Strangers from a Different Shore: A History of Asian Americans* (New York: Penguin, 1987), 80–121.

36. Takaki, *Strangers from a Different Shore*, 124–31.

37. Takaki, *Strangers from a Different Shore*, 179–229.

38. Iris Chang, *The Chinese in America: A Narrative History* (New York: Viking, 2003), 173–98.

39. Chang, *The Chinese in America*, 175–78.

40. Chang, *The Chinese in America*, 175–78.

41. Takaki, *Strangers from a Different Shore*, 201–3.

42. Chang, *The Chinese in America*, 177–78.

43. Chang, *The Chinese in America*, 185–92; Takaki, *Strangers from a Different Shore*, 218–21.

44. Arthur Schlesinger Jr., *The Disuniting of America: Reflections on a Multicultural Society* (New York: Norton, 1998), 41; Nathan Glazer, *We Are All Multiculturalists Now* (Cambridge, Mass.: Harvard University Press, 1997), 102, 105–9; Ravitch, "Minority Group Education in the United States," 188–89.

45. Ravitch, "Minority Group Education in the United States," 190.

46. Thomas Jefferson, *Notes on the State of Virginia* (Chapel Hill, N.C.: University of North Carolina Press, 1995).

47. Fawn Brodie, *Thomas Jefferson: An Intimate History* (New York: Norton, 1974); Annette Gordon-Reed, *Thomas Jefferson and Sally Hemings: An American Controversy* (Charlottesville, Va.: University Press of Virginia, 1998); Jan Lewis and Peter Onuf, eds., *Sally Hemings and Thomas Jefferson: History, Memory, and Civic Culture* (Charlottesville: University Press of Virginia, 1999).

48. Paul Finkelman, "Jefferson and Slavery: Treason against the Hope of the World," in *Jeffersonian Legacies*, edited by Peter S. Onuf (Charlottesville: University Press of Virginia, 1993), 185–86; Brodie, *Thomas Jefferson*, 158, 423; Gordon-Reed, *Thomas Jefferson and Sally Hemings*, 139.

49. Donnarae MacCann, *White Supremacy in Children's Literature: Characterizations of African Americans, 1830–1900* (New York: Garland, 1998), 69–77, 185–207.

50. MacCann, *White Supremacy in Children's Literature*, 70, 174–77, 201–7.

51. MacCann, *White Supremacy in Children's Literature*, 197–99, 206–7.

52. MacCann, *White Supremacy in Children's Literature*, 197–99, 206–7.

53. MacCann, *White Supremacy in Children's Literature*, 3–69.

54. MacCann, *White Supremacy in Children's Literature*, 83–144, 150–76, 179–84.

55. MacCann, *White Supremacy in Children's Literature*, 145–49, 176–79.

56. MacCann, *White Supremacy in Children's Literature*, 83–121.

57. MacCann, *White Supremacy in Children's Literature*, 123–44, 150–52, 179–81, 233–42.

58. Winthrop Jordan, *White Over Black: American Attitudes Towards the Negro, 1550–1812* (Chapel Hill: University of North Carolina Press, 1995).

59. George M. Fredrickson, *The Black Image in the White Mind: The Debate on Afro-American Character and Destiny, 1817–1914* (Hanover, N.H.: Wesleyan University Press, 1971).

60. Donald Bogle, *Toms, Coons, Mulattoes, Mammies, and Bucks: An Interpretive History of Blacks in American Films*, third edition (New York: Continuum, 1994).

61. Arnoldo De Leon, *They Called Them Greasers: Anglo Attitudes Toward Mexicans in Texas, 1821–1900* (Austin: University of Texas Press, 1983).

62. Eugene H. Jones, *Native Americans as Shown on the Stage: 1753–1916* (Metuchen, N.J.: Scarecrow Press, 1988).

63. Raymond William Stedman, *Shadows of the Indian: Stereotypes in American Culture* (Norman: University of Oklahoma Press, 1982).

64. Donnarae MacCann and Gloria Woodard, *The Black American in Books for Children* (Metuchen, N.J.: Scarecrow, 1972).

65. Donnarae MacCann and Gloria Woodard, eds., *Cultural Conformity in Books for Children* (Metuchen, N.J.: Scarecrow Press, 1977).

66. Clint C. Wilson II and Félix Gutiérrez, *Minorities and Media: Diversity and the End of Mass Communication* (London: Sage, 1985).

67. Shirley Biagi and Marilyn Kern-Foxworth, eds., *Facing Difference: Race, Gender, and Mass Media* (Thousand Oaks, Calif.: Pine Forge Press, 1997).

68. Karin Badt, *Charles Eastman: Sioux Physician and Author* (New York: Chelsea House, 1995).

69. Violet J. Harris, "African American Children's Literature: The First One Hundred Years," *Journal of Negro Education* 59, no. 4 (Fall 1990): 543; Dianne Johnson-Feelings, "Children's and Young Adult Literature," in *The Oxford Companion to African American Literature*, ed. William L. Andrews, Frances Smith Foster, and Trudier Harris (New York: Oxford University Press, 1997), 135.

70. Harris, "African American Children's Literature," 546–47; Johnson-Feelings, "Children's and Young Adult Literature," 135.

71. Harris, "African American Children's Literature," 547–48.

72. Harris, "African American Children's Literature," 548–49.

73. Centro de Estudios Puertorriqueños at Hunter College City University of New York, "Historical/Biographical Note," in *Guide to the Pura Belpré Papers*, http://www.centropr.org/lib-arc/faids/belpreb.html (26 June 2006); Martha Eads Ward, *Authors of Books for Young People* (Metuchen, N.J.: Scarecrow, 1990).

74. Centro de Estudios Puertorriqueños. "Historical/Biographical Note," in *Guide to the Pura Belpré Papers*.

75. "The Augusta Baker Collection of African American Children's Literature and Folklore," http://www.sc.edu/library/spcoll/kidlit/baker.html (26 June 2006); The Bulletin of the Center for Children's Books, "Gone but Not Forgotten: Augusta Braxton Baker," http://alexia.lis.uiuc.edu/puboff/bccb/1000gone.html (26 June 2006); "Speaking of History: The Words of South Carolina Librarians — Augusta Baker," http://www.libsci.sc.edu/histories/oralhistory/bakerpage.htm (26 June 2006).

76. Champagne, "Education," 858–59.

77. Gloria Emerson, "Foreword," in *Native American Picture Books of Change: The Art of Historic Children's Editions*, by Rebecca C. Benes (Santa Fe: Museum of New Mexico Press, 2004), ix–xiv.

78. Emerson, "Foreword," xi.

79. Rosalinda B. Barrera, Olga Liguori, and Loretta Salas, "Ideas a Literature Can Grow On: Key Insights for Enriching Children's Literature about the Mexican American Experience," in *Teaching Multicultural Literature in Grades K–8*, ed. Violet J. Harris (Norwood, Mass.: Christopher-Gordon, 1993), 219.

80. Arlene Hirschfelder, "Native American Literature for Children and Young Adults," *Library Trends* 41, no. 3 (Winter 1993): 414.

81. Johnson-Feelings, "Children's and Young Adult Literature," 136; Harris, "African American Children's Literature," 548–50.

82. Nathan Glazer, "The Problem of Ethnic Studies," in *Ethnic Dilemmas: 1964–1982* (Cambridge, Mass.: Harvard University Press, 1983), 103–7.

83. Southern Poverty Law Center, "Teaching Tolerance," http://www.tolerance.org/teach/ (16 Nov. 2006).

84. Augusta Baker, "The Negro in Literature," *Child Study* 22 (Winter 1944–1945): 58, 63.

85. Eva Knox Evans, "The Negro in Children's Fiction," *Publishers Weekly* 140 (August 30, 1941): 650–53.

86. Helen Trager, "Intercultural Books for Children," *Childhood Education* 22 (November 1945): 138–45; Daphne Muse, "Introduction," in *The New Press Guide to Multicultural Resources for Young Readers* (New York: New Press, 1997), 3.

87. Charlemae Rollins, et al., *We Build Together: A Reader's Guide to Negro Life and Literature for Elementary and High School Use* (Champaign, Ill.: National Council of Teachers of English, 1941, 1954, 1967).

88. Augusta Baker, *Books about Negro Life for Children* (New York: New York Public Library [NYPL], 1963).

89. Baker, *The Black Experience in Children's Books* (New York: NYPL, 1971).

90. Barbara Rollock, *The Black Experience in Children's Books* (New York: NYPL, 1974, 1984, 1994).

91. Rudine Sims (Bishop), *Shadow and Substance: Afro-American Experience in Contemporary Children's Fiction* (Urbana, Ill.: National Council of Teachers of English, 1982), 33–48; Harris, "African American Children's Literature," 548–50.

92. Johnson-Feelings, "Children's and Young Adult Literature," 136.

93. Sims, *Shadow and Substance*, 17–32.

94. Sims, *Shadows and Substance*, 17–32; Harris, "African American Children's Literature: The First Hundred Years," 548–50.

95. Rose E. Warder, "Multicultural Children's Literature Historical Timeline," http://home.wi.rr.com/valonkent/timeline.htm; Muse, "Introduction," 3; Lyn Miller-Lachmann, "Introduction," in *Our Family, Our Friends, Our World* (New Providence, N.J.: Bowker, 1992), 6; Nancy Larrick, "The All-White World of Children's Books," *Saturday Review* 48 (September 11, 1965): 63–65, 84–85. Also in *The New Press Guide to Multicultural Resources for Young Readers*, ed. Daphne Muse (New York: New Press, 1997), 19–25.

96. Beryl Banfield, "Commitment to Change: The Council on Interracial Books for Children and the World of Children's Books," *African American Review* 32, no. 1 (1998): 17–22; Johnson-Feelings, "Children's and Young Adult Literature," 137.

97. Muse, "Introduction," 3; Miller-Lachmann, "Introduction," 6.

98. Banfield, "Commitment to Change," 17–22.

99. Banfield, "Commitment to Change," 17–22; Johnson-Feelings, "Children's and Young Adult Literature," 137.

100. Council on Interracial Books for Children, Racism and Sexism Resource Center for Educators, *Human and Anti-Human Values in Children's Books: Guidelines for the Future* (New York: The Center, 1976).

101. Barbara Bader, "How the Little House Gave Ground: The Beginnings of Multiculturalism in a New Black Children's Literature," *The Horn Book Magazine* 78 (Nov./Dec. 2002): 657–73; Bader, "Multiculturalism Takes Root," *The Horn Book Magazine* 79 (Mar./Apr. 2003): 143–62; Diane Ravitch, *The Language Police: How Pressure Groups Restrict What Children Learn* (New York: Knopf, 2003).

102. Bader, "Multiculturalism Takes Root," 143–62.

103. Council on Interracial Books for Children, Racism and Sexism Resource Center for Educators, *Unlearning "Indian" Stereotypes: A Teaching Unit for Elementary Teachers and Children's Librarians* (New York: The Racism and Sexism Resource Center for Educators, 1977).

104. Council on Interracial Books for Children, Racism and Sexism Resource Center for Educators, *Unlearning Asian Stereotypes* (New York: The Center).

105. Council on Interracial Books for Children, Racism and Sexism Resource Center for Educators, *Stereotypes, Distortions, and Omissions in U.S. History Textbooks* (New York: The Center, 1977).

106. Council on Interracial Books for Children, "10 Quick Ways to Analyze Children's Books for Racism and Sexism," in *The New Press Guide to Multicultural Resources for Young Readers*, ed. Daphne Muse (New York: The New Press, 1997), 17–19. Also http://www.birchlane.davis.ca.us/library/10quick.htm (26 June 2006).

107. Sims, *Shadow and Substance*, 49–78; Harris, "African American Children's Literature," 550–53.

108. Barrera, Liguori, and Salas, "Ideas a Literature Can Grow On," 219.

109. Carmen L. Medina and Patricia Enciso, "'Some Words Are Messengers/Hay Palabras Mensajeras': Interpreting Sociopolitical Themes in Latino/a Children's Literature," *The New Advocate* 15, no. 1 (Winter 2002): 35–47.

110. Susan Freiband and Consuelo Figueras, "Understanding Puerto Rican Culture: Using Puerto Rican Children's Literature," *MultiCultural Review* 11, no. 2 (June 2002): 31.

111. Sherry York, "Introduction," in *Children's and Young Adult Literature by Latino Writers: A Guide for Librarians, Teachers, Parents, and Students* (Worthington, Ohio: Linworth Publishing, 2002), 7.

112. Rosalinda B. Barrera, Ruth E. Quiroa, and Cassiette West-Williams, "Poco a Poco: The Continuing Development of Mexican American Children's Literature in the 1990s," *The New Advocate* 12, no. 4 (Fall 1999): 321.

113. "Immigration Act of 1965," http://campus.northpark.edu/history/WebChron/USA/ImmigrationAct.CP.html (22 Aug. 2005).

114. Sandra Yamate, "Asian Pacific American Children's Literature: Expanding Perceptions about Who Americans Are," in *Using Multiethnic Literature in the K–8 Classroom*, ed. Violet J. Harris (Norwood, Mass.: Christopher-Gordon, 1997), 95–128.

115. Mary G. Byler, *American Indian Authors for Young Readers: A Selective Bibliography* (New York: Association of Indian Affairs, 1973).

116. Champagne, "Education," 859–63.

117. Barbara Bader, "Multiculturalism in the Mainstream," *The Horn Book Magazine* 79 (May/June 2003): 283–84.

118. Miller-Lachmann, "Introduction," 8; Kathleen T. Horning, "The Contributions of Alternative Press Publishers to Multicultural Literature for Children," *Library Trends* 41, no. 3 (Winter 1993): 524–40; Chris Liska Carger, "Harriet Rohmer on New Voices and Visions in Multicultural Literature," *The New Advocate* 14, no. 2 (Spring 2001): 119–26.

119. Gary B. Nash, "American History Reconsidered: Asking New Questions about the Past," in *Learning from the Past: What History Teaches Us about School Reform*, edited by Diane Ravitch and Maris A. Vinovskis (Baltimore, Md.: Johns Hopkins University Press, 1995), 137–42.

120. Nash, "American History Reconsidered," in *Learning from the Past*, 143.

121. Nash, "American History Reconsidered," in *Learning from the Past*, 143–144.

122. John Hope Franklin, *Mirror to America: The Autobiography of John Hope Franklin* (New York: Farrar, Strauss, and Giroux, 2005), 227–29.

123. Franklin, *Mirror to America*, 229–31.

124. Muse, "Introduction," 4–5; Miller-Lachmann, "Introduction," 7–8.

125. Miller-Lachmann, "Introduction," 7–8; "Children's Books By and About People of Color Published in the United States: Statistics Gathered by the Cooperative Children's Book Center," School of Education—University of Wisconsin, Madison, http://www.education.wisc.edu/ccbc/books/pcstats.htm (23 Aug. 2005).

126. Walter Dean Myers, "I Actually Thought We Would Revolutionize the Industry," *New York Times Book Review*, 9 Nov. 1986, p. 50.

127. Miller-Lachmann, "Introduction," 7–8.

128. Sims (Bishop), *Shadow and Substance*.

129. Nash, "American History Reconsidered," 144–45.

130. Nash, "American History Reconsidered" in *Learning from the Past*, 145.

131. Glazer, *We Are All Multiculturalists Now,* 22–31, 64–65.

132. *History–Social Science Framework for California Public Schools: Kindergarten Through Grade Twelve* (Sacramento: California State Board of Education, 1988).

133. Glazer, *We Are All Multiculturalists Now*, 64–65.

134. University of the State of New York, *A Curriculum of Inclusion: Report of the Commissioner's Task Force on Minorities: Equity and Excellence* (Albany, N.Y.: Task Force on Minorities, 1989).

135. Glazer, *We Are All Multiculturalists Now*, 23–25.

136. New York State Social Studies Review and Development Committee, *One Nation, Many Peoples: A Declaration of Cultural Interdependence* (Albany, N.Y.: New York State Education Department, 1991).

137. Glazer, *We Are All Multiculturalists Now*, 25–31.

138. Charlotte A. Crabtree, National Council for History Standards, and National Center for History in the Schools, *Lessons from History: Understandings and His-*

torical Perspectives Students Should Acquire (Los Angeles, Calif.: UCLA National Center for History in the Schools, 1992).

139. Glazer, *We Are All Multiculturalists Now*, 66–69.

140. Glazer, *We Are All Multiculturalists Now*, 69–71; Council for Basic Education, *History in the Making: An Independent Review of the Voluntary National History Standards* (Washington, D.C.: The Council, 1996).

141. Glazer, *We Are All Multiculturalists Now,* 70–77.

142. Miller-Lachmann, "Introduction," 8–9.

143. Miller-Lachmann, "Introduction," 9.

144. Barahona Center for the Study of Books in Spanish for Children and Adolescents//Centro Barahona para el Estudio de Libros Infantiles y Juveniles en Español, http://www.csusm.edu/csb (22 Aug. 2005).

145. University of San Francisco, Department of International and Multicultural Education, Center for Multicultural Literature for Children and Young Adults, 2130 Fulton St., San Francisco, Calif. 94117, http://www.soe.usfca.edu/institutes/childlit (22 Aug. 2005).

146. Violet J. Harris, ed., *Teaching Multicultural Literature in Grades K–8* (Norwood, Mass.: Christopher-Gordon, 1993.).

147. Violet J. Harris, *Using Multiethnic Literature in the K–8 Classroom* (Norwood, Mass.: Christopher-Gordon, 1997).

148. Merri V. Lindgren, ed., *The Multicolored Mirror: Cultural Substance in Literature for Children and Young Adults* (Fort Atkinson, Wisc.: Highsmith, 1991).

3

General Trends in the Field

MAINSTREAM RESPONSES TO MULTICULTURALISM

There are several major issues related to multicultural and ethnic children's literature, including mainstream responses, issues specific to children's literature, and structural issues in publishing and other fields. All of these issues are related to the historical trends and events described in chapter 2. White professionals have responded to multiculturalism in several ways: a few have been especially committed to it, a number have criticized multiculturalism in general, and others have stressed cultural literacy and the core curriculum. All of these responses will be further described in this chapter.

Debate on the issue of multiculturalism in the field of children's literature has focused on how to evaluate materials written about people of color. Debate has taken the following forms: the "insider/outsider" debate over cultural authenticity, the question of whether the criteria for authenticity are too strictly enforced, how to treat "socially conscious" and "melting-pot" literature, and debate resulting from the conflicting professional cultures of people from different fields. A major question is who should be writing about whom, and what qualifies any writer to write about any group. All of these issues, including the use of different kinds of evaluation criteria, will be discussed in this chapter.

Committed Support

Supporters of multicultural and ethnic children's literature from all backgrounds have contributed to this field by doing marketing, promotion, programming, outreach, and teaching to bring this literature to the attention of young people and their families. Other efforts have included production, dissemination, and criticism. Production includes writing books and other materials, but also establishing and managing alternative publishing houses. Dissemination entails getting materials to customers, establishing and maintaining collections in libraries and bookstores, cataloging and classifying materials for libraries, and documenting the existence of materials through bibliographies and other guides and through research-oriented library collections.

Criticism is a huge area, encompassing reviews, scholarly criticism, and the creation and use of prizes, evaluation criteria, and alternative review media. Criticism can also include traditional literary criticism; criticism of racism, ethnocentrism, or other biases in the media; tracing themes in the literature; and creating themes and theories of criticism itself.

A few mainstream professionals have been especially committed to the promotion of multicultural and ethnic books for children. At different times, Nancy Larrick,[1] Virginia Moore Kruse, and Kathleen Horning[2] have published pivotal articles and statistics describing the lack of works on and by people of color. Dorothy Broderick,[3] Arlene Hirschfelder,[4] and Donnarae MacCann[5] have published extensive works on stereotyping in children's literature. Lyn Miller-Lachmann,[6] Frances Ann Day,[7] and Sherry York[8] have each published several bibliographies describing this literature. Miller-Lachmann is now the editor of *The MultiCultural Review*, and Harriet Rohmer is the founder of the Children's Book Press, a major multicultural publisher of children's books in San Francisco.

General Criticism of Multiculturalism

Several major critics of multiculturalism have emerged, including Arthur Schlesinger Jr., Nathan Glazer, and Diane Ravitch. These critics are in favor of some aspects of multiculturalism but opposed to other aspects. They raise provocative questions, and most of them bring something valuable to this discussion. Arthur Schlesinger Jr. was for thirty years a member of the executive council of the *Journal of Negro History*, and has long advocated the study of the history of many cultures. His father, Arthur Schlesinger Sr., was the last white member of the Association for the Study of Negro Life and History and was a close friend of Carter G. Woodson.[9] Nathan Glazer raises many thoughtful questions as he observes the interactions of people from many ethnic groups, in and out of school settings, over a long period of time. Diane Ravitch also raises many serious concerns in her work in educational history and with educational standards and curricula. Issues they discuss include the following:

- Whether multiculturalism promotes fragmentation and separation, and whether it can mutate into cultural separatism
- The self-esteem of children of color in relation to the curriculum
- The significance of model minorities
- Afrocentrism

Both Schlesinger and Glazer are very concerned that multiculturalism might undermine civic harmony by replacing assimilation with fragmentation, and integration with separation.[10] Glazer in particular asks how much educators should stress national unity in creating school curricula.[11] Schlesinger states that multiculturalism should promote ethnic understanding between groups rather than ethnic chauvinism.[12] Schlesinger, Glazer, and Ravitch[13] are all seeking a middle ground between complete assimilation and a very traditional European curriculum, on the one hand, and cultural separatism, on the other. I believe that multiculturalism can be an agent for unity *or* division, depending on what is taught or communicated and how this is done.

Glazer[14] questions whether students must "see themselves" in the curriculum if they are to learn effectively. Schlesinger[15] writes that history should not be taught specifically to raise the self-esteem of minority children. He claims that the traditional "Eurocentric" curriculum does *not* necessarily wreak havoc on the psyches of children of color. Yet, in a different context, he also briefly discusses black students who view any intellectual activity as "acting white." I suspect that young people who think this way do not know their history in general, and their culture's intellectual history in particular. Schlesinger also states that it does not matter where role models come from.[16] Actually, it does matter. Children of all backgrounds need a variety of role models, some of whom look like them and come from their cultures. Schlesinger does provide an excellent discussion of the uses and abuses of both exculpatory history, which is written to justify the status quo, and compensatory history, designed to focus more on formerly excluded people.[17]

Related to the issue of self-esteem and role models are Schlesinger's[18] and Glazer's[19] discussions of "model minorities" who made it in society and assimilated, even though they never "saw themselves" at public school. However, all ethnic groups that have done well, such as Jewish, Chinese, Japanese, Greek, and Armenian Americans, came to the United States as voluntary immigrants and brought their cultures with them. All of these groups were able to start language schools, religious training, and other programs on their own time and their own dime to pass on their cultures. On the other hand, two of the ethnic groups with the most severe problems, African Americans and Native Americans, were separated from their original cultures in various ways and are recovering from cultural amnesia! Schlesinger is quite correct in stating that the failure of groups and individuals rests on many more factors than those discussed here, but I still maintain that knowing one's own cultural roots and having choices about how to deal with those can really help also.

Cultural Literacy and the Core Curriculum

Advocates of cultural literacy[20] and the core curriculum are reacting to the multicultural curricula in elementary and secondary schools and to ethnic studies courses and programs at the college level. They are also reacting to other phenomena, including a K–12 curriculum offering a "cafeteria approach" to required subjects instead of a sequence of required courses for everybody. E. D. Hirsch[21] and other advocates of cultural literacy are very concerned with the following three issues:

- Maintaining a common base of knowledge for better communication and to create better citizens
- The importance of providing real information, not just techniques. There must also be enough related information to provide students with a broader context of subjects under discussion
- The lack of a standardized uniform or systematic curriculum (Hirsch and other advocates of cultural literacy and core knowledge are concerned about a fragmented "cafeteria styled" curriculum, as well as a lack of shared knowledge among the public.)

Cultural literacy is not diametrically opposed to multiculturalism, nor vice versa. Proponents in both camps agree on the importance of shared content and context in school curricula. Hirsch's points about the importance of background knowledge in the teaching of reading[22] can apply well to both traditional Western curricula and multicultural curricula.

There is sharp disagreement between the two on several issues, however, including whose content and context should be taught, how much to teach, and how to integrate all of these things. Proponents of multiculturalism and cultural literacy also disagree on whether the Western canon is truly universal or mainly Western. In addition, proponents of cultural literacy stress literature from the past, whereas ethnic and multicultural research and literature are still emerging.

Proponents of cultural literacy argue that if all are literate in the Western canon, all can advance in Western society.[23] This is the cultural and educational version of the Anglo conformity approach to race relations that is described in chapter 1. While knowing Western civilization is essential for everybody to function in a white-dominated world, it is not enough. Everybody also needs to know the contributions and wisdom of people whose roots are not in the West. Successful people of color have always needed to be bicultural. People of obvious European descent have been able to be more monocultural until recently, but can no longer afford this luxury in such a rapidly changing world. Everybody will need to know how to find out about groups of people who have been neglected in the past or who are new to them.

To determine "what literate Americans know" and probably should know, Hirsch, Joseph Kett, and James Trefil, all professors from the University of Virginia,[24] generated a list of undefined terms that they took from indexes, reference books, textbooks, general books, magazines, and a major dictionary. After combining and critiquing their results among themselves, they submitted their list to over one hundred consultants outside the academic world. They found strong consensus about "significant elements in our core literate vocabulary" from educated Americans of different ages, sexes, races, and national origins. Out of this research has come an appendix to *Cultural Literacy: What Every American Needs to Know* entitled "What Literate Americans Know,"[25] as well as two dictionaries of cultural literacy[26] and a "core knowledge" series for students in grades 1–6.[27] They have published two editions of *The Dictionary of Cultural Literacy*. While most of their information has come from the West, they have included some content from elsewhere, and increased this content between editions of their dictionary.

There have been several reactions from multiculturalists. Kwame Anthony Appiah and Henry Louis Gates Jr. asked scholars from many cultures around the world, including Western scholars of those cultures, about information people need in order to understand those cultures. They asked these experts to suggest fifty of the most important cultural contributions from the regions in which they are knowledgeable. Appiah and Gates collated these suggestions, "producing for each region a master list of the top fifty or so topics mentioned more than once." They then worked with another group of researchers to investigate these topics, and those written results were received and modified by scholars in the field. This led to the publication of *The Dictionary of Global Culture*.[28] In addition, Gates also published *Loose Canons*,[29] a book of essays exploring some African American perspectives on the evolving literary canon.

Rick Simonson and Scott Walker compiled *The Graywolf Annual Five: Multicultural Literacy*[30] in 1988 in reaction to both the work of E. D. Hirsch and the publication of *The Closing of the American Mind* by Allan Bloom.[31] They published several essays by people from a wide variety of ethnic groups who also reacted to the Western canon. Simonson and Walker[32] criticized both Hirsch and Bloom for being too static, for giving shallow definitions of culture, and for their outdated worldviews. They state that most

Americans are becoming aware of the contributions of repressed cultures, are more aware of how history has always been written and rewritten, and believe that we should all be more sensitive to cultural changes. They also maintain that because at least one fourth of all Americans are "of color" (as of 1988), none of us can afford to remain ignorant of any part of our population. Simonson and Walker also compiled a list of words and concepts that were omitted by Hirsch.

The essays, which had all been published previously, also criticized the Western canon and made suggestions for changes in curricula. Wendell Berry[33] raises two provocative questions about knowledge—how and what should we learn, and how should we use that knowledge? Some of the other contributors to this volume—Paula Gunn Allen,[34] Ishmael Reed,[35] Guillermo Gomez-Pena,[36] Eduardo Galeano,[37] David Mura,[38] and Michele Wallace[39]— wrote on four themes: a melting world (where assimilation takes place in both directions), contributions from non-Western cultures, problems encountered by people of color, and interactions between people of color and the West and white people.

Reed called the United States "a cultural bouillabaisse," and stated that the melting world is already here. Gomez-Pena mentioned melting borders, with Latin Americans moving north to the United States and Africans and people from the Middle East moving west to Europe. Allen discussed the contributions of Native Americans to the United States, as well as the advantages and values of traditional Native American cultures. The authors mentioned the following problems facing people of color: stereotypes in Western culture (Allen), writing in a repressed society (Galeano), the lack of diversity or minority control in the media, poor educational histories, and attempts at assimilation that have not succeeded (Wallace). In discussing interactions with white people and the West, Mura and Wallace mention different cultural worldviews, "color blindness," ignorance and lack of recognition of the past, the relevance of Western culture to all, and what they believe white people can do to solve these problems. All of these essays provide food for thought for anybody considering cultural literacy, multiculturalism, and how to combine the two.

Some critics of multiculturalism have quickly mentioned and dismissed critical thinking,[40] and proponents of multiculturalism have not mentioned this topic at all. Critical thinking,[41] which is based on Western philosophical thought, can be used as a way to teach students and the public how to evaluate both the traditional teachings of Western culture and newer multicultural teachings. Yet nobody mentions teaching in such a way that students are hungry for more, which may include using bibliographies and pathfinders (mini-bibiliographies on research subjects), library programming, homework assignments, independent study, projects, or information literacy instruction to encourage students to find out more about topics that interest them. Critical thinking can cause students to really consider pros and cons of all that they are learning. In fact, for critical thinking to work, students would have to have something to think critically about. Both the traditional Western canon and newer multicultural curricula would provide that.

Information literacy instruction is used by librarians and instructors to teach patrons and students how to do library, computer, and other research and how to find information on topics that interest them. The emphasis here is on determining a person's information needs and then finding, evaluating, and using that information. It is impossible to teach everything about everyone in school. However, educators can determine an integrated framework of information to teach, both about the West and about other cultures. Beyond that, information literacy can be used to teach students how to find out more information or find more literature related to topics that interest them. The traditional Western canon, multicultural curricula, critical thinking, and information literacy can all be combined to create a dynamic curriculum.

Advocates of cultural literacy have been criticized by multiculturalists for not recognizing how limited Western traditional curricula has been, or the racism and stereotypes that have long been part of the curricula. However, Western culture is also respected by many people of color for its more positive aspects, such as the promotion of democracy and freedom and for being the lingua franca or cultural glue that ties everything else together. The Western canon has also gradually changed over hundreds of years. Proponents of cultural literacy have made two contributions to the field of multiculturalism. First, they are beginning to define the most important things that everyone should know about Western civilization. Second, and probably more important, they stress the importance of background knowledge for people to be able to put words and other information into context. In addition, knowing about the West is important for all children. But so is knowing about other cultures. Disagreements between proponents of multiculturalism and of cultural literacy have been more a matter of degree than opposites. Finding a combination of approaches that all can agree with is vital, and will be a challenge for some time.

Afrocentrism, Multiculturalism, and the Treatment of Intellectuals of Color

Arthur Schlesinger[42] is to be highly commended for his attention to African American intellectuals. He mentions a wide range of scholarship, briefly differentiates between diverse kinds of research on Africa and the black diaspora, and also states that Afrocentrism is *not* multiculturalism. In addition, he also briefly mentions a number of more mainstream African American scholars. Critics of multiculturalism have every reason to be suspicious of the worst of Afrocentric research, considering their experience with Afrocentrists in New York. However, critics use the worst of this research to cast doubt on all black scholarship and on multiculturalism in general. So far, there is a lack of discussion of emerging scholarship from Latino/as, Asian Americans, or Native Americans.

Schlesinger mentions several streams of research relating to Africa and the African diaspora and quickly dismisses them all. However, like research on and from the West, this research varies widely in quality. Critics of the worst of Afrocentric work are right in questioning research not supported by hard evidence, as well as any signs of cultural chauvinism.

But one can write from an African-centered point of view and observe the rules of scholarly and literary discourse. Some of this work is by African scholars. For instance, John Mbiti[43] describes traditional African religions and how they function in African societies, without being chauvinistic. One can describe the empires of east and west Africa, describe tribal life for ordinary people, and present good and bad aspects of all of these things, and still write from an African perspective.

Afrocentric scholars have been criticized for calling ancient Egyptians black and for claiming Alexander Pushkin and the family of Alexandre Dumas as black. However fifty to one hundred years ago, all of these people would have been classified as black under the "one drop" rule prevailing in the United States, if any of them had been living in this country at that time. African Americans classified them as they themselves were classified—anybody with any black ancestry in this country was considered black. In addition, claiming the mixed-race Egyptians as black is no more absurd than pretending that they were white or that north Africa has little or nothing to do with the rest of the continent.

Schlesinger[44] quickly dismisses the work of African American scholars who discuss unique cultural and learning styles of black children. He is very justified in questioning a genetic basis for this. However, he also has difficulty with the concept that there may be any cultural differences. He cites Janice Hale[45] where she agrees with him, but says nothing about her research that presents these learning and relational styles not as genetic, but as cultural.

He also ridicules the work of scholars of various backgrounds who study the similarities between Black English and African languages, quoting an African journalist who saw no simlarities.[46] What Schlesinger does not mention is that many of these scholars are linguists who have observed similarities between Ebonics and the various Creoles of the Caribbean.

These similarities are based not on vocabulary (which the African journalist was probably commenting on) but on the structure and grammar of the languages.

Schlesinger does not discuss research in anthropology or in folklore on possible surviving "Africanisms" or African cultural traits in the West, a subject of debate among scholars of different ethnic backgrounds and from several academic disciplines since the mid-twentieth century. Information crucial to this debate includes research not only on Africans and African Americans, but also on black people in the Caribbean and Latin America as well. Possible Africanisms in the West include not only the structural use of language, but also "call and response" in conversation, song, worship, and other public events; religious practices; cooking styles; hairstyles; crafts, such as basketry; architectural styles, where applicable; and the spread of folklore. An example of this last is the existence of Anansi stories in West Africa, the Caribbean, and Belize, as well as the presence of Br'er Rabbit and other trickster tales in the United States. One book that does discuss Africanisms as they affect black and white people is *Africanisms in American Culture*, which is edited by Joseph Holloway.[47]

Schlesinger questions the amount of African American interest in Africa without mentioning either the gross stereotyping that has historically been prevalent in the Western media about that continent, or the impact of the end of colonization on African American attitudes toward Africa. It is true that when the African continent was colonized, most African Americans did not necessarily identify with west Africa, but there was always an undercurrent of interest in the African diaspora. Colonial African Americans called themselves Africans. A small minority of African Americans did colonize Liberia. Black denominations such as the African Methodist Episcopal (AME) Church sent missionaries to Africa. A literary movement, Negritude, which originated in the French-speaking countries of west Africa, also had an influence on Caribbean and African American writers. Some African Americans have been fascinated by Egypt, Nubia, and Ethiopia and were outraged when Italy invaded Ethiopia in the 1930s. While a lot of the African American middle class did not support Marcus Garvey, he was seen as charismatic and influential to others, and he has more influence than Schlesinger and others would guess. Artists, politicians, and activists in a variety of fields, such as Harry Belafonte, Malcolm X, and Shirley Chisholm, were children of Garveyites. W. E. B. DuBois, who was definitely *not* influenced by Garvey, attended several major pan-African conferences throughout the twentieth century. Later in life, he married Shirley Graham, an early African American children's book author with a strong interest in Africa, who was the daughter of AME missionaries to Liberia. DuBois would spend his last few years in Ghana. If everybody else can claim their original heritage, why is it so controversial for African Americans to do the same?

Schlesinger and Hirsch both cite Orlando Patterson when he defends the teaching of Western civilization, but neither discuss Patterson's scholarship and how it may be relevant to either a multicultural or a traditional curriculum. Schlesinger treats scholars like John Hope Franklin, Henry Louis Gates, and Kenneth Clark in similar ways. He also does not consider more theoretical researchers like Cornel West or Vine Deloria. It would have been helpful if Schlesinger had paid more attention to what a multicultural curriculum based on the work of these scholars might look like.

Schlessinger lists "A Baker's Dozen—Books Indispensable to an Understanding of America" in the appendix of his book.[48] All thirteen of the writers are white, and only one is a woman. Works like *The Life and Times of Frederick Douglass*, *The Souls of Black Folk* by W. E. B. DuBois, *Up from Slavery* by Booker T. Washington, and *The Invisible Man* by Ralph Ellison are not listed. Maybe he should have expanded his list to twenty-five or fifty titles and been more inclusive. However, Schlesinger must be given credit for mentioning more and a far wider range of black scholars than does almost anybody else.

In the "Atkinson-Ravitch Sampler of Classic Literature for Home and School,"[49] Diane Ravitch does recommend the titles by DuBois, Washington, and Ellison that are mentioned above and a similar one by Frederick Douglass for high school readers. For younger readers, she recommends selected poems (no anthologies) by Paul Laurence Dunbar, Langston Hughes, and Arna Bontemps. In her essay "Literature: Forgetting the Tradition,"[50] Ravitch questions the inclusion of Sandra Cisneros, Nikki Giovanni, Toni Cade Bambara, Lawrence Yep, Pat Mora, Julia Alvarez, Walter Dean Myers, Naomi Shihab Nye, and Rudolfo A. Anaya because "they are not well-known to the public." Ravitch does not mention Newbery Award winners such as Mildred Taylor or Virginia Hamilton, who was also an internationally recognized winner of the Hans Christian Andersen Award for lifetime achievement as a children's book author. While her emphasis on established writers of the past may be understandable, she is missing the best writers in an emerging multicultural literature, and most of these authors write for young children. Ravitch states that students may never encounter Melville, Emerson, Conrad, or Hawthorne. Ironically, the emergence of the current writers listed above and their struggle for recognition and study in schools and colleges are very similar to the emergence of a separate and general U.S. literature 150 years ago, when this literature was first studied in schools. Many of the nineteenth-century authors whom Ravitch cites, as well as writers such as Twain and Poe, are also still being assigned in high schools and colleges, though possibly not as much as they once were. Schools are combining the traditional and the new.

Glazer is more concerned in his research with the complex reactions of professionals, parents, and community people to developments in education than to those of intellectuals, even as he cites researchers, mostly in the social sciences. Two scholars of color whom he mentions are Glenn Loury and Ronald Takaki. For the most part, critics of multiculturalism do not fully know, recognize, or understand the contributions of scholars, intellectuals, or writers of color. Awareness of black intellectuals is limited, and awareness of intellectuals from other groups, nearly nonexistent at this time. Admission to the Western canon for scholars of color has been very slow, and not all are readily assimilating.

However, there are at least two exceptions to this. Gary Nash[51] extensively considers the many kinds of literature related to Afrocentrism, and he thoroughly describes black scholarship, even as he comes to the same conclusions as Schlesinger. Donnarae MacCann also makes extensive use of black scholarship in her book *White Supremacy in Children's Literature*.[52]

MORE SPECIFIC ISSUES IN CHILDREN'S LITERATURE

There are more specific issues in the field of multicultural and ethnic children's literature. A very important one is who the literature is written for. Who can and who should write children's literature about people of color? How should this literature be evaluated? These questions are reflected in several controversies—the "insider/outsider" debate over cultural authenticity; the possible overuse of criteria meant to prevent stereotyping; debate over socially conscious, melting-pot, and culturally conscious children's literature; conflicts between professional cultures; and the use of different kinds of criteria. Some differences between the fields of education and of children's literature will also be briefly mentioned.

The "Insider/Outsider" Debate

The insider/outsider debate over cultural authenticity is a very spirited one. Related to this are disagreements about what evaluative criteria should be used to determine the quality of this literature. A great deal of research and literature has been written on these issues.

There are three schools of thought on cultural authenticity:

Multicultural literature should be written by all. The author's own background should not make a difference.

Write what you know. People not belonging to a culture should not write on that culture. *Only members of a culture should write their own story*. A writer's background will determine how well he or she describes the culture under consideration.

Background makes a definite difference as people write about a culture new or unknown to them. Most of the time, works by members of cultural groups are much more authentic than those from the outside. *However, people not indigenous to a group can learn enough about a culture new to them to do a good job.* How much or what kind(s) of preparation necessary for this is open to much debate. *Also, some cultural group members may not know their own culture that well* and may make errors writing about or illustrating a story about their own culture or a related one.

Even though there are exceptions on all sides, there are the following tendencies. People of color have been more likely to believe (often justifiably) that cultural outsiders do not understand their cultures well enough to authentically write about them. They want to be sure that writers do the appropriate research and preparation sufficient to adequately write about or illustrate a different culture. These views are described in articles by Woodson;[53] Mikkelson;[54] Cai;[55] Seto;[56] Fang, Fu, and Lamme;[57] and McNair.[58] White writers are more likely to state that background does not matter, and all should be able to write on all groups, as long as they write well and have a good imagination. Examples of essays reflecting this viewpoint are those by Campbell[59] and one by Salle[60] entitled "Ethnicity and Authenticity, or How Black (Hispanic, Native American, etc.) Do I Gotta Be?"

To answer *that* question, Moreillon[61] describes her experience writing about a Native American nation as a white teacher and author. She taught at the Tohono O'odham reservation for a period of time, and as she wrote, she consulted with people in this community to be sure that her writing was authentic. Ironically, she was repeating the experiences of Ann Nolan Clark and others working with Native Americans in the 1920s, 1930s, and 1940s. Hopefully, many authors learning about a culture new to them at least do some library research and visit the group under discussion. However, depending on the author's background, the situation of the group under consideration, and the subject covered, this may or may not be enough (and in many cases, it would not be). It may be necessary to work or live with the group for a long time and consult with elders, leaders, and other group members before one can really begin to understand the culture.

Many of the essays mentioned above, plus some others, were compiled, updated, and published in an anthology, *Stories Matter: The Complexity of Cultural Authenticity in Children's Literature.*[62] The purposes of this collection are to provide a sense of history on this issue, to promote a broad understanding of current issues and debates, and to get a glimpse of possible new conversations and questions. This work includes thoughtful essays from people with all points of view on this subject, and there is some consensus that authenticity is a very vital issue—as well as a very complicated one. Fox and Short[63] maintain that all children should be able to see themselves accurately portrayed in books, and that ethnic authors have a right to tell their own stories and to pass on their values to their own (and the neighbors') children. They view culturally authentic books as more engaging for children from the culture described and a source of cultural understanding for other children.

However, cultural authenticity is not as straightforward as it appears. While members of cultural groups are usually much more knowledgeable about their own cultures than outsiders, they vary greatly in their general opinions, as well as in how they evaluate a work. For example, Smolkin and Suina[64] describe the different reactions of Pueblo people to Gerald McDermott's *Arrow to the Sun*, which was praised and used by some group members and criticized and avoided by others. In addition, not all group members know or identify with all aspects of their own culture, and some may produce stereotypes of their own. Mo and Shen[65] make the point that just because a cultural practice is authentic does not mean that it is acceptable to all members of a culture. They also state that authors should not promote inhuman values from *any* culture. In addition, they state that all cultures have some overlapping values appropriate to all.

Henry Louis Gates[66] mentions that authenticity can be "faked" well enough to fool some cultural insiders, and he cites the case of *The Education of Little Tree* by Forrest Carter and the presence of false slave narratives. He believes that no human culture is inaccessible to people who make the effort to understand, learn, or inhabit another world.

Critics of cultural authenticity raise some very thoughtful points in *Stories Matter*. Aronson[67] mentions that pretending that "*a* culture has *a* view that belongs to *a* people" is wrong. Both he and Lasky[68] ask whether anyone can tell what elements come from any particular culture and what was borrowed from elsewhere. Aronson also wonders how people can easily allow cultural crossing in music but not in books. Rochman[69] raises some excellent concerns about the portrayal of ethnic characters in children's books, and asks whether they must always be "strong, dignified, loving, sensitive, and wise." She maintains that the best of literature is rich in ambiguity and "glories in conflict." Rochman also mentions that bland, didactic stories will chase readers away. While she believes that authenticity matters, she also states that there is no sure formula for acquiring it, and that it would be best to combat inaccuracy with accuracy.

One way around many of these issues is to teach children, professionals, and parents critical thinking and encourage them to approach literature in this spirit. However, there is one very important fact that is seldom mentioned in this debate. Publishing is often a zero-sum game. As mainstream authors' works about previously neglected or maligned groups are published, people from these groups have great difficulty in getting published by mainstream presses and must choose between not publishing or seeking alternatives. One result is that children seldom get to hear worldviews of people from many ethnic groups, and they miss themes that are important to everyone. Also, as Smith points out in an article entitled "A Different Drum,"[70] worldview includes not only how people perceive their reality, but how they describe their perceptions and the styles they use in doing this. Bishop's[71] points in *Stories Matter* are very important. She urges all authors to pay serious attention to good writing by ethnic authors and to look for themes, textual features, and predominating ideologies or worldviews. She also mentions that people who write about other groups should be willing to deal with criticism from that group.

Stories Matter also discusses many other questions related to cultural authenticity, including what experiences authors need to have to write authentic books, how a book's purpose and use may relate to this question, the relationship between cultural authenticity and literary excellence, and the issue of social responsibility versus writers' freedom of expression.

Criteria as Dogma?

In her book *The Language Police*,[72] Diane Ravitch criticizes critics and "censors" from both the left and the right who influence U.S. textbook publishers. According to her, censors on the right want to restore an idealized vision of the past, and those from the left believe in an idealized vision of the future. Neither side wants children and adolescents to read material that challenges their view of the world. The right wing tries to control topics covered by books, while the left wing tries to control language and images. The right wing has had the most success on the publication of trade books, while the left wing has influenced text publishing companies through the use of evaluation guidelines. She concludes that the guidelines combine "left-wing political correctness with right wing religious fundamentalism."

Ravitch[73] pays the most attention to evaluating guidelines meant to prevent stereotyping that are now used in many textbooks. They originated with guidelines that were created by the Council on Interracial Books for Children, and are now devised by educational publishers, test development companies, states, and scholarly and professional associations. She describes the kinds of stereotyping discussed in the guide from Riverside Publishing—emotional stereotyping (of men and women), occupational stereotyping, stereotyping of activities or behaviors, role stereotyping (for example the use of Asian

American scholars or African American athletes), stereotyping of community settings, and stereotyping of physical attributes or abilities.

Ravitch makes a number of points that should be seriously considered. Can guidelines to prevent stereotyping be taken too far when rigidly applied? Can women still be described or shown as housewives or African Americans as urban people? I think so. If authors leave out all language and pictures that can offend the left or subjects that can offend the right, students will be left with some very dull and irrelevant textbooks. Rochman makes similar arguments about multicultural children's books. If negative people or negative aspects of different cultures can never be portrayed, books can become distorted and very dull.

Ravitch[74] makes her strongest points when she describes inoffensive books influenced by the left and right as stories with no geographic locations; little conflict (which can be readily resolved); obedient, respectful children who are never in danger; healthy and active older people who never die; disabled people who need no assistance; no fantasy or magic; and in the case of scientific stories, no reference to evolution or prehistoric times. Or as Garrison Keillor puts it on *The Prairie Home Companion,* "where the women are strong, the men good-looking, and the children all above average." Some of the guidelines for avoiding stereotypes can also lead to historic inaccuracy, if adhered to too strictly, defeating the purpose of much of this literature.

However, Ravitch seems very reluctant to deal with the viewpoints of people of color unless they agree with her, stating that "the very existence of guidelines" that may limit words or ideas is offensive, and she views any work with ethnic organizations as self-censorship.[75] Ravitch believes that the Council on Interracial Books for Children (CIBC) was a good organization as long as it stressed the inclusion of formerly neglected groups, encouraged publishers to include more realistic stories and more accurate historical treatment about diverse groups, and awarded prizes for the best new children's books by minority writers.[76] On the other hand, she criticizes the CIBC for being influenced by racial separation and black power and for their angry criticism about past and present education practices and stereotypes in children's books. While she criticizes the CIBC for their insistence that only minority group members are qualified to write about their own experiences, she never addresses either the lack of minority writers being published or stereotypes still existing, especially in children's literature. She was also unsympathetic to CIBC's "demand" that publishers subsidize minority-owned bookstores, printers, and publishers. Yet, if people of color have difficulty being published by major mainstream presses and do not control major presses of their own—is *that* censorship? What say, if any, should people have in how they are portrayed? These issues are not resolved.

Ravitch does note some valid problems with publishers working with ethnic organizations. A community-based group, such as the Council on Islamic Education, may have one representative working with several textbook publishers, leading to very similar information in all textbooks. People from ethnic groups are often very reluctant to say anything negative about their own group, especially when most information on them has been negative. However in my opinion, Ravitch's reluctance to accept publishers working with these organizations at all is further evidence that varied viewpoints from diverse groups are not always particularly welcomed.

Melting-Pot, Socially Conscious, and Culturally Conscious Literature

According to the critic Rudine Sims,[77] authors writing on a culture not their own have a tendency to write melting-pot and socially conscious literature. Melting-pot literature consists mostly of picture books describing everyday routines and events in the lives of children of color, without being culturally specific. At worst, a white character may be "colored in." Socially conscious books can be compared to the well-meaning movie from the 1960s *Guess Who's Coming to Dinner?* Usually written for older children, socially conscious books on African Americans tend to be either about slavery or the civil rights movement. The main character is usually white, either trying to help a black child or reacting to black people in the story. These books portray people of color, but do so through a white lens. The main point of these books is the reaction of white people to people of color, who are seen as problems or challenges to be solved. These books mean well, but include subtle stereotypes of their own. Sims also described culturally conscious books, usually written on people of a group by authors from the group. These books are written from the points of view of ethnic children, include more specific cultural details than do the melting-pot books, and hopefully include fewer stereotypes than the socially conscious books. Many reflect the perspectives of ethnic writers writing for their own children, as well as those from other groups. They are both confirming their cultures to their own children and explaining it to others.

Socially conscious literature about African Americans first appeared in the 1950s and early 1960s as they were first attempting to integrate society in large numbers. Socially conscious novels about this particular group were not published as often in the late 1960s and 1970s, and they were replaced by culturally conscious literature, more often written by African Americans themselves. However, socially conscious novels about black people made a reappearance in the 1990s, and some critics of color[78] raised the issue of why this was happening at that time. I question whether socially conscious literature on Latino/as, Native Americans, or Asian Americans has ever been totally replaced by culturally conscious literature from these groups, even though the latter literature definitely exists.

Conflicts in Professional Cultures

This is not strictly a racial or ethnic debate. Debbie Reese[79] describes two cultures, one of authors, editors, and reviewers, and another of teachers and librarians. After surveying people from these professions, she concludes that authors, editors, and reviewers represent a culture of literature, and that they tend to believe that reviews and criticism should focus on a book's literary quality *only*. They focus on *how well* something is said, and they promote intellectual freedom. Teachers and librarians represent a culture of education, and tend to believe that reviews should consider both literary quality and the sociopolitical realities behind a book. *What is said* matters as much to them as *how it is said*. While authors, editors, and reviewers are likely to promote intellectual freedom, teachers and librarians are just as serious about social responsibility. They are very concerned about the impact of books on all of their diverse students or patrons.

While many issues related to multiculturalism are equally relevant to school texts and trade books, there are also some differences. As Ravitch has noted, the left wing has been able to influence textbook publishers with the use of evaluation guidelines. The right wing has more of an influence on trade books. While some Afrocentric materials with questionable content have been adopted by a few school systems, this type of material is *not* being published by the mainstream, multicultural, or ethnic presses mentioned in this work. While the books published deal with difficult subjects, such as slavery or the Middle Passage, we are not seeing the worst excesses of Afrocentric scholarship in school texts. However, questions about who should write what, whether to evaluate books for cultural authenticity, and how to do this are still very important issues.

If Diane Ravitch and other critics of multiculturalism are correct, textbooks, especially in literature and the social sciences, are thoroughly integrated. However, the percentage of trade books about children of color is still consistently low (no more than 10 percent) and the percentage of writers of color even lower. There is still much work to be done.

Who Is Qualified to Write?

There are at least three kinds of criteria to use in evaluating multicultural and ethnic children's literature—traditional literary criteria, criteria related to cultural authenticity, and evolving ethnic criteria.

Nobody is questioning the use of traditional literary quality in evaluating children's books. However, some proponents of multicultural children's literature question whether these criteria are enough. A book can be an imaginative work of high literary quality and still distort and stereotype the culture that it portrays.[80] This is especially problematic when there is little else published on the culture, especially by people from the group represented.

When criteria for preventing stereotyping are used too rigidly, this can lead to dull materials with their own distortions. However, considering the long history of both stereotyping of many groups in children's literature and other media and the lack of writers from diverse cultures being published, these criteria are necessary, at least as guidelines. They can help authors to avoid the worst stereotyping about people.

A third set of criteria is emerging from ethnic critics analyzing their own literature, both for children and for adults. These analysts can bring aspects of their own cultures to the subject at hand that others would not be aware of. Some of this form of criticism may transfer and translate very well to other settings. One may have to be selective here, but this opens up another channel of thought on this issue. For instance, MacCann[81] discusses "the Black Aesthetic," a literary theory proposed by Addison Gayle[82] in 1970. Advocates of the Black Aesthetic combine traditional literary criteria with general guidelines to avoid both cultural misrepresentation and a multitude of rigid rules.

I believe that writers' backgrounds make a definite difference, especially as they write about cultures new to them. Usually group members can describe their own group better than others can—but not always. Authors and illustrators do not always know their own cultures very well, and some writers and illustrators can learn enough about a culture not their own to do a good job. Some types of literature, such as history, biography, folklore collections, or literary anthologies may be more accessible to writers and illustrators not from groups portrayed.

There are two issues related to qualifications that should probably be pursued separately. One is the issue of cultural authenticity itself. Joseph Bruchac,[83] Philip Lee,[84] and the supporters of the Americas Award[85] all evaluate materials for cultural authenticity regardless of the author. What qualifies any author to write about any group is a complex issue. How well do group members know their own cultural groups? And for people writing on or illustrating those from other groups, how did they find out about the culture under consideration? Did they do extensive library research; consult ethnic media, leaders, organizations, or institutions; or live and work in the community for a period of time? All of these questions are relevant.

Another issue is the recruitment of many more ethnic writers. At this time, many new writers of color are being published largely by minority-owned alternative presses. Other publishers also need to work more with new writers. A few presses are hiring editors of color and starting new multicultural and ethnic imprints. This can also help. These developments will be further described in the next section.

The Flesh-Colored Band-Aid: Diversity in Publishing and Related Fields

It may be time to reconsider the way publishing houses, review media, and library collection development procedures are structured. Like the flesh-colored Band-Aids of the 1950s, all of these institutions and procedures were created by white people for white people. In some ways they still reflect the integrated cultural world of a century ago, when publishers, creators of children's literature, educators, librarians, cultural institutions, and the media strongly influenced one another. Major changes are needed in all of these fields to more truly reflect the diversity of America. Publishing houses, review media, jobbers, libraries, and other institutions need to not only hire many more people of color, but also promote them and incorporate many more ways of thinking and doing. They should also collaborate more with alternative organizations that already exist. Some of this may now be happening with Lectorum acting as the Spanish-language division of Scholastic and with the acquisition of Libros Sin Fronteras, a major Spanish-language distributor, by Baker and Taylor. Hyperion has also created a black-oriented line, Jump at the Sun.

Several editors of color have produced children's books for mainstream publishers. Bernette Ford is a pioneer in this area, starting her career at Random House in 1972 and working at Golden Books, Grosset and Dunlap, and Putnam. Between 1988 and 2004, Ford founded Cartwheel Books for the Very Young at Scholastic and launched Just For You!, a series of books for readers in Kindergarten through grade 2, for the same publisher in 2004. Since then, she has founded the Color-Bridge Books for All Children, a multicultural imprint of African American and Latino titles for children from infants to age six. Other editors include Andrea Davis Pinckney, Scholastic's new picture book editor, and Phoebe Yeh, the executive editor at the Harper Collins Books for Children, who had earlier been at Scholastic.

Taxel[86] describes structural developments in the publishing world that could have a negative impact, for the most part, on multicultural and ethnic children's literature. They include fast capitalism, structural changes in the industry, marketing trends, and other tensions between commerce and culture. He defines *fast capitalism* as a stress on "competition and markets centered on change, flexibility, quality, and distinctive niches."

He notes major changes in the industry, including the replacement of independent bookstores with chains and online vendors, the acquisition of small publishers by large multimedia conglomerates, and the replacement of traditional literary-oriented managers with more bottom line–oriented executives from retailing. This has led to a shift from an editorial focus to marketing and financial growth strategies and more emphasis on the bottom line than the public good. There is also a search for synergy, with books being merchandized and tied to other media, as exemplified by the Pleasant Company, Scholastic, and especially Disney. Changes in copyright and tax laws also make it difficult for publishers to maintain backlogs of high-quality but unconventional or low-selling books. In addition, there has been an emphasis on selling to bookstores, discount stores, supermarkets, and drugstores and a deemphasis on the public or school library market. However, I believe that under some conditions, creators of multicultural materials may be able to benefit from these and other trends, including niche marketing, selling to various stores, media tie-ins, and the whole-language movement in schools.

As a result of all of the issues described above, and in spite of some positive developments, it has been a real necessity for multicultural and ethnic authors, editors, publishers, and other professionals to build alternative publishing companies and institutions; to find creative ways to market, distribute, and promote their materials; to have a strong base in their specific communities; and to reach out to other people. These efforts will be described in more detail at the end of this chapter and in chapters 4 and 5.

Using and Promoting the Material

Other issues related to multicultural children's literature include how to use and promote this material and how children and their families react to it. Libraries and other institutions have created a variety of programs and activities to promote multicultural literature, and some initiatives are reported in the professional library media and on the Internet. Library approaches can be divided into two types. One type involves the general techniques of multicultural and ethnic librarianship described in guidebooks and other library literature, including administration, planning, surveying, collection development, and information literacy instruction. Another type includes specific programs and activities that libraries, bookstores, community agencies, and organizations can do for the public, either on their own or in combination with other agencies, organizations, and businesses; these include story hours, creative writing, performances, and family or intergenerational programs.

Teachers also promote this material by using it in classes with students of all ages, and much of this activity is reported in the professional education literature. They create classroom activities, curricula, and learning kits or web quests to encourage their students to read and appreciate literature and to understand and appreciate different cultures. Educators also publish books and articles on educational issues and learning styles in their target community that can be helpful to all. In addition, some publish research and more general articles on how children and teenagers react to this literature. All of these trends will be discussed in more detail in chapters 4 and 5.

LOUD, PROUD, AND CURRYING THE HOT SAUCE: A MULTICULTURAL REACTION TO THE MAINSTREAM

As stated in chapter 1, Western culture is a banquet where most people of color have been slaves and servants until recently, not invited guests. It is also a party, a conversation, and a family reunion. Professionals of color are now crashing the party, bringing the hot sauce of criticism, interrupting the conversation by supplying their own answers and insights to questions, raising their own questions, and sometimes even changing the subject!

People of color in the West are also children of the West—adopted children, stepchildren, and sometimes "outside children," and they are crashing a family reunion—and being treated accordingly, at least at times. The Thomas Jefferson family reunion is both a metaphor and a reality for too many people. People of color are not always viewed as part of the family—but they are, and the Western canon is theirs. They paid for it! To quote a song made famous by Billie Holiday, people of color have "the right to sing the blues." They should be able to comment on and criticize Western culture and make suggestions for changes. This is not only a right, but a duty and a responsibility.

Professionals of color have the right to sing or play not only the blues, but also jazz, soul, hip-hop, reggae, calypso, salsa, bossa nova, meringue, spirituals, gospel, mariachi, and world—as well as folk, country, rock, arias, art songs, and opera when moved to do so. While criticism is very important, it is also important for professionals of color to take a more nuanced look at Western culture and canons. What is good there and worth preserving for all? What are the different ways that one can combine traditional Western stories and information with both classic and emerging materials that are rooted elsewhere?

Professionals of color are demanding not only the "right to sing the blues," but also the right to be seated at the banquet table as guests—and without having to "pass" psychologically, culturally, or physically. This can be very upsetting to some people already comfortably established at the table. In addition, many of these intellectuals of color would also like to bring the cornbread, black-eyed peas, fry bread, beans and rice, enchiladas, tamales, moo-shi, and curries of their own research and literature to share with all. New perspectives may very well emerge that will be helpful to all.

Professionals of color are canaries in the mineshaft of the West, and some of their observations have been painful to all.[87] Pain is a warning that all is not right with the body, and it should not be ignored, covered over, or silenced. The way to deal with pain is to eliminate what is causing it. Then the body's health can be restored. Listening to both the pain and the song of previously neglected and oppressed people can help to restore both the West and the world in general.

WHAT ALL SHOULD DO

Some issues in multicultural and ethnic children's literature will be resolved over time, and other issues will exist for quite awhile. Based on the discussion in this chapter, I make the following recommendations for all professionals.

Combine the use of guidelines for cultural authenticity with an application of the Golden Rule. All authors writing for children from other groups (which includes everybody) should keep this uppermost in their minds. If authors and illustrators do not want their own children exposed to demeaning images or stories, they should have the same consideration for the neighbors' children. One can be honest yet fair. There may still be cultural misunderstandings as people write about groups new to them, but this should eliminate the worst of the cultural chauvinism on all sides.

Prevent or resolve conflict between groups. This is one place where multicultural materials can be very helpful, if written carefully. However this is a responsibility not only for multicultural and ethnic writers, but for everybody. Peacekeeping, reconciliation, restorative justice,[88] and conflict negotiation techniques from the Quakers, Martin Luther King Jr., Mahatma Gandhi, and the Diné (Navajo) people are some initial places to look for more information.

Increase diversity in publishing and in the related fields of the media, education, and library and information science (LIS). The lack of diversity in this field leads to a lack of diverse authors, a lopsided perspective, and stereotypes about minorities and ethnic people. It leads to good materials not being published, or if published, poorly marketed. But as more diverse employees are hired and promoted, they become gatekeepers. They are then in a better position to find and nurture diverse authors and illustrators, eliminating many of the problems described in this chapter.

Leave young people and children "hungry for more." Teachers and librarians can encourage students to use booklists, pathfinders, websites, and children's literature through homework, projects, independent study, library programming, and other challenges. This will encourage young people to take advantage of the more "optional" joy of reading to find out more.

Where possible, books should be reviewed by members of the group represented as well as by people from outside of the group. All can check titles for both literary quality and cultural authenticity. The Coretta Scott King and Pura Belpré award committees do this, resulting in culturally authentic books that can appeal to a broad audience.

Take people of color and their research more seriously. Some of this research, especially in professional fields such as education, can have direct application to working with children in the classroom or library. More theoretical research and the use and reading of media and literature for both adults and children can also provide all professionals with more background information. Professionals working with groups new to them should also become aware of social, economic, cultural, and political issues affecting the communities that they serve. Resources that can help are listed in chapter 4.

Education is related to the Latin word educere, *which means "to lead out."*[89] Most children's books and educational methods and materials have been designed for middle-class white children and begin where these children are. *Professionals need to be encouraged to use more creative and effective ways to start with all children where they are (in their languages, dialects, and relational and learning styles) in order to teach them about themselves and about the rest of the world.*

Children in the "majority" also need to be "led out" to realize that their culture is not the only one. There are many ways to create a world, to look at issues, and to solve problems. How to learn about other people is an important skill for everybody.

Is the glass half empty or half full? Use a combination of honesty, fairness, and hope. Be honest about problems and issues in literature, but hold out some solutions or challenge young people to deal with issues. Life does not always present happy endings, but neither is it hopeless. We are *all* works in progress.

Recreate "a blast from the past." It may be worthwhile to redesign social studies curricula in grades 5–12 so that history and geography are taught as separate subjects for eight years, and to deemphasize other social sciences at this level. This would give educators plenty of time to more thoroughly cover the geography and history of all continents, to pay more attention to diverse ancient civilizations, and to continue to stress U.S. political history and traditions.

A ROOM WITH A VIEW:
WHAT SHOULD AMERICA LOOK LIKE AND BE?

One can argue that the United States is a Creole country in a Creole hemisphere. Like most other countries in the Americas, it was settled by indigenous people first; then by Europeans, who brought African slaves; and then later, by immigrants from other European, Asian, and in some cases, Middle Eastern countries. The Americas are not Europe, Africa, or Asia; neither are they *in* Europe, Africa, or Asia, but they are *of* all of these places, as well as being of the indigenous peoples from this hemisphere. A more inclusive approach to any assimilation may be to see this country (and this hemisphere) as not just a child of Europe, but a child of the world. This point is worth pondering. Some countries in Latin America and the Caribbean are already Creolized.

As we continue to integrate perspectives from a wider variety of people, I believe that Western civilization will be a potent force in the world for a long time. The Latin language has outlasted the Roman Empire by about fifteen hundred years. European languages are still being used as lingua francas in many African countries and in India. Western civilization will probably dominate for a long time, but not necessarily forever. However, I believe that it is also highly unlikely to ever totally disappear.

Changes are likely to occur to ethnic institutions and media as our society becomes more integrated and more diverse. Good multicultural curricula can introduce everyone to a wide variety of people, but cannot give in-depth or very specialized information on all groups. Using pathfinders, libraries, and selected ethnic material will enable people from the group described to learn much more about themselves, and other interested people to learn more about the group.

In a truly integrated world where all can assimilate, some organizations, like the National Negro Baseball League, will go out of business. Some, like black newspapers, will look for new purposes, and others, like tribal Indian colleges, will do for their own audience what mainstream colleges cannot do as well.

Some ethnic institutions and media are likely to last awhile, for several reasons. They can usually provide much more detailed information than their mainstream and multicultural counterparts. They can deal with local issues not necessarily of concern to the broader community. They are very important starting places for many ethnic leaders and writers. Last, they depend on the initiatives of the people being served or described themselves. This next section will describe multicultural and international literature and other resources for children. Chapters 4 and 5 will focus on more specific ethnic resources.

CHARACTERISTICS OF U.S. MULTICULTURAL BOOKS

Multicultural and ethnic children's books in the United States are still relatively few and rare. Since 1985, the Cooperative Children's Book Center at the University of Wisconsin in Madison has been collecting statistics on this subject. In 1985, they documented the number of books written by and about African Americans, and in 1993, they expanded this activity to include books by and about all peoples of color. Of the approximately 5,000 children's books published in the United States every year since 1998, 10 percent or fewer are about people of color, and 5 percent are by people of color. The number of books published about each group has been very consistent across this time period. Each year, between 150 and 200 books are published about African Americans and between 40 and 100 books each about Asian Americans, Native Americans, and Latino/as. The number of books being published by people of color and the proportion relative to all books published has also not changed for either the better or the worse since the late 1980s.[90]

Statistics also show that in too many categories, a large proportion of books written on people of color are by authors not from the culture portrayed. For instance, in 2005, 149 books were written about African Americans, 75 of them by African Americans. Of the 64 books published about Asian Americans, 60 were written by people from those cultures. Out of 34 books published about Native Americans, only 4 were by people from the relevant cultures. Out of 76 books about Latino/as, 50 were by Latino/as.[91]

New ethnic writers still have difficulty getting published, especially by the mainstream. In too many cases they must still fight for the privilege of telling their own stories.[92] Many of these writers are published by alternative ethnic or multicultural presses. Until recently, authors of color have tended not to get the "lunchbox" or movie deals to promote their books, and they still often have small print runs.

However, that may be changing. The Pleasant Company publishes a series called the American Girl Books that features protagonists from many backgrounds, who all live in the American past. These books are thoroughly merchandized with dolls, clothing, cherished items from the series, and a retail store and restaurant.[93] The author of the series about Addy, a young ex-slave, is African American.[94]

Scholastic has one of the best records of any of the mainstream publishers for publishing multicultural children's books. It has published four series of historical fiction—Dear America, My Name Is America, My America, and the Royal Diaries. All of these books are about children or young people living in historical times and are written in a diary format, and books by and about people of color are included in these series. The Dear America series, with 37 books, is for girls in grades 5–8, and My Name Is America (18 books) is for boys in the same age group. My America (17 books) is for a slightly younger audience in grades 3–5. The Royal Diaries, for young people in grades 4–8 (20 books), is a world historical fiction series based on the lives of real princes and princesses.[95] While these series have been well reviewed by most critics, there has been a more mixed response from some critics of color. On the one hand, *I Thought My Soul Would Rise and Fly* by Joyce Hanson[96] is a Coretta Scott King Honor Book. On the other hand, *My Heart Is on the Ground* by Ann Rinaldi has been thoroughly criticized by a panel of librarians and critics for appropriation, stereotyping, and a lack of both historical and cultural accuracy.[97]

MULTICULTURAL AND INTERNATIONAL RESOURCES

Useful multicultural resources that either discuss multiculturalism in general or deal with diverse groups include the following:

- Multicultural bibliographies
- Organizations
- Major periodicals, review media, and websites
- Prizes
- Publishers and presses
- Ethnic authors
- Library collections
- Education materials
- Multicultural histories
- International resources

Multicultural Bibliographies

Most multicultural bibliographies list materials about people of color. Most are annotated, and they tend to discuss criteria that should be used in evaluating materials listed, and some give historical and other types of background on multiculturalism. Current bibliographies have been compiled by Kruse, Horning, and Schliesman;[98] Miller-Lachmann;[99] Rochman;[100] Helbig;[101] Marantz and Marantz;[102] Lind;[103] and Muse.[104] Two recent bibliographies from Europe are *Cross-Currents: A Guide to Multicultural Books for Young People*,[105] from Ireland, and *Outside In: Children's Books in Translation*,[106] from the United Kingdom. Bishop compiled and published several editions of *Kaleidoscope: A Multicultural Booklist for Grades K–8* for the National Council of Teachers of English.[107] This series is no longer being updated. Previously, she wrote the more critical *Shadow and Substance: Afro-American Experience in Contemporary Children's Fiction.*[108]

Organizations

Some of the major organizations in this field have included the Council on Interracial Books for Children,[109] the Ethnic and Multicultural Information Exchange Round Table (EMIERT) of the American Library Association (ALA), the National Association for Multicultural Education (NAME), and more recently, the Center for Multicultural Literature for Children and Young Adults at the University of San Francisco.[110] A number of these organizations publish newsletters and other periodicals, maintain a website, and do other activities. EMIERT[111] publishes the *EMIE Bulletin*,[112] which is now incorporated into the *MultiCultural Review*, and NAME[113] publishes *Multicultural Perspectives.*[114] The *Council on Interracial Books for Children Bulletin* is no longer published, but existing issues are important and useful for historical information. It has been replaced by the *MultiCultural Review.*

Major Periodicals, Review Media, and Websites

Other major periodicals in this field include the *MultiCultural Review*,[115] *Teaching Tolerance*,[116] and *Multicultural Education Journal.*[117] *The New Advocate*[118] was a general scholarly periodical on children's literature that included a lot of information on multiculturalism. Some multicultural periodicals for children are *Faces: The Magazine about People*[119] and *Skipping Stones: A Multicultural Children's Quarterly.*[120] General multicultural review media include the *MultiCultural Review* and *Teaching Tolerance.* Good websites include *Multicultural Education and the Internet*[121] and *Multicultural Kids.*[122]

Prizes

Prizes in multicultural children's literature include the Skipping Stones Award from the children's magazine, the American Book Award from the Before Columbus Foundation, and the Lee and Low New Voices Award. More specific ethnic prizes are described in chapters 4 and 5. A recent book that lists prizewinning literature is *Ethnic Book Awards: A Directory of Multicultural Literature for Young Readers*[123] by Sherry York.

Publishers and Presses

The two major publishers of U.S. multicultural literature are Lee and Low[124] and the Children's Book Press.[125] Groundwood Books[126] is a comparable press from Canada. PaperTigers.org[127] is an organization with a specific ethnic focus that also offers materials from a variety of other groups. There are several lists of publishers. One is Horning's *Alternative Press Publishers of Children's Books.*[128] In her article "The Contribution of Alternative Press Publishers to Multicultural Literature for Children,"[129] she further describes these presses. The Cooperative Children's Book Center has also published *Small Presses Owned and Operated by People of Color: Publishers of Children's Books.*[130]

Ethnic Authors

There are several general lists of ethnic authors. They include a bio-bibliography by Day,[131] a 1994 article by Bishop,[132] and good web pages from the library of Slippery Rock University[133] and Scholastic/Instructor.[134] Commentary by authors and other people of color in this field can be most easily found in Lindgren's *The Multicolored Mirror*, Harris's *Teaching Multicultural Literature in Grades K–8* and *Using Multiethnic Literature in the K–8 Classroom*, and some issues of *The New Advocate*.

Library Collections

There are public library systems around the country that have collected materials on very diverse peoples for years, including publications for children. Some of these libraries include the public libraries of New York City, Queens Borough (N.Y.), Brooklyn (N.Y.), Cleveland, Chicago, Los Angeles (the city), and the County of Los Angeles, and they are often good places to start. These libraries tend to have diverse collections at their main libraries and strong collections on specific groups at branches serving these groups. Most of these collections circulate current materials used by the youth, as well as their parents, teachers, and other interested adults. It is not clear what becomes of potentially valuable books as they wear out. These collections do reflect what people are reading and using now.

Research collections are more likely to collect books that are of interest to adult scholars and specialists, and each has its own philosophy, purposes, and procedures. They are usually noncirculating collections for the historical record and for research. Those focusing specifically on multicultural children's literature are rare. A few examples include the Cooperative Children's Book

Center (CCBC) at the University of Wisconsin, Madison, the Amistad Research Center collection at Tulane University, and the Effie Lee Morris Historical and Research Collection of Children's Literature at the San Francisco Public Library. The CCBC has been collecting books on and about people of color since the 1980s, keeping statistics on the number of books published every year, publishing a bibliography, and keeping information on alternative publishers. The Amistad collection at Tulane is a multicultural one that depends upon donations. They collect children's books. The Effie Lee Morris Collection is a general children's research library that also collects books on the "changing portrayals of ethnic and social groups with an emphasis on Pacific Rim peoples."

There are several special collections that focus more on specific groups. They include the James Weldon Johnson Collection at the Countee Cullen Branch of the NYPL, the William Tucker Collection of Black Authors and Black Illustrators at North Carolina Central University, the Langston Hughes Library at the Alex Haley Farm in Tennessee, and the Augusta Baker Collection of African American Children's Literature and Folklore at the University of South Carolina, for African American materials; the Barahona Center in California for Spanish-language, Latino/a, and related materials; and the Mashantucket Pequot Children's Library in Connecticut for Native American materials. All will be further described in chapter 4.

Education Materials

Materials from the field of education discuss philosophical issues in this field, suggest subjects to include in curricula for all children, and provide information on educational issues and successful teaching and learning styles in a variety of cultures. A few examples will be mentioned here.

Books discussing more philosophical aspects of multicultural education include *Comprehensive Multicultural Education* by Bennett,[135] *Multicultural Education of Children and Adolescents* by M. Lee Manning and Leroy G. Baruth,[136] *Other People's Children* by Lisa Delpit,[137] and *Multicultural Education: Issues and Perspectives* by James Banks.[138] A few examples of materials on some multicultural subjects that can be taught to all children include *Freedom's Plow*, a book by Theresa Perry and James W. Fraser;[139] the periodical *Teaching Tolerance*, and Facing History and Ourselves,[140] an organization with an impressive website. The general books on multicultural education by Bennett and by Manning and Baruth discuss successful teaching and learning styles in diverse classrooms. Other books by educators who have successfully taught diverse students in demanding circumstances include Deborah Meier's *The Power of Their Ideas*[141] and Herbert Kohl's *The Discipline of Hope*.[142]

Multicultural Histories

There are now several histories of multicultural America written for older students and adults. An eleven-volume set for middle school readers is *A History of Us* by Joy Hakim.[143] She has also published a one-volume history for older readers, *Freedom: A History of Us*.[144] Two important scholarly histories for adults and advanced readers are *A Different Mirror: A History of Multicultural America* by Ronald Takaki[145] and *A People's History of the United States* by Howard Zinn.[146] Zinn and Anthony Arnove have also published the documentary *Voices of a People*.[147] A more recent title is *Natives and Strangers: A Multicultural History of Americans*, edited by Leonard Dinnerstein, Roger L. Nichols, and David M. Reimers.[148]

International Resources

International resources are relevant for several reasons. Many ethnic children and youth in the United States are recent immigrants, and literature from their home countries may still be relevant. In addition, many specific ethnic groups, such as Jews, Chinese, Latino/as, and people of South Asian or African descent, have had diasporas, or people from their group of origin live in many countries around the world. For some young people born in the United States and their elders, this heritage is still relevant. It is also very advantageous for all children to have some exposure to the best of the world's literature. Important and relevant international resources include the organization International Board on Books for Young People (IBBY)[149] and their periodical, *Bookbird*.[150] Bibliographies include works by Evelyn B. Freeman and Barbara A. Lehmann,[151] Carl M. Tomlinson,[152] Miller-Lachmann,[153] and more recent work from Europe by Liz Morris and Susanna Coghlan[154] and Deborah Hallford and Edgardo Zaghini.[155] There are also two major prizes in this area, which can direct people to the best of international literature. One prize is the Mildred L. Batchelder Award for the best children's book to be translated into English. Another is the Hans Christian Andersen, a lifetime achievement award given by IBBY for the world's best juvenile writers. More specific ethnic materials and institutions will be discussed in chapters 4 and 5.

REFERENCES

1. Nancy Larrick, "The All-White World of Children's Books," *Saturday Review* 48 (September 11, 1965): 63–65, 84–85. Also in *The New Press Guide to Multicultural Resources for Young Readers*, ed. Daphne Muse (New York: New Press, 1997), 19–25.

2. *Children's Books by and about People of Color Published in the United States*, http://www.education.wisc.edu/ccbc/books/pcstats.htm (16 Nov. 2006).

3. Dorothy Broderick, *Image of the Black in Children's Fiction* (New York: Bowker, 1973).

4. Arlene B. Hirschfelder, *American Indian Stereotypes in the World of Children: A Reader and Bibliography* (Metuchen, N.J.: Scarecrow, 1999).

5. Donnarae MacCann, *White Supremacy in Children's Literature: Characterizations of African Americans, 1830–1900* (New York: Routledge, 2000); Donnarae MacCann and Gloria Woodard, *The Black American in Books for Children* (Metuchen, N.J.: Scarecrow, 1972); Donnarae MacCann and Gloria Woodard, *Cultural Conformity in Books For Children: Further Readings in Racism* (Metuchen, N.J.: Scarecrow, 1977); Donnarae MacCann and Yulisa Amadu Maddy, *Apartheid and Racism in South African Children's Literature, 1985–1995* (New York: Routledge, 2001).

6. Lyn Miller-Lachmann, *Global Voices, Global Visions: A Core Collection of Multicultural Books* (New Providence, N.J.: Bowker, 1995); Miller-Lachmann, *Our Family, Our Friends, Our World* (New Providence, N.J.: Bowker, 1992).

7. Frances Ann Day, *Latina and Latino Voices in Literature: Lives and Works Updated and Expanded* (Westport, Conn.: Greenwood, 2003); Day, *Multicultural Voices in Contemporary Literature: A Resource For Teachers* (Portsmouth, N.H.: Heinemann, 1994).

8. Sherry York, *Children's and Young Adult Books By Latino Writers: A Guide For Librarians, Teachers, Parents, and Students* (Worthington, Ohio: Linworth Publishing, 2002); York, *Children's and Young Adult Literature by Native Americans* (Worthington, Ohio: Linwood Publishing, 2003); York, *Ethnic Book Awards: A Directory of Multicultural Literature For Young Readers* (Worthington, Ohio: Linworth Publishing, 2005); York, *Picture Books by Latino Writers: A Guide for Librarians, Teachers, Parents, and Students* (Worthington, Ohio: Linworth Publishing, 2002).

9. Arthur M. Schlesinger Jr., *The Disuniting of America* (New York: W.W. Norton and Company, 1998), 80–81.

10. Schlesinger, *The Disuniting of America*, 21; Nathan Glazer, *We Are All Multiculturalists Now* (Cambridge, Mass: Harvard University Press, 1997), 45–49.

11. Glazer, *We Are All Multiculturalists Now*, 41–45.

12. Schlesinger, *The Disuniting of America*, 22.

13. Diane Ravitch, *The Language Police: How Pressure Groups Restrict What Students Learn* (New York: Knopf, 2003).

14. Glazer, *We Are All Multiculturalists Now*, 49–56.

15. Schlesinger, *The Disuniting of America*, 22, 93–94, 108–109.

16. Schlesinger, *The Disuniting of America*, 94–95.

17. Schlesinger. *The Disuniting of America*, 54–58.

18. Schlesinger, *The Disuniting of America*, 94.

19. Glazer, *We are All Multiculturalists Now*, 87, 49–52.

20. E.D. Hirsch Jr., *Cultural Literacy: What Every American Needs to Know* (New York: Vintage, 1987).

21. Hirsch, *Cultural Literacy,* xiii–32.

22. Hirsch, *Cultural Literacy,* 33–69.

23. E.D. Hirsch Jr., Joseph F. Kett, and James Trefil, *The Dictionary of Cultural Literacy: What Every American Needs to Know* (Boston: Houghton Mifflin, 1993), xv.

24. Hirsch, *Cultural Literacy,* 134–139.

25. E.D. Hirsch Jr., Joseph Kett, and James Trefil, "What Literate Americans Know: A Preliminary List," in *Cultural Literacy: What Every American Needs to Know,* by E.D. Hirsch (New York: Random House, 1987), 146–215.

26. E. D. Hirsch Jr., Joseph F. Kett, and James Trefil, *The Dictionary of Cultural Literacy: What Every American Needs to Know* (Boston: Houghton Mifflin, 1993); E.D. Hirsch Jr., *A First Dictionary of Cultural Literacy* (Boston: Houghton Mifflin, 1989).

27. Hirsch, *What Your First Grader Needs to Know: Fundamentals of a Good First-Grade Education* (Garden City, N.Y.: Doubleday, 1998); Hirsch, *What Your Second Grader Needs to Know: Fundamentals of a Good Second-Grade Education Revised* (Garden City, N.Y.: Doubleday, 1999); Hirsch, *What Your Third Grader Needs to Know: Fundamentals of a Good Third-Grade Education* (Garden City, N.Y.: Doubleday, 2002); Hirsch, *What Your Fourth Grader Needs to Know: Fundamentals of a Good Fourth-Grade Education* (Garden City, N.Y.: Doubleday, 2004); Hirsch, *What Your Fifth Grader Needs to Know: Fundamentals of a Good Fifth-Grade Education* (Garden City, N.Y.: Doubleday, 2005); Hirsch, *What Your Sixth Grader Needs to Know: Fundamentals of a Good Sixth-Grade Education* (Garden City, N.Y.: Doubleday, 1995).

28. Kwame Anthony Appiah and Henry Louis Gates Jr., eds., *The Dictionary of Global Culture* (New York: Knopf, 1997), xi–xiv.

29. Henry Louis Gates Jr., *Loose Canons: Notes on the Culture Wars.* (New York: Oxford University Press, 1992).

30. Rick Simonson and Scott Walker, eds., *The Graywolf Annual Five: Multicultural Literacy—Opening the American Mind* (St. Paul, Minn: Graywolf Press, 1988).

31. Allan Bloom, *The Closing of the American Mind: How Higher Education Has Failed Democracy and Impoverished the Souls of Today's Students* (New York: Simon and Schuster, 1987).

32. Simon and Walker, eds., *The Graywolf Annual Five: Multicultural Literacy,* ix–xv.

33. Wendell Berry, "People, Land, and Community," in *The Graywolf Annual Five: Multicultural Literacy—Opening the American Mind,* eds. Rick Simonson and Scott Walker (St. Paul, Minn.: Graywolf Press, 1988), 41–56.

34. Paula Gunn Allen, "Who Is Your Mother? Red Roots of White Feminism," in *The Graywolf Annual Five: Multicultural Literacy—Opening the American Mind,* eds. Rick Simonson and Scott Walker (St. Paul, Minn.: Graywolf Press, 1988), 13–27.

35. Ishmael Reed, "America: The Multinational Society," in *The Graywolf Annual Five: Multicultural Literacy—Opening the American Mind,* eds. Rick Simonson and Scott Walker (St. Paul, Minn.: Graywolf Press, 1988), 155–160.

36. Guillermo Gomez-Pena, "Documented/Undocumented," in *The Graywolf Annual Five: Multicultural Literacy—Opening the American Mind,* eds. Rick Simonson and Scott Walker (St. Paul, Minn.: Graywolf Press, 1988), 127–134.

37. Eduardo Galeano, "In Defense of the Word: Leaving Bueno Aires, June, 1976," in *The Graywolf Annual Five: Multicultural Literacy—Opening the American Mind,* eds. Rick Simonson and Scott Walker (St. Paul, Minn.: Graywolf Press, 1988), 113–125.

38. David Mura, "Strangers in the Village," in *The Graywolf Annual Five: Multicultural Literacy—Opening the American Mind,* eds. Rick Simonson and Scott Walker (St. Paul, Minn.: Graywolf Press, 1988), 135–153.

39. Michele Wallace, "Invisibility Blues," in *The Graywolf Annual Five: Multicultural Literacy—Opening the American Mind,* eds. Rick Simonson and Scott Walker (St. Paul, Minn.: Graywolf Press, 1988), 161–172.

40. Hirsch, *Cultural Literacy,* 132–133, 15, 28.

41. The Critical Thinking Community, *A Brief History of the Idea of Critical Thinking,* http://www.criticalthinking.org/aboutCT/briefHistoryCT.shtml (26 June 2006).

42. Schlesinger, *The Disuniting of America,* 63–71, 79–85.

43. John Mbiti, *African Religion and Philosophy* (Garden City, N.Y.: Doubleday, 1970).

44. Schlesinger, *The Disuniting of America,* 68–69.

45. Janice E. Hale, *Black Children: Their Roots, Culture, and Learning Styles* (Baltimore, Md.: Johns Hopkins University Press, 1986).

46. Schlesinger, *The Disuniting of America,* 69–70.

47. Joseph E. Holloway, ed., *Africanisms in American Culture* (Bloomington, Ind.: Indiana University Press, 1990).

48. Schlesinger, *The Disuniting of America,* 87–90

49. Diane Ravitch, "The Atkinson-Ravitch Sampler of Classic Literature For Home and School," in *The Language Police: How Pressure Groups Restrict What Students Learn* (New York: Knopf, 2003), 203–234.

50. Ravitch. "Literature: Forgetting the Tradition," in *The Language Police: How Pressure Groups Restrict What Students Learn* (New York: Knopf, 2003), 112–132.

51. Gary B. Nash, "American History Reconsidered: Asking New Questions About the Past," in *Learning From the Past: What History Teaches Us About School Reform,* edited by Diane Ravitch and Maris A. Vinovskis. (Baltimore, Md.: Johns Hopkins University Press, 1995), 147–157.

52. Donnarae McCann, *White Supremacy in Children's Literature: Characterizations of African Americans, 1830–1900* (New York: Garland, 1998).

53. Jacqueline Woodson, "Who Can Tell My Story," *The Horn Book Magazine* 74 (Jan/Feb., 1998): 34–38. Revised and updated in *Stories Matter* 41–45.

54. Nina Mikkelson, "Insiders, Outsiders, and the Questions of Authenticity: Who Shall Write for African American Children?" *African American Review* 32 no. 1 (1998): 33–49.

55. Mingshui Cai, "Can We Fly Across Cultural Gaps on the Wings of Imagination?" *The New Advocate* 8, no. 1 (Winter, 1995): 1–16. Revised and updated in *Stories Matter*, 167–181.

56. Thelma Seto, "Multiculturalism is Not Halloween," *The Horn Book Magazine* 71 (March/April, 1995): 169–174. Revised and updated in *Stories Matter* pp. 93–97.

57. Zhihui Fang, Danling Fu, and Linda L. Lamme, "Rethinking the Role of Multicultural Literature in Literacy Instruction: Problems, Paradox, Possibilities," *The New Advocate* 12, no. 3 (Summer, 1999): 259–276. Revised and updated as "The Trivialization and Misuse of Multicultural Literature: Issues of Representation and Communication," in *Stories Matter*, 284–303.

58. Jonda McNair, " 'He May Mean Good, But He Do So Doggone Poor!': A Critical Analysis of Recently Published 'Social Conscious' Children's Literature," *MultiCultural Review* 12, no. 1 (March, 2003): 26–32.

59. Patty Campbell, "The Sand in the Oyster," *The Horn Book Magazine* 40 (July–August, 1994): 491–497.

60. Ellen Salle, "Ethnicity and Authenticity, or How Black (Hispanic Native American, etc.) Do I Gotta Be?" *Emergency Librarian* 27, no. 2 (Nov/Dec. 1994): 22–27.

61. Judy Moreillon, "The Candle and the Mirror: One Author's Journey as an Outsider," *The New Advocate* 12, no. 2 (Spring, 1999): 127–140. Revised and updated in *Stories Matter*, 61–77.

62. Dana L. Fox and Kathy G. Short, eds., *Stories Matter: the Complexity of Cultural Authenticity in Children's Literature* (Urbana, Ill.: National Council of Teachers of English, 2003).

63. Dana L. Fox and Kathy G. Short, "The Complexity of Cultural Authenticity in Children's Literature: Why the Debates Really Matter," In *Stories Matter*, 20–22.

64. Laura B. Smolkin and Joseph H. Suina, "Artistic Triumph or Multicultural Failure? Multiple Perspectives on a 'Multicultural' Award-Winning Book," in *Stories Matter*, 213–230.

65. Mo Weimin and Wenju Shen, "Accuracy is Not Enough: the Role of Cultural Values in the Authenticity of Picture Books," in *Stories Matter,* 202–203.

66. Henry Gates, " 'Authenticity', or the Lesson of Little Tree," In *Stories Matter*, 135–142.

67. Marc Aronson, "A Mess of Stories," in *Stories Matter*, 78–83.

68. Kathryn Lasky, "To Stingo With Love: An Author's Perspective on Writing Outside One's Culture," in *Stories Matter*, 87.

69. Hazel Rochman, "Beyond Political Correctness." In *Stories Matter*, 101–115.

70. Cynthia Leitich Smith, "A Different Drum: Native American Writing," *The Horn Book Magazine* 78, no. 3 (July/Aug., 2002): 409–412.

71. Rudine Sims Bishop, "Retraining the Debate about Cultural Authenticity," in *Stories Matter*, 25–37.

72. Diane Ravitch, *The Language Police: How Pressure Groups Restrict What Students Learn* (New York: Knopf, 2003), 62–96.

73. Ravitch, *The Language Police*, 79–96, 19–49.

74. Ravitch, *The Language Police*, 29–30.

75. Ravitch, *The Language Police*, 49, 147.

76. Ravitch, *The Language Police*, 81–87, 147.

77. Rudine Sims (Bishop), *Shadow and Substance: Afro-American Experience in Contemporary Children's Fiction* (Urbana, Ill.: National Council of Teachers of English, 1982).

78. McNair, "'He May Mean Good, But He Do So Doggone Poor!'"; Cai, "Can We Fly Across Cultural Gaps on the Wings of Imagination?"

79. Debbie Reese, "Contesting Ideology in Children's Book Reviewing," *Studies in American Indian Literatures* 12, no. 1: 51–53.

80. Jacqueline Shachter Weiss, *Prizewinning Books For Children: Themes and Stereotypes in U.S. Prizewinning Prose Fiction For Children* (Lexington, Mass.: Lexington Books, 1983).

81. MacCann, *White Supremacy in Children's Literature*, 212.

82. Addison Gayle, *The Black Aesthetic*.

83. Joseph Bruchac, "All Our Relations: Native-American Multicultural Understanding," *The Horn Book Magazine* 71 (March/April, 1995): 158–162.

84. Philip Lee, *Multicultural Book Publishing* (Children's Book Council), http://www.cbcbooks.org/cbcmagazine/perspectives/multicultural_book_publishing.html (26 June 2006).

85. Consortium of Latin American Studies Programs (CLASP), *Americas Award*, http://www.uwm.edu/Dept/CLACS/pdf/aa05.pdf

86. Joel Taxel, "Children's Literature at the Turn of the Century: Toward a Political Economy of the Publishing Industry," *Research in the Teaching of English* 37, no. 2 (November 2002): 168–171.

87. Lani Guinier and Gerald Torres, *The Miner's Canary: Enlisting Race, Resisting Power, Transforming Democracy* (Cambridge, Mass.: Harvard University Press, 2003).

88. Robert Yazzie, "Navajo Justice," *Winds of Change* (August, 2000): 88–91.

89. J.A. Simpson and E.S.C. Weiner, comps., *The Oxford English Dictionary Vol. 5* (Oxford: Clarendon Press, 1989), 73,74.

90. *Children's Books by and about People of Color Published in the United States*, http://www.education.wisc.edu/ccbc/books/pcstats.htm (26 June 2006); Kathleen T. Horning, Merri V. Lindgren, Hollis Rudiger, Megan Schliesman, with Tana Elias, *CCBC Choices 2006* (Madison, Wis.: Cooperative Children's Book Center, School of Education, University of Wisconsin, 2006), 13–14.

91. *Children's Books by and about People of Color Published in the United States.*

92. Daphne Muse, "Introduction," in *The New Press Guide to Multicultural Resources For Young Readers* (New York: New Press, 1997).

93. Joel Taxel, "Children's Literature at the Turn of the Century: Toward a Political Economy of the Publishing Industry," *Research in the Teaching of English* 37, no. 2 (November 2002): 168–171.

94. Pleasant Company Publications, *Meet Authors and Illustrators: Connie Porter*, http://www.childrenslit.com/f_connieporter.htm (26 June 2006).

95. Taxel. "Children's Literature at the Turn of the Century," 168–171; Scholastic, "Authors," http://www.scholastic.com/dearamerica/books/authors.htm (26 June 2006).

96. Joyce Hansen, *I Thought My Soul Would Rise and Fly: The Diary of Patsy, a Freed Girl* (New York: Scholastic, 2003).

97. "My Heart Is on the Ground and the Indian Boarding School Experience," in *A Broken Flute: The Native Experience in Books for Children*, edited by Doris Seale and Beverly Slapin (Berkeley, Calif.: Oyate, 2005). Also in *MultiCultural Review* (Sept., 1999): 41–46 and *Alternative Library Literature, 1998/1999* (Jefferson, N.C.: McFarland, 2001): 205–210.

98. Ginny Moore Kruse, Kathleen T. Horning, and Megan Schliesman, *Multicultural Literature for Children and Young Adults: A Selected Listing of Books by and about People of Color* (Madison,Wis.: Cooperative Children's Book Center, 1991), ED 418 710.

99. Lyn Miller–Lachmann, *Our Friends, Our Family, Our World: An Annotated Guide to Significant Multicultural Books for Children and Teenagers* (New Providence, N.J.: Bowker, 1992).

100. Hazel Rochman, *Against Borders: Promoting Books for a Multicultural World* (Chicago, Ill.: ALA, 1993).

101. Alethea K. Helbig, *This Land Is Our Land: A Guide to Multicultural Literature for Children and Young Adults* (Westport, Conn.: Greenwood, 1994).

102. Sylvia Marantz and Kenneth Marantz, *Multicultural Picture Books: Art for Understanding Others* (Worthington, Ohio: Linworth Publishing, 1994).

103. Beth Beutler Lind, *Multicultural Children's Literature: An Annotated Bibliography K–8* (Jefferson, N.C.: McFarland, 1996).

104. Daphne Muse, ed., *The New Press Guide to Multicultural Resources for Young Readers* (New York: New Press, 1997).

105. Liz Morris and Susanna Coghlan, eds., *Cross-Currents: A Guide to Multicultural Books for Young People* (Dublin: IBBY Ireland, 2005).

106. Deborah Hallford and Edgardo Zaghini, eds., *Outside In: Children's Books in Translation* (London: Milet Publishing, 2005).

107. Rudine Sims Bishop, *Kaleidoscope: A Multicultural Booklist for Grades K–8* (Urbana, Ill:: National Council of Teachers of English, 1994, 1997, 2001, 2003).

108. Rudine Sims (Bishop), *Shadow and Substance: Afro-American Experience in Contemporary Children's Fiction* (Urbana, Ill.: National Council of Teachers of English, 1982).

109. The Council on Interracial Books for Children, 1841 Broadway, New York, N.Y. 10023.

110. University of San Francisco, School of Education, Department of International and Multicultural Education, Center for Multicultural Literature for Children and Young Adults, 2130 Fulton St., San Francisco, Calif. 94117, http://www.soe.usfca.edu/departments/ime/index.html (26 June 2005).

111. American Library Association (ALA), Ethnic Materials and Information Exchange Round Table (EMIERT), http://www.ala.org/template.cfm?section=emiert (26 June 2006).

112. ALA, EMIERT, *EMIE Bulletin*. Now an insert in the *MultiCultural Review*, 14497 N. Dale Mabry Highway, Suite 205N, Tampa, Fla. 33618.

113. National Association for Multicultural Education (NAME), 733 Fifteenth St. NW, Suite 430, Washington, D.C. 20005, http://www.nameorg.org (26 June 2006).

114. NAME, *Multicultural Perspectives*, Lawrence Erlbaum Associates, 10 Industrial Ave., Mahwah, N.J. 07430.

115. *The MultiCultural Review*, 14497 N. Dale Mabry Highway, Suite 205N, Tampa, Fla 33618, http://www.mcreview.com/ (26 June 2006).

116. *Teaching Tolerance*, Southern Poverty Law Center, 400 Washington Ave., Montgomery, Ala., http://www.tolerance.org/teach/ (26 June 2006).

117. *Multicultural Education Journal*, Alberta Teachers' Association, Multicultural Education, 11010-142nd. St., Edmonton, T5N 2R1 Alberta, Canada.

118. *The New Advocate*, Christopher-Gordon Publishers, 1502 Providence Highway, Suite 12, Norwood, Mass. 02062.

119. *Faces: The Magazine about People*, Cobblestone Publishing, Carus Publishing Company, 30 Grove St., Suite C, Peterborough, N.H. 03458, http://www.cricketmag.com/ProductDetail.asp?pid=16 (26 June 2006).

120. *Skipping Stones: A Multicultural Children's Quarterly*, P.O. Box 3939, Eugene, Ore., http://www.skippingstones.org/ (26 June 2006).

121. Paul Gorski, *Multicultural Education and the Internet*, http://www.mhhe.com/socscience/education/multi_new/ (26 June 2006).

122. Multicultural Kids, http://www.multiculturalkids.com/ (26 June 2006).

123. Sherry York, *Ethnic Book Awards: A Directory of Multicultural Literature for Young Readers* (Worthington, Ohio: Linworth Publishing, 2005).

124. Philip Lee, "Multicultural Book Publishing," Children's Book Council, http://www.cbcbooks.org/cbcmagazine/perspectives/multicultural_book_publishing.html (26 June 2006); Lee and Low Books, 95 Madison Ave., Suite #606, New York, N.Y. 10016, http://www.leeandlow.com/home/index.html (26 June 2006).

125. Chris Liska Carger, "Harriet Rohmer on New Voices and Visions in Multicultural Literature," *The New Advocate* 14, no. 2 (Spring, 2001): 119–126; Children's Book Press, 2211 Mission St., San Francisco, Calif. 94110, http://www.childrensbookpress.org/ (26 June 2006).

126. Groundwood Books, 720 Bathhurst St., Suite 500, Toronto, Ontario M5S 2R4, Canada, http://www.groundwoodbooks.com/ (26 June 2006).

127. Pacific Rim Voices, PaperTigers.org, Kiriyama Pacific Rim Institute, 650 Delauncey St., San Francisco, Calif. 92107, http://www.papertigers.org/index.html (26 June 2006).

128. Kathleen Horning, *Alternative Press Publishers of Children's Books: A Directory* (Madison, Wis. Friends of the Cooperative Children's Book Center, 1992).

129. Horning, "The Contributions of Alternative Press Publishers to Multicultural Literature for Children," *Library Trends* 41, no. 3 (Winter, 1993): 524–40.

130. *Small Presses Owned and Operated by People of Color: Publishers of Children's Books*, http://www.soemadison.wisc.edu/ccbc/books/pclist.htm (26 June 2006).

131. Frances Ann Day, *Multicultural Voices in Contemporary Literature; A Resource for Teachers* (Portsmouth, N.H.: Heinemann, 1994).

132. Rudine Sims Bishop, "Books from Parallel Cultures: What's Happening?" *The Horn Book Magazine* 70 (Jan./Feb., 1994): 105–109.

133. Slippery Rock University of Pennsylvania, "Multicultural Children's Authors," http://www.sru.edu/pages/8912.asp (26 June 2006).

134. Scholastic/Instructor, "How to Choose the Best Multicultural Books," http://teacher.scholastic.com/products/instructor/multicultural.htm (26 June 2006).

135. Christine Bennett, *Comprehensive Multicultural Education: Theory and Practice* (Boston: Pearson, 2007).

136. M. Lee Manning and Leroy G. Baruth, *Multicultural Education of Children and Adolescents* (Boston: Allyn and Bacon, 2003).

137. Lisa Delpit, *Other People's Children: Cultural Conflict in the Classroom* (New York: New Press, 1995).

138. James Banks, *Multicultural Education: Issues and Perspectives* (Hoboken, N.J.: Wiley, 2002).

139. Theresa Perry and James W. Fraser, *Freedom's Plow: Teaching in the Multicultural Classroom* (NY: Routledge, 1993).

140. Facing History and Ourselves, National Foundation, 25 Kennard Rd., Brookline, Mass. 02146, (617) 734–1111, http://facinghistory.org/ (26 June 2006).

141. Deborah Meier, *The Power of Their Ideas: Lessons For America from a Small School in Harlem* (Boston: Beacon Press, 1995).

142. Herbert Kohl, *The Discipline of Hope: Learning From a Lifetime of Teaching* (NY: New Press, 1998).

143. Joy Hakim, *A History of Us*, 11 vols. (New York: Oxford University Press, 2003).

144. Hakim, *Freedom: A History of Us* (New York: Oxford University Press, 2003).

145. Ronald Takaki, *A Different Mirror: A History of Multicultural America* (Boston: Little Brown, 1993).

146. Howard Zinn, *A People's History of the United States* (New York: Harper Perennial, 2003).

147. Howard Zinn and Anthony Arnove, *Voices of a People: History of the United States* (New York: Seven Stories Press, 2004).

148. Leonard Dinnerstein, Roger L. Nichols, and David M. Reimers, eds., *Natives and Strangers: A Multicultural History of America* (New York: Oxford University Press, 2003).

149. International Board on Books for Young People (IBBY), Nonnenweg 12, Postfach, CH-4003, Basel, Switzerland, http://www.ibby.org/ (26 June 2006).

150. IBBY, *Bookbird*, Anne Marie Corrigan, Bookbird Subscriptions, U. of Toronto Press, 5201 Dufferin St., North York, Ontario M3H 5T8, Canada.

151. Evelyn B. Freeman and Barbara A. Lehman, *Global Perspectives in Children's Literature* (Boston: Allyn and Bacon, 2001).

152. Carl M. Tomlinson, *Children's Books from Other Countries* (Lanham, MD: Scarecrow, 1998).

153. Lyn Miller-Lachmann, *Global Voices, Global Visions: A Core Collection of Multicultural Books* (New Providence, N.J.: Bowker, 1995); Miller-Lachmann, *Our Family, Our Friends, Our World: An Annotated Guide to Significant Multicultural Books For Children and Teenagers* (New Providence, N.J.: Bowker, 1992).

154. Morris and Coglan, eds., *Cross-Currents.*

155. Hallford and Zaghini, eds., *Outside In.*

4

Specific Ethnic
Initiatives and Conclusions

People from all groups are involved in writing, publishing, criticizing, distributing, stocking, and collecting ethnic and multicultural children's literature. However, each major group has also emphasized certain activities. African Americans have been *documenting* works by African American writers in the form of bibliographies and criticism of the literature. A number of black research libraries have been established around the country, and most of them also collect children's materials.

People working with the Latino/a community have also *documented* literature related to their community in the form of bibliographies, articles, and library collections. They have especially excelled in the *marketing of programming, outreach, services, and other activities* in libraries, schools, and elsewhere. Many books have been written on planning library collections and services for Latino/as, and there have been very successful national programs like *El Dia de los Niños: El Dia de los Libros/Day of Children: Day of Books*. Most of these activities have been spearheaded by Latino/a librarians, authors, and professionals.

For many reasons, it has been very necessary for Native Americans and their supporters to emphasize the *criticism* of children's materials written about indigenous Americans. Over time, the bulk of all materials on Native Americans has been written by non-indigenous authors who do not know or understand the specific group that they are writing about, and misinformation and stereotypes abound. This is a problem with all groups, but it is a particularly sensitive one for Native Americans. However, the percentage of Native American authors publishing materials about themselves has improved in recent years.

Asian Americans have emphasized *the accessibility, dissemination, and distribution* of their materials, whether these are written in English or in other languages. Materials are available in traditional bookstores and at a number of sites on the Internet to make ordering easier. For libraries collecting a lot of Asian American materials for children, thorough cataloging of the materials has also been important, especially when the materials are in various languages. This enables librarians who do not speak or read the other languages to still find appropriate materials for their patrons.

PAN-AFRICAN

African American

There is a long and strong bibliographic tradition in the African American community, going all the way back to the general bibliographies compiled by Monroe Work in the 1920s, and continuing with similar works on children's literature compiled by Augusta Baker and Charlemae Rollins in the 1940s and 1950s. Bibliographies like Baker's *Books about Negro Life for Children*, Baker's and Rollock's *The Black Experience in Children's Books*, and Rollins's *We Build Together* listed the best material available at the time *about* black people. More recent bibliographies focus more specifically on African American authors and illustrators. Book-length bibliographies include works by Deborah Kutenplon and Ellen Olmstead,[1] Osayimwense Osa,[2] Barbara Thrash Murphy,[3] Henrietta Smith,[4] Pamela Toussaint,[5] and Helen E. Williams,[6] as well as the *Black Books Galore!* bibliographies and buying guides published by Donna Rand, Toni Trent Parker, and Sheila Foster.[7] There are bibliographical articles in reference books and periodicals by Rudine Sims Bishop,[8] Daphne Muse,[9] and Violet J. Harris.[10] More critical books and articles are by Donnarae MacCann and Gloria Woodard,[11] Dorothy Broderick,[12] Muse,[13] Gail Singleton Taylor,[14] and Kutenplon and Olmstead,[15] but most of the criticism has been done by Sims Bishop,[16] Dianne Johnson-Feelings,[17] and Harris.[18] Bishop and Jonda McNair[19] and Dianne Johnson[20] have also written specific information on the early authors Arna Bontemps and Langston Hughes. In addition, the University of Missouri has published *The Collected Works of Langston Hughes*, an eighteen-volume set that includes his works for children.[21]

There are at least four noncirculating research collections specializing in black children's literature. One is the William Tucker Collection of Black Authors and Illustrators at the North Carolina Central University in Durham, N.C. Another collection is the private Langston Hughes Library at the Alex Haley Farm in Tennessee, which is maintained by the Children's Defense Fund. A third is the Augusta Baker Collection of African American Children's Literature and Folklore at the University of South Carolina. The fourth is the

James Weldon Johnson Collection at the Countee Cullen Regional Library of the New York Public Library (NYPL) that was established by Baker. In addition, most other black research collections also collect children's materials. They include the Schomberg Center for Research in Black Culture of the NYPL, the Auburn Avenue Research Library of the Atlanta-Fulton Public Library, the African American Museum and Library of the Oakland (California) Public Library, and the Black Resource Center at the A. C. Bilbrew Library, a branch of the County of Los Angeles Public Library. Many public library branches serving black communities, especially in larger cities, are likely to have current and circulating collections as well, some integrated into the rest of their general collections, and some freestanding.

Alternative presses that specialize in black children's literature include Writers and Readers/Black Butterfly Press[22] and Just Us Books.[23] Hyperion, a major publisher, has established "Jump at the Sun," a specialized African American line.[24] In addition, Carus, the publisher of *Cobblestones* and *Cricket* also produces *Footsteps*, a periodical of African American history. Review media covering children's books include *Black Issues Book Review*[25] and Black Books Galore,[26] which is a website and ordering service. Parker, Rand, and Foster have published the *Black Books Galore!* bibliographies, and their company does book fairs in many locations. Representatives from Black Books Galore, Wiley Press, and the Black Caucus of the American Library Association also work together to give an award for the best public and school library programming promoting black children's books.

Vanesse Lloyd-Sgambati of Philadelphia has created the African American Children's Book Project, an organization that encourages children to read and that preserves African American books. She gives a book fair annually and plans to eventually start a children's book museum. In addition, the Black Caucus of the National Council of Teachers of English sponsors an annual National African American Read-in to celebrate Black History Month. They encourage bookstores, churches, community and professional organizations, and schools to do read-ins from books by African American authors, and they also urge participating organizations to report their activities on the Black Caucus's website.[27]

Other important people working in this area include Henrietta Smith, Rudine Sims Bishop, Daphne Muse, Violet J. Harris, Dianne Johnson-Feelings, Khafre Abif, and Rand, Parker, and Foster. Educators who have published books on educational issues in the African American community include Gloria Ladson-Billings,[28] Janice E. Hale,[29] Michele Foster,[30] Barbara Sizemore,[31] and Joyce E. King.[32] The Commission on Research in Black Education in the American Education Research Association also contributes to this area of research. Black periodicals related to education include the *Journal of Negro*

Education,[33] *The Journal of Blacks in Higher Education*,[34] and until recently, *Black Issues in Higher Education*,[35] issued by the publisher of *Black Issues Book Review*. *Black Issues in Higher Education* has changed its name and focus and now publishes as *Diversity—Issues in Higher Education*. Another relevant periodical is *The Black Collegian*,[36] a career-oriented publication for young people. Several college guides specifically for African Americans have also been published. The Coretta Scott King Award is an annual prize for the best children's book by an African American author or illustrator, and two guides on teaching about these books have been published by Claire Gatrell Stephens[37] and Nancy J. Polette.[38]

For professionals and older readers who want to know more about African Americans, supplementary materials from the popular to the scholarly abound. General histories include the classic *From Slavery to Freedom* by John Hope Franklin[39] and *Before the Mayflower* by Lerone Bennett.[40] More recent histories include *To Make Our World Anew*, edited by Robin D. G. Kelley and Earl Lewis,[41] and *Creating Black Americans* by Nell Irvin Painter.[42] The very diverse lives of ordinary African Americans are described in *Drylongso* by John Langston Gwaltney,[43] *Walking on Water* by Randall Kenan,[44] and *In Search of Black America* by David J. Dent.[45] Problems and solutions described and proposed by black leaders can be found in *Like It Is*, which is edited by Emily Rovetch;[46] *Black Genius*, edited by Walter Mosley and several others;[47] *How to Make Black America Better*, edited and compiled by Tavis Smiley;[48] and the recently published bestseller, *The Covenant with Black America*,[49] which has also been spearheaded by Smiley.

Links to African American websites include the "African American Web Connection,"[50] "Black History Quest: African American Resources,"[51] and "Help By Subject—Resources in Black Studies" by Sylvia Curtis.[52] Some popular magazines are *Ebony*,[53] *Jet*,[54] *American Legacy*,[55] *Black History Bulletin*,[56] and *The Crisis*.[57] Scholarly journals include *Black Scholar*,[58] *Callaloo*,[59] *Obsidian III*,[60] and *Western Journal of Black Studies*.[61]

African American scholars represent many schools of thought. For general histories of black intellectual life, start with *Black Intellectuals* by William Banks[62] and consider the more Afrocentric *Black Intellectuals, Black Cognition, and a Black Aesthetic* by William D. Wright.[63] *In the Vineyard* by Perry A. Hall[64] and *Africana Studies* by James C. Conyers[65] are both histories of black studies programs. These departments have gone in several directions, reflecting the schools of thought of their faculties. One school of thought is Afrocentrism, which is represented by Molefi Kete Asante in works such as *The Afrocentric Idea*[66] and *Afrocentricity*.[67] "Philosophy born of struggle" is described in an anthology of that name compiled by Leonard Harris,[68] and black conservatism is presented in books such as *Black Conservatism* by P.

Eisenstadt,[69] *Black and Right* by Stan Faryna,[70] and *Authentically Black* by John McWhorter.[71]

Black feminism is described in titles such as *The Black Feminist Reader* edited by Joy James;[72] *All the Women Are White, All the Blacks Are Men, But Some of Us Are Brave* by Gloria Hull, Patricia Bell Scott, and Barbara Smith;[73] *Ain't I a Woman* by Bell Hooks;[74] and *Black Feminist Thought* by Patricia Hill Collins.[75] Womanism, the theological counterpart of black feminism, is described in books such as *Katie's Canon: Womanism and the Soul of the Black Community* by Katie Geneva Cannon[76] and *Introducing Womanist Theology* by Stephanie Y. Mitchem.[77] Other aspects of black theology are described by *Introducing Black Theology of Liberation* by Dwight Hopkins,[78] the two-volume *Black Theology: A Documentary History* edited by James Cone and Gayraud Wilmore,[79] and "Black Theology: Schools of Thought," an article by Donna L. Gilton.[80] Blyden Jackson has written volume one of *A History of Afro-American Literature*,[81] which covers the period up to 1895, and reference books on this subject include *The Oxford Companion to African American Literature*[82] and *Masterpieces of African American Literature*.[83] Not specifically mentioned here is more specialized social science, humanities, and professional research by these scholars. African American scholarship is extremely diverse.

African

Children's literature in Africa and the Caribbean have developed separately from each other and from African American literature. These literatures are not only documented separately, but this documentation is also widely scattered and not always easy to find. *The Black Experience in Children's Books* has always included books about Africa and the Caribbean, which for the most part have been written by U.S. authors and published by U.S. publishers, but other documentation is very necessary.

As is true of other ethnic literature in the United States, African literature available in the United States was written mostly by Europeans and Americans (including African Americans) and others viewing the continent from the outside. Africans have gradually developed their own body of literature (especially youth literature), and the works mentioned here reflect this.

The foremost authorities writing about African children's literature in the United States are Nancy Schmidt, Osayimwense Osa, Meena Khorana, and more recently, Donnarae MacCann and Yulisa Amadu Maddy. Schmidt[84] did pivotal work in the 1970s documenting children's materials about Africa published in the United States. She also discussed literature produced in Africa and elsewhere, described the problems with this literature, and made recommendations for the best books. Osa,[85] Khorana,[86] Raoul Granqvist,[87] and Maddy and MacCann[88] have contributed other book-length bibliographies and critical works that in a number of ways update the work of Schmidt. The African Studies Association gives an annual Children's Book Award for the best children's book on Africa.

Currently scholars have produced quite a bit of work specific to various regions of Africa. While Osa has discussed English-language works by African writers, Cecile Lebon[89] does the same for literature from French-speaking countries. Vivian Yenika-Agbaw[90] analyses stereotypes in books about West Africa written by Africans, white Europeans and Americans, and African Americans; and Jeffrey Garrett[91] discusses the treatment of Islam and other religions in West African children's literature.

Until the 1990s, South Africa was ruled by a minority white population under the system of apartheid, and most of that country's literature reflects the views of this ruling group. Carol Littlejohn and the team of Maddy and MacCann have written on this subject. Littlejohn[92] simply describes the best literature that she found, while MacCann and Maddy[93] take a much more critical stance, describing stereotypes that continue to exist in children's literature since the end of apartheid. A website showing and describing South African writers of different backgrounds is "South African Children's Literature,"[94] which is from the University of South Africa.

There are also several current developments in Ethiopia, where local authors, such as Tesfaye Gabre-Mariam,[95] are currently publishing. Gebre-Mariam has organized a group called Writers for Ethiopian Children. In addition, Down Home Books (http://www.downhome.com/featured.htm) is publishing books for Ethiopian children in English, Amharic, and other languages.[96] The British writer Elizabeth Laird[97] has been collecting traditional stories from around the country in order to write reading textbooks in simplified English for children in grades 3 and 4. Ethiopian children's books are expected to educate as well as entertain.

Caribbean

Caribbean literature for children can be especially challenging to find. Some materials are published in the Caribbean, but many of them are published abroad in the United States, Canada, and Great Britain. The companies that have produced the most have been Macmillan, Longman, and Heinemann. Yahaya Bello[98] writes about themes and trends in Caribbean children's literature, providing a good overview of the topic. There is a brief bibliography by Annette Wallace[99] and a children's book list from Macmillan Caribbean.[100] Information on Puerto Rican literature will be described in the next section on Latino/a literature.

LATINO/A

Unique Characteristics of This Literature

Latin American, Latino, and Spanish-language literature covers a number of nationalities—and languages. One part of this material is by *Latino/a authors residing in the United States*, and many lists include other Latin American authors as well. Within the United States, most of this literature is written by Mexican Americans or Chicanos, but there are also writers from Puerto Rico, Cuba, the Dominican Republic, and Central and South America. These works are in Spanish or English, and in some cases they are bilingual.

Second, there is the world of Spanish-language literature. This includes *materials from all countries where Spanish is the primary language*. The biggest publishing centers are in Spain, Mexico, and Argentina. Some materials translate well across Latino/a cultures and nationalities, but not all. There are some differences in Spanish grammar and vocabulary from country to country. While it is important to acquire some of the best materials from a variety of Latin American countries and Latino/a cultures, it is vital to consider the demographics of one's local service area. Traditionally, most Latino/as in the Southwest have been Chicano or Mexican American; most in Florida, Cuban Americans; and most in the Northeast, Puerto Ricans and, to some extent, Cuban Americans. However, it appears that people from the Dominican Republic are now becoming the dominant Latino group in much of the Northeast, and Latino/as from different groups are settling everywhere. Local areas may vary widely over time in this regard.

Third, *many Anglo publications, as well as classics from around the world, have been translated into Spanish*. In fact, there are more translations than original Spanish-language works, at least in the United States, though this may be gradually changing.

The professional people, organizations, materials, and resources mentioned below are aware of all of these trends and realities. Some try to track all of the literature described here. Some are bringing a much-needed focus to Latino/a writers who live in the United States, and others are concerned about how to acquire the best Spanish-language or bilingual materials.

Keeping Track: Bibliographies, Evaluative Materials, Library Collections, and Publishers

By far, the most important person keeping track of all these resources has been Isabel Schon, who has been publishing bibliographies for almost thirty years. She has not only written series of book-length bibliographies,[101] but more recently she has also continued to write bibliographical articles and columns for the *MultiCultural Review, Booklist, Childhood Education, Science and Children, Young Children, Voice of Youth Advocates (VOYA), Multicultural Education, The Social Studies,* and *American Libraries.* Schon is the director of the Barahona Center for the Study of Books in Spanish for Children and Adolescents/Centro Barahona para el Estudio de Libros Infantiles y Juveniles en Espanol,[102] the world's only library devoted specifically to children's books in Spanish about Latin Americans and Latino/as in the United States and to works by Latin American and Latino/a writers, regardless of language. The Barahona Center has an excellent website that can help people to find relevant resources on the Internet, and it offers several workshops a year on related topics.

A more recent initiative is the review publication *Criticas,*[103] which has been published since 2001 by the *School Library Journal. Criticas* reviews Spanish-language and Spanish-English books published in the United States, including translations of Anglo and other materials. They also cover books translated from Spanish into English; to some extent, Spanish, Latino/a, and Latin American writers; and both children's and adult materials. The periodical has recently made a transition from print to a mostly online format, which is now free. Other bibliographies of children's books about Latino/as include a book-length bibliography about Latino/a and Asian American children by Patricia Beilke and Frank J. Sciara[104] and an article on trade books by Judy A. Leavell, Barbara Hatcher, Jennifer Battle, and Nancy Ramos-Michael.[105]

However, finding information specifically on Latino/a authors who write or illustrate for children has been difficult until recently. During the 1990s, REFORMA, the National Association to Promote Library and Information Services to Latinos and the Spanish Speaking and the American Library Association's Association of Library Services to Children (ALA-ALSC) established the Pura Belpré Award to recognize these writers and the best of their work. Other awards established with different criteria but that still encourage Latino/a writers include the Americas Award and the Tomás Rivera Mexican American Children's Book Awards. One can also find some U.S. Latino writers on the Barahona website by choosing an age group to be investigated and choosing the United States under the country field on the search screen, but this is not totally dependable. In addition, Carmen L. Medina and Patricia Encisco[106] have published a very interesting article that critically analyzes themes in the works of Latino/a writers from all groups. Several publications (mostly by non-Latino/as) have specifically focused on Latino/a writers from all groups. They include the work of Schon,[107] Sherry York,[108] Frances Ann Day,[109] and Christine M. Hill.[110]

Rosalinda Barrera with several other researchers[111] have published several articles on Mexican American or Chicano literature. There has also been a small body of works about and by Puerto Ricans published on the U.S. mainland over the years, but the size of this literature has *declined since the 1970s!* Sonia Nieto describes this situation and important characteristics of Puerto Rican culture in the continental United States.[112]

On the other hand, Puerto Rican literature published and disseminated on the island of Puerto Rico has flourished since the 1950s and 1960s, according to Susan Freiband and Consuelo Figueras.[113] The Puerto Rican Institute for Children's and Young People's Books/Instituto Puertorriqueño del Libro Infantil y Juvenil awards the Ester Feliciano Mendoza and the Isabelita Freites de Matos awards for the best books. These materials seem to be heavily promoted and used in Puerto Rican schools.

Another concern is where to find and how to evaluate books *in* the Spanish language. A bibliography published by International Board on Books for Young People (IBBY)—Mexico[114] lists the best of world children's and young adult literature in Spanish translation and available from Mexican publishers. Yvonne S. Freeman[115] and Margarita Gonzalez-Jensen[116] have written articles on choosing Spanish-language books, and Schon has also addressed the quality of Spanish-language books and their English translations in her reviews. Barrera and Ruth E. Quiroa[117] have also published a recent article describing in detail issues that arise when Spanish is used in bilingual or English-based texts.

Most materials for children by Latino/a authors are published by Arte Publico Press/Piñata Books, the Children's Book Press, and Lee and Low. Some other relevant publishers include the Cinco Puntos Press, Red Crane Books, and Curbstone Press. Some important vendors or distributors of Spanish-language materials are now part of mainstream firms. Lectorum, the country's oldest Spanish-language bookstore and Spanish-language distributor, is now the Spanish-language division of Scholastic. Baker and Taylor has recently acquired another major distributor, Libros Sin Fronteras (Books without Borders). Some librarians who collect Spanish-language materials also take advantage of international book fairs, such as La Feria Internacional del Libro de Bogotá in Colombia; La Feria de del Libro de Buenos Aires in Argentina; LIBER in Madrid, Spain; and the Guadalajara International Book Fair in Mexico.[118]

While there is now a very small but growing body of young adult (YA) literature for and about Latino/a teenagers, this group of young people continues to do assigned and recreational reading from related adult classics. Nicolás Kanellos, the founder of Arte Publico and Piñata Books, has been publishing a series entitled *Recovering the Hispanic Literary Heritage* that

includes historical titles of interest to young adults. There are also readers and
other books that were published as a result of the Bilingual Education Act of
1968, including the *Serie Tierra de Encanto* by Ernest Galarza, the *Raintree
Hispanic Stories Series*, and children's books by Nathaniel Archuleta. Some
of these materials may still be found in curriculum centers.[119]

Promoting the Materials: Initiatives in Libraries, Schools, and Other Institutions

While Latino/as and other people with a strong interest in Latino/a cultures
have worked very hard to *document* and criticize works by and about La-
tino/as, they have especially excelled at *marketing programming, outreach,
services, curricula, and other activities in libraries, schools, and other institutions*. These activities can be roughly divided into library and community
initiatives and school initiatives.

Library initiatives include creating handbooks and manuals on planning
library services for Latino/as and executing programs for the community.
I know of thirteen such guides to serving Latino/a communities—nine
books and four websites. Three sources especially useful for children are
books by Adela Artola Allen,[120] Barbara Immroth and Kathleen de la Peña
McCook,[121] and a web page written by Maria Mena and published by the
Children's Book Council.[122] Mena's page gives an excellent overview
on library services for Latino/a children, Allen focuses on services for
children, and Immroth and de la Peña McCook focus on services for adolescents. A good example of library services for Latino/a communities is
the Multnomah County Library's Library Outreach in Spanish (LIBROS)
in Oregon.

Library programming for the whole family and community has been
very important in promoting Latino/a and other literature. Historically, this
practice dates back to the programming and community outreach activities
of Pura Belpré during most of the twentieth century. Programming includes
bilingual or Spanish-language story hours, programming for families, Spanish-language or bilingual collections, library card campaigns, and library
tours and other forms of information literacy instruction. It also incorporates
community assessment, working with community agencies, and creating bilingual or Spanish signage and websites.

El Dia de los Niños: El Dia el los Libros/Day of Children: Day of Books,[123]
which is celebrated in libraries on April 30 with the cooperation of RE-
FORMA, the National Association of Bilingual Educators, and MANA, a
national Latina organization, has been a vital national program. The author
Pat Mora and her family have been awarding prizes to libraries offering the

best programs on that day. Some libraries also celebrate National Hispanic Heritage Month (September 15–October 15).

Educators have contributed to this field in two ways: by creating curricula and classroom activities to promote Latino/a literature and culture and by writing books and other materials on Latino/a issues in the field of education. Examples of curricula and activities for the classroom can be found in articles by Lynn Atkinson Smolen and Victoria Ortiz-Castro,[124] James Jupp,[125] Bess A. Isom and Carolyn P. Casteel,[126] Maria A. Perez-Stable and Mary H. Cordier,[127] and Medina.[128] Books on issues in Latino/a education include titles by Antonia Darder, Rodolfo D. Torres, and Henry Gutiérrez;[129] Eugene E. Garcia;[130] JoAnn Crandall;[131] Stanton Wortham, Enrique G. Murillo Jr., and Edmund T. Hamann;[132] and Victoria-Maria MacDonald.[133] A Latino/a educational periodical is *The Hispanic Outlook in Higher Education*,[134] and a relevant organization and website is Aspira,[135] "the only national nonprofit organization devoted solely to the education and leadership development of Puerto Rican and other Hispanic youth."

Supplementary Materials for Professionals and Older Readers

Historical books on Latino/as in America include *Harvest of Empire* by Juan Gonzalez[136] and *The Columbia History of Latinos in the United States since 1960* by David Gutiérrez.[137] Lives of a variety of ordinary Latino/as in the United States are portrayed in *Americanos: Latino Life in the United States* by Edward James Olmos, Carlos Fuentes, and Lea Ybarra;[138] *Living in Spanglish* by Ed Morales;[139] *Strangers among Us* by Roberto Suro;[140] and *Growing Up Latino* by Ilan Stavans.[141] More scholarly introductions to Latino/as include *Hispanic Nation: Culture, Politics, and the Constructing of Identity* by Geoffrey Fox,[142] *The Latino Studies Reader* edited by Antonia Darder and Rodolfo Torres,[143] *The Latino/a Condition* edited by Richard Delgado,[144] *Latinos: A Biography of the People* by Earl Shorris,[145] *Herencia: The Anthology of Hispanic Literature of the United States* edited by Nicolás Kanellos,[146] and *The Handbook of Hispanic Cultures in the United States* edited by Kanellos and Claudio Esteva-Fabregat.[147]

Links to Latino/a websites include the Latin American Network Information Center (LANIC),[148] Andanza al Web Latino,[149] *Hispanic Magazine*,[150] and Hispanic Online.com.[151] Popular periodicals include *Hispanic: The Magazine For and About Hispanics*,[152] *Latino Leaders: The National Magazine of the Successful Hispanic American*,[153] and *Contacto: A Magazine for Today's Latino*.[154] More scholarly journals include the *Latino(a) Research Review*,[155] which reviews scholarly materials for adults; *Aztlan: A Journal of Chicano Studies*;[156] the *Bilingual Research Journal*; and the *Bilingual Review. Aztlan* has published a couple of articles about Chicano studies programs,[157] and there are good introductions to Latino/a theology by Eduardo C. Fernández[158] and Justo Gonzalez.[159]

All of the resources listed here lead to information on more specific groups, such as Mexican Americans or Chicanos, Puerto Ricans, Cuban Americans, Dominican Americans, Salvadoran Americans, etc. Consult library catalogs, Amazon.com, and Internet search engines for more information on specific groups.

NATIVE AMERICAN

All groups described at length in this book have experienced racism in the United States. All have lacked books published about them, all have struggled to be able to write and disseminate their own stories, and all must deal with stereotypes and misinformation in children's and other literature written about them. When writers from all of these groups finally have a chance to write and to publish, they bring perspectives never seen before to children's literature. Most of these trends are particularly evident in looking at children's literature by and about Native Americans. There is an abundance of materials about Native Americans, but most of it is poor in quality. For many reasons, *criticism* and *establishing criteria* for this literature have been major focuses of Native American writers, librarians, educators, publishers, and their supporters. This section will look at critical literature, media, and organizations; initiatives specifically from Native American writers; and resources for teachers, librarians, professionals, and older readers.

Of Critical Importance

A tremendous amount of work has been done over the years by a few people—Arlene Hirschfelder, Donnarae MacCann, Beverly Slapin and Doris Seale, Naomi Caldwell and Lisa Mitten, and more recently, Cynthia Leitich Smith and Debbie Reese. Work by others will also be cited below. Most, but not all, of these researchers are Native Americans.

Overviews of the treatment of Native Americans in children's literature have been written by Reese[160] and Smith.[161] The literature on stereotypes about Native Americans in children's literature is especially extensive. It is a shameful state of affairs, not that these evaluative materials exist, but that their information is so necessary.

The first criticism on literature written about Native Americans was the Council on Interracial Books for Children (CIBC) study *Unlearning Indian*

Stereotypes: A Teaching Unit for Elementary Teachers and Children's Librarians.[162] R. W. Stedman,[163] Elizabeth Noll,[164] MacCann,[165] and Reese[166] also undertook similar research. While Stedman did not specifically discuss children's literature, his descriptions of stereotypes of Native Americans elsewhere in U.S. culture prove to be all too relevant to this field.

There are three major streams of research, coming from several analysts, which include the following:

- The bibliographies and work of Hirschfelder
- The research, commentary, and activities of Caldwell and Mitten and reactions to these
- The bibliography and work of Slapin and Seale, and their organization, Oyate

Hirschfelder has published several critical works and bibliographies through the years, including *American Indian Stereotypes in the World of Children: A Reader and Bibliography*[167] in 1982, which she revised in 1999. She also published a critical article in *Library Trends*[168] in 1993. In addition to the usual criteria for evaluating materials, Hirschfelder commented more at length on how to evaluate folklore.

Caldwell and Mitten published an article, "'I' Is Not for Indian," in the *MultiCultural Review* in 1992.[169] Their article describes some criteria for evaluating materials on Native Americans and provides lists of books recommended and not recommended. They have given workshops on this subject and published their bibliography on the web. Caldwell also did an article on stereotypes in picture books for *School Library Journal*,[170] and was soon interviewed by MacCann and Olga Richard on this subject for the *Wilson Library Bulletin*.[171] Ten years later, Nina Lindsay published an update, "'I' Still Isn't for Indian," in the *School Library Journal*.[172]

Seale had been a reviewer for the CIBC before editing *Books without Bias: Through Indian Eyes* with Slapin in 1988.[173] In 1996, they produced a pamphlet entitled *How to Tell the Difference: A Guide to Evaluating Children's Books for Anti-Indian Bias*.[174] This guide and other materials were folded into *Through Indian Eyes: The Native Experience in Books for Children* in 1998.[175] More recently, they published *A Broken Flute* in 2004.[176] In addition, they established an organization and website, Oyate,[177] which list their criteria for evaluating materials about Native Americans, list books recommended and not recommended, and offer some books and curriculum materials for sale. All of these publications have amply demonstrated stereotypes in books about Native Americans as well as criteria for evaluating the quality of good and poor materials.

Not only is there criticism, but there are now sources that describe the critical literature. These include brief guides by Kay Marie Porterfield and Emory Dean Keoke[178] and by Joan Berman.[179] In her article "Native American Literature for Children and Young Adults,"[180] Hirschfelder cites dissertations and other scholarly research on this topic not found elsewhere.

Because of the many problems with literature about Native Americans, alternative review media and programs have been very necessary. In addition to Oyate, they include the *Akwesasne Notes*,[181] *Wicazo Sa Review*,[182] and more recently, the *Independent American Indian Review*.[183]

In addition, the Children's Library at the Mashantucket Pequot Museum has been collecting as many materials on Native Americans as they can, as well as recommended materials and books by Native American authors. Library activities include workshops and programs for children and adults that promote the best of the literature and discuss how to evaluate all of this material.[184] The D'Arcy McNickle collection of the Newberry Library[185] also collects children's books related to Native Americans, but the Mashantucket Pequot Museum has done more critical work on this particular issue. The Native Studies Collection at the Ethnic Studies Library of the University of California, Berkeley,[186] also buys and collects recommended children's materials.

Impact of Native American Authors

It is, of course, extremely necessary for Native Americans to be able to write, tell, and publish their own stories and to present their own worldviews. It is also vital that they be able to define their own world and take a critical look at Western cultures. A few examples of critical materials from diverse fields outside of children's literature, but with information and insights germane to that subject, include work by Cornel Pewewardy,[187] Craig S. Womack,[188] and the Alaska Native Knowledge Network.[189] There are Christian materials by Richard Twiss[190] and Craig Stephen Smith,[191] and more philosophical works by Jerry H. Gill,[192] Donald Fixico,[193] and Vine Deloria.[194] Devon A. Mihesuah,[195] Linda Tuhiwai Smith,[196] and Cheryl Crazy Bull[197] discuss issues in "de-colonizing research" with an emphasis on research tied to spiritual values and the importance of using research and its results to benefit the community under consideration. Susan C. Faircloth, and John W. Tippeconnic[198] have published a brief guide for language teachers and teachers of other subjects who wish to indigenize their teaching methods, making them more relevant to Native American students. I believe that current Native American authors who write for young people have two goals that are very similar to those of their counterparts of one hundred years ago—to affirm and further explain their specific cultures to their own children, and to teach others about the same.

Mary G. Byler,[199] Cynthia Leitich Smith,[200] Hap Gilliland,[201] and more recently, York[202] have all compiled lists and bibliographies of Native American authors who write for children. Smith[203] has also written a more critical article for *The Horn Book Magazine* on Native American writing, and authors like George Littlefield[204] and Debbie Reese[205] have been interviewed. Organizations and listings of Native American writers in general include the Wordcraft Circle,[206] the Native Writers Circle of the Americas,[207] and Storytelling: Native American Authors Online.[208]

Resources for Librarians and Teachers

Because of the ironic abundance of materials on Native Americans but the lack of *good* materials on this group, it is very necessary to be aware of reliable resources for teachers and librarians. These resources can be divided into four groups:

• Sources of good nonfiction works about Native Americans
• Resources on how to teach all children about Native Americans
• Information on specific programs and curricula by and for Native Americans
• More general information on Native American education, including teaching guides, philosophical works, and other information

Sources of good nonfiction works include a list by Kuipers[209] of recommended books on Native Americans that can be used in the library for reference work and the *American Indian Resource Manual for Public Libraries*[210] published by the Wisconsin Department of Public Education. Several mainstream publishers have created series of books about historical and contemporary Native Americans. Examples include *We Are Still Here: Native Americans Today* from the Lerner Publishing Group and *Indians of North America* and *North American Indians of Achievement* from Chelsea House. Guides on how to teach all children about Native Americans have been compiled by Karen D. Harvey, Lisa D. Harjo, and Lynda Welborn;[211] Harvey, Harjo, and Jane K. Jackson;[212] Hirschfelder and Yvonne Beamer;[213] Reese and Jean Mendoza;[214] and Reese.[215]

Native American librarians and educators have been creating programs and curricula particularly for Native American children and youth. If I Can Read, I Can Do Anything[216] is a national library and literacy program created by Loriene Roy to encourage schoolchildren to read. The Cradleboard Project[217] is a science education curriculum created by educator and musician Buffy Sainte-Marie to be used in Native American and other schools. A new electronic periodical for young people is *Native Youth Magazine*,[218] which encourages reports and other contributions from young people. The Council for Indian Education[219] provides in-service training and instructional materials, such as readers, to teachers of Native Americans. Their president, Hap Gilliland, has lived and worked with indigenous peoples from all over the world, taught at all levels, directed teacher training in reading, and written many college texts and several children's books as well as other materials.

Materials in the field of Native American education come in three forms—sources on how to teach Native Americans in the classroom, general and philosophical commentary from educators, and related education periodicals. Sources on teaching Native Americans include works by Gilliland,[220] Jon Reyhner,[221] Gregory Cajete,[222] and Marylou Schultz and Miriam Kroeger.[223] More general works by educators include books by Deloria[224] and by Linda Miller Cleary and Thomas D. Peacock.[225]

Four educational periodicals in the United States and Canada are the *Journal of American Indian Education*,[226] which is published by the Center for Indian Education at Arizona State University's College of Education; *Tribal College Journal: The Voice and Vision of American Indian Higher Education*, which is published by the American Indian Higher Education Consortium;[227] the *Canadian Journal of Native Education*,[228] which is published by the University of Alberta; and *Winds of Change*,[229] an education and career periodical published by the American Indian Science and Engineering Society (AISES). *Winds of Change* also publishes an annual college guide especially for Native American youth.

Publishers and distributors of Native American materials include the Children's Book Press, Oyate, Daybreak Star,[230] Canyon Records,[231] Indian Historian Press,[232] Theytus Book, Ltd.,[233] and the Cinco Puntas Press. Some materials can be ordered from the Mashantucket Pequot Museum Bookstore in Connecticut. Many tribes are now building their own libraries, starting tribal colleges, making K–12 education more culturally relevant, and developing museums,[234] education centers, and publishers. For information on a particular nation, it is well worth it to ask the tribe itself about resources. Mitten lists nations on her website.[235] Some other important organizations are the American Indian Library Association (AILA)[236] and the Mashantucket Pequot Museum and Research Center.[237] AILA is currently in the process of establishing the American Indian Children's Book Awards. The first presentation was given at the Joint Librarians of Color conference in Dallas, Texas, in October 2006. Recipients of the first awards included Joseph Bruchac for *Hidden Roots* and Louise Erdich for *The Birchbark House*.

Supplementary Materials for Professionals and Older Readers

Histories of Native Americans include *500 Nations: An Illustrated History of North American Indians* by Alvin M. Josephy,[238] *A Companion to American Indian History* by Philip Deloria and Neal Salisbury,[239] and *A Forest of Time: American Indian Ways of History* by Peter Nabokov.[240] Other introductory materials include *Native American FAQ Handbook* by George Russell;[241] *Custer Died for Your Sins* by Vine Deloria Jr;[242] *Native Voices: American Indian Identity and Resistance,* edited by Richard A. Grounds, George E. Tinker, and David E. Wilkins;[243] *Native American Literature: An Introduction* by Suzanne Evertsen Lundquist;[244] and *The Cambridge Companion to Native American Literature* by Joy Porter and Kenneth M. Roemer.[245]

Popular periodicals include *American Indian,*[246] *Indian Country Today,*[247] *Native American Times,*[248] and *Native Peoples: Arts and Lifeways.*[249] Scholarly journals include *American Indian Culture and Research Journal,*[250] *American Indian Quarterly,*[251] *Canadian Journal of Native Studies,*[252] *Native Americas: Hemispheric Journal of Indigenous Issues,*[253] *Studies in American Indian Literatures,*[254] and *Wicazo Sa Review: A Journal of Native American Studies.*[255]

ASIAN AMERICAN

Like the other groups described here, Asian Americans have been involved in all aspects of children's literature—as authors, publishers, distributors, librarians, teachers, and so forth. They have produced, documented, and criticized literature by and about Asian Americans. They have also done programming in and outside of libraries. However, Asian Americans have especially excelled in the area of *access and distribution* with their network of publishers, stores, and web-based companies. This section will discuss their documentation and evaluation activities and then will describe publishers, bookstores, distributors, and other organizations, programs, and websites Asian American contributions to the general field of multicultural children's literature will also be briefly mentioned. Some South Asian sources will be mentioned throughout, but more detailed discussion of voices from the South Asian diaspora will be found at the end of this chapter.

Bibliographies and Criticism

Shu-Hsien Lai Chen[256] and Sandra S. Yamate[257] have written articles giving excellent overviews of the field of Asian American children's literature, especially useful for those new to the field. Bibliographies listing books about Asian Americans are written by Beilke and Sciara;[258] Craig Heller, Bruce Cunningham, Ginny Lee, and Hannah H. Heller ;[259] Esther Jenkins and Mary C. Austin ;[260] Khorana;[261] NYPL's Chinese Heritage Booklist Committee;[262] Barbara A. Black,[263] and Zheng Ye Yang.[264]

The bibliography by Jenkins and Austin is especially useful. It describes literature on Asians and Asian Americans by authors of all backgrounds; provides extensive information on original folklore and literature from Asia; discusses themes of folklore and stories, describes the characteristics of storytelling and style; and gives extensive background on the literature described. Literature about Chinese, Japanese, Korean, and Southeast Asians and their U.S. descendants is all listed, annotated, and described. Jenkins and Austin also list quite a few Asian American authors, considering the 1989 copyright date.

Khorana's book is about children's literature from the Indian subcontinent (or South Asia). The bibliography from the New York Public Library on the Chinese American experience in the United States was published in the *EMIE Bulletin*, and Black's bibliography looks at children's books about Asian Americans from a British perspective.

Many Asian Americans and others have written very scholarly articles on stereotypes in U.S. literature depicting Asians and Asian Americans. The earliest studies were by the CIBC[265] and Asian Americans for Fair Media.[266] Suzanne Lo and Ginny Lee;[267] Valerie Oaka Pang, Carolyn Colvin, My Luang Tran, and Roberta H. Barba;[268] Elaine Aoki;[269] Mingshui Cai;[270] Violet H. Harada;[271] and Shao-yi Leu[272] have conducted more recent studies, and many of these articles establish criteria for evaluating materials. Uma Krishnaswami[273] describes errors and stereotypes in books about South Asia and South Asian Americans. Yamate criticizes not only the literature, but also some of the criticism, and finds that many established criteria are not specific enough, especially for people new to the cultures described. She raises many questions about how materials should be critiqued.[274]

Greg Leitich Smith[275] and Nancy Garhan Attebury[276] describe the works of Asian American authors in their respective articles, and ALA-ALSC has published "Sharing Cultures," a brief bibliography on books by Asian American children's authors, which is available in different forms from the *EMIE Bulletin* as well as on the web.[277] Khorana[278] and Cheri Jones[279] both discuss materials on South Asian Americans in their articles. There are also several articles that specifically discuss an early Asian American author, Yoshiko Uchida.[280]

Some relevant articles and reviews appear in the Chinese American Librarians' Association (CALA) and the Asian Pacific American Librarians' Association (APALA) newsletters, and a few have appeared in the *EMIE Bulletin*, but many more previews and reviews of materials are on Internet sites, some of which focus on specific ethnic groups or geographic areas. Goldsea's "Asian American Bookview—Kids' Book Page"[281] includes short excerpts of books under consideration. Good sources of book review information on many Asian nationalities and ethnic groups are available from PaperTigers.org,[282] which is part of Pacific Rim Voices and the Asian American Curriculum Project (formerly the Japanese American Curriculum Project).[283] Krishnaswami has created a web page entitled "South Asia in Children's Books."[284]

There is currently one prize being offered for writers of Asian American children's literature, which has been created by APALA and CALA—the Asian Pacific American Award for Literature. There is a serious shortage of Asian American writers who have been published by mainstream presses. Some seem to have trouble breaking into this arena. Many publish with alternative presses, such as Lee and Low, Children's Book Press, and Polychrome Publishers, the only press in the United States that publishes strictly Asian American books for children.[285]

Bookstores and distributors abound, both in real public space and on the web. They include Asia for Kids,[286] the Asian American Curriculum Project, Bess Press,[287] China Books,[288] Shen's Books and Supplies,[289] South Asian Children's Books and Software,[290] the shop at the Japanese American Cultural and Community Center,[291] Press Pacifica,[292] Asian American Booksellers,[293] and Multicultural Distribution Center.[294] Bess Press and Press Pacifica are Hawaiian publishers.

There are excellent library collections for Asian American children at the Chinatown Branch of the San Francisco Public Library and the Asian Branch of the Oakland Public Library in California. Other cities that may also have good collections include Seattle, Chicago, New York City, Queens Borough (N.Y.), and Boston. I was not able to find a separate research library for Asian American children's literature comparable to some other collections mentioned in this work. However, the San Francisco Public Library has at their main library a general research children's collection called the Effie Lee Morris Historical and Research Collection of Children's Literature. It collects books on many subjects and multicultural books in general, but one of their areas of emphasis is old and new books reflecting both the Asian American and the general Pacific Rim experience in children's books. Its staff tries to trace the history of how these experiences have been handled over the years in children's literature.

Community Programming Initiatives

A number of organizations promote Asian American books for children and young people. Some publish materials, some have programs working with young writers, and some work with librarians and other groups concerned with this issue. The Asian American Writers' Workshop in New York City[295] offers several programs and activities for Asian and other youth. Some of these programs teach Asian American adult literature to high school students. Some of their other activities include workshops for young, new writers. Another important cultural group is Riksha[296] in Chicago, which promotes the arts by publishing a literary magazine, producing plays, and attempting to deal with issues in the community. A number of individuals also work on projects with organizations. For example, Sandra Yamate compiled an anthology, *Children of Asia America* (published by Polychrome), on behalf of the Asian American Coalition. Books on the educational needs of young Asian Americans have been published by Li-Rong Lilly Cheng,[297] Don T. Nakanishi and Tina Yamano Nishida, [298] and Clara C. Park and Marilyn Mei-Ying Chi.[299]

Asian Americans have also made contributions to the general field of multicultural children's literature. Lee and Low is a multicultural publishing firm owned by two Chinese American families. Researchers like Cai and Yamate have raised serious theoretical and philosophical questions that should be of concern to the whole field.

Voices from the South Asian Diaspora

The continent of Asia incorporates about fifty countries and nationalities. A challenge for pan-Asian groups in the United States is to be able to represent well the interests of all of these diverse groups. One group of people which is becoming very vocal includes those from India, Pakistan, Sri Lanka, Bangladesh, and other countries in that area. They have been called many names in the United States, for example, *Indian* or *East Indian*. The worst was *Indian Americans*; this is especially confusing if Native Americans are called American Indians, and also compounds Columbus's original mistake! Recently, the term *South Asian* has been used to refer to people from this part of the world.

There have been two waves of immigration to the United States by South Asians. The first was in the late nineteenth and early twentieth centuries. Then legislation to restrict Asian immigration in general was applied to South Asians, and the small, scattered communities, mostly of men, all but died out. Dhan Gopal Mukerji, an immigrant who came to the United States in the early twentieth century, won a Newbery Award in 1928.[300]

A second wave of immigration came, starting in the mid-1960s, as a result of the Immigration Act of 1965. Many of these immigrants were middle class, professional, and well educated. Their children went to U.S. schools and libraries and read Western literature. Children of South Asian immigrants in the United States also read English-language literature from the subcontinent, as well as some religious (mostly Hindu) materials produced in the United States[301] However, in recent years, a very small English-language Western-style literature with South Asian roots has started to develop in the English-speaking Western countries. Writers of South Asian descent who write in English include Uma Krishnaswami, Tanuja Desai Hidier, and Mitali Perkins in the United States; Rachna Gilmore and Rukhsana Khan in Canada; and Jamila Gavin in Great Britain. All of these writers now have websites of their own. Their books seem to be popular all over the South Asian diaspora.[302]

The two main writers who are keeping track of trends in this field are Meena G. Khorana (who has also done bibliographies on African children's literature) and Uma Krishnaswami. Khorana has done an extensive book-length bibliography on books from South Asia.[303] She has also written an article on the history of South Asian and related literature in the United States.[304]

Krishnaswami has created several novels, an extensive website, and one additional article. Two of her web pages[305] are on literature on South Asia in general. Both Krishnaswami and Khorana discuss books written in South Asia as well as books about this geographic area written elsewhere in the world, such as the United Kingdom or the United States, and they criticize many of these books for having stereotypes. Krishnaswami, however, focuses more on children's writers of South Asian descent who now write in the United States, Canada, and England in her web page, "South Asia Voices—With North American Accents." She has also written "On the Seashore of Worlds: Selected South Asian Voices from North America and the United Kingdom" for *Bookbird*. Mitali Perkins has created a website especially for young immigrants.[306] Rukhsana Khan, a Muslim originally from Pakistan, has also created an extensive website which will be discussed in chapter 5. There is already a tremendous amount of adult literature from the South Asian diaspora, and it is probable that much more of a children's literature will also develop. One indication of this is that *Kahani: A South Asian Literary Magazine for Children*[307] debuted in the fall of 2004 and promises to be an excellent addition to this literature. This periodical focuses on the experiences of South Asian Americans. In addition, there is an *EMIE Bulletin* article on "East Indian Children in America" by Cheri Jones[308] and a website entitled "South Asian Children's Books and Software."[309]

Supplementary Materials for Professionals and Older Readers

Historical books on Asian Americans include *Strangers from a Different Shore* by Ronald Takaki,[310] *The Columbia Guide to Asian American History* by Gary Y. Okihiro,[311] and *Asian American Dreams: The Emergence of an American People* by Helen Zia.[312] Introductory information on contemporary

Asian Americans can be found in *Yellow: Race in America Beyond Black and White* by Frank H. Wu,[313] *YELL-Oh Girls: Emerging Voices Explore Culture, Identity and Growing Up Asian American* by Vickie Nam,[314] *Asian American X: An Intersection of Twenty-First Century Asian American Voices* edited by Arar Han and John Hsu,[315] *The Accidental Asian: Notes of a Native Speaker* by Eric Liu,[316] *Forever Foreigners or Honorary Whites? The Asian Ethnic Experience Today* by Mia Tuan,[317] and *Invitation to Lead: Guidance for Emerging Asian American Leaders* by Paul Tokunaga.[318]

More scholarly information can be found in *Contemporary Asian America: A Multidisciplinary Reader*, edited by Min Zhou and James V. Gatewood;[319] *Margins and Mainstreams: Asians in American History and Culture* by Gary Okihiro;[320] and *Asian American Studies: A Reader*, edited by Jean Yu-Wen Shen Wu and Min Song.[321] Books on Asian American literature include *An Interethnic Companion to Asian American Literature* by King-Kok Cheung,[322] *Reading Asian American Literature* by Sau-ling Cynthia Wong,[323] and *Asian American Literature* by Elaine Kim.[324] Works on Asian American Christian theology include *Journeys at the Margin: Toward an Autobiographical Theology in American-Asian Perspective*, edited by Peter C. Phan and Jung Young Lee,[325] and *Realizing the America of Our Hearts*, edited by Fumitaka Matsuoka and Eleazar S. Fernandez.[326]

Links to Asian American websites include "Asian-Nation: The Landscape of Asian America,"[327] "Goldsea: Asian American Supersite,"[328] "Help by Subject—Asian American Studies" by Gerardo Colmenar,[329] the Association for Asian American Studies website,[330] and the entertainment e-magazine for young people *YOLK: Generasian Next.*[331] Popular periodicals include *Monolid Magazine,*[332] and more scholarly journals include *Amerasia Journal,*[333] *Journal of Asian American Studies,*[334] *Asian American Movement Ezine,*[335] and *Asian American Policy Review.*[336] *Amerasia Journal* has published several special issues on developments in Asian American studies,[337] and Kandice Chuh and Karen Shimakawa have edited the book *Orientations: Mapping Studies in the Asian Diaspora.*[338] Asian Americans originally came from approximately fifty countries that vary widely. Consult library catalogs, Amazon.com, and Internet search engines for information on more specific groups, such as Chinese Americans, Japanese Americans, Filipino Americans, Hmong Americans, Pacific Islanders, South Asians, and many other groups.

REFERENCES

1. Deborah Kutenplon and Ellen Olmstead, *Young Adult Fiction by African American Writers, 1968–1993* (New York: Garland, 1996).

2. Osayimwense Osa, *The All-White World of Children's Books and African American Children's Literature* (Trenton, N.J.: Africa World Press, 1995).

3. Barbara Thrash Murphy, *Black Authors and Illustrators of Books for Children and Young Adults: A Biographical Dictionary* (New York: Garland, 1999).

4. Henrietta Smith, ed., *The Coretta Scott King Awards Books: 1970–1999* (Chicago: ALA, 1999).

5. Pamela Toussaint, *Great Books for African American Children* (New York: Penguin, 1999).

6. Helen E. Williams, *Books by African American Authors and Illustrators* (Chicago: ALA, 1991).

7. Donna Rand, Toni Trent Parker, and Sheila Foster, *Black Books Galore! Guide to Great African American Children's Books* (Stamford, Conn.: Wiley, 1998); Donna Rand, Toni Trent Parker, and Sheila Foster, *Black Books Galore! Guide to African American Children's Books about Boys* (Stamford, Conn.: Wiley, 2000); Donna Rand, Toni Trent Parker, and Sheila Foster, *Black Books Galore! Guide to Great African American Books about Girls* (Stamford, Conn.: Wiley, 2000); Donna Rand, Toni Trent Parker, and Sheila Foster, *Black Books Galore! Guide to More Great African American Books* (Stamford, Conn.: Wiley, 2001).

8. Rudine Sims Bishop, "Books from Parallel Cultures: New African American Voices," *The Hornbook Magazine* 68 (Sept./Oct. 1992): 616–20.

9. Daphne Muse, "Ebony Voices and Cowrie Shell Dreams: Black American Classics in Fiction and Poetry for Young Readers," in *The New Press Guide to Multicultural Resources for Young Readers* (New York: New Press, 1997), 320–26.

10. Violet J. Harris, "Contemporary Griots: African American Writers of Children's Literature," in *Teaching Multicultural Literature in Grades K–8* (Norwood, Mass.: Christopher Gordon, 1993), 55–108.

11. Donnarae MacCann and Gloria Woodard, *The Black American in Books for Children* (Metuchen, N. J.: Scarecrow, 1972).

12. Dorothy Broderick, *Image of the Black in Children's Fiction* (New York: Bowker, 1973).

13. Daphne Muse, "Black Children's Literature: The Birth of a Neglected Genre," *The Black Scholar* 7, no. 4 (December 1975):11–15.

14. Gail Singleton Taylor, "Pass It On: The Development of African American Children's Literature," *The Negro Educational Review* 50, no. 2 (Jan.–Apr. 1999): 11–17.

15. Kutenplon and Olmstead, *Young Adult Fiction by African American Writers.*

16. Rudine Sims (Bishop), *Shadow and Substance: Afro-American Experience in Contemporary Children's Fiction* (Urbana, Ill: National Council of Teachers of English, 1982); Rudine Sims Bishop, "Walk Tall in the World: African American Literature for Today's Children," *Journal of Negro Education* 59, no. 4 (1990): 556–65; Bishop, "Evaluating Books By and About African Americans," in *The Multicolored Mirror: Cultural Substance in Literature for Children and Young Adults,* ed. Merri Lindgren (Fort Atkinson, Wis.: Highsmith, 1991): 31–34.

17. Dianne Johnson, *Telling Tales: The Pedagogy and Promise of African American Literature for Youth* (New York: Greenwood, 1990); Dianne Johnson-Feelings,

"Children's and Young Adult Literature," in *The Oxford Companion to African American Literature*, ed. William L. Andrews, Frances Smith Foster, and Trudier Harris (New York: Oxford University Press, 1997), 133–40.

18. Violet J. Harris, "African American Children's Literature: The First One Hundred Years," *Journal of Negro Education* 59, no. 4 (1990): 540–55; Harris, "Children's Literature Depicting Blacks," in *Using Multiethnic Literature in the K–8 Classroom* (Norwood, Mass.: Christopher Gordon, 1997), 21–58.

19. Rudine Sims Bishop and Jonda McNair, "A Centennial Salute to Arna Bontemps, Langston Hughes, and Lorenz Graham," *The New Advocate* 15, no. 2 (Spring 2002): 109–19.

20. Dianne Johnson, "The Langston Hughes, Arna Bontemps Legacy: Historical Fiction, Realistic Fiction and the American Dream," in *Telling Tales: The Pedagogy and Promise of African American Literature for Youth* (New York: Greenwood, 1990), 39–79.

21. Langston Hughes, *The Collected Works of Langston Hughes—Works for Children and Young Adults: Poetry, Fiction and Other Writing* (Columbia, Mo.: University of Missouri, 2003); Hughes, *The Collected Works of Langston Hughes—Works for Children and Young Adults: Biographies* (Columbia, Mo.: University of Missouri, 2001).

22. Writers and Readers/Black Butterfly Books, Box 461, Village Station, New York, N.Y. 19914.

23. Just Us Books, 356 Glenwood Ave., East Orange, N.J. 07017, http://www.justusbooks.com/ (26 June 2006).

24. Hyperion Books for Children, "Jump at the Sun," 114 Fifth Ave., New York, N.Y. 10011, http://www.hyperionbooksforchildren.com/jump/moreabout.asp (26 June 2006).

25. *Black Issues Book Review,* Cox, Matthews and Associates, 10520 Warwick Ave., Suite B-8, Fairfax, Va. 22030-3136, http://www.bibookreview.com/ (26 June 2006).

26. Black Books Galore, 65 High Ridge Rd. #407, Stamford, Conn. 06905, http://www.blackbooksgalore.com/ (26 June 2006).

27. National Council of Teachers of English (NCTE). "The Seventeenth National African American Read-In," http://www.ncte.org/prog/readin/107901.htm (26 June 2006).

28. Gloria Ladson-Billings, *The Dreamkeepers: Successful Teachers of African American Children* (San Francisco: Jossey Bass, 1994); Ladson-Billings, *Beyond the Big House: African American Educators on Teacher Education* (New York: Teachers College Press, 2005).

29. Janice E. Hale, *Black Children: Their Roots, Culture, and Learning Styles* (Baltimore: Johns Hopkins, 1982); Hale, *Learning While Black: Creating Educational Excellence for African American Children* (Baltimore: Johns Hopkins, 2001).

30. Michele Foster, *Black Teachers on Teaching* (New York: New Press, 1997).

31. Barbara Sizemore, *An Abashing Anomaly: The High Achieving Predominantly Black Elementary School*, ERIC Education Resources Information Center, ED 236274.

32. Joyce E. King, *Black Education: A Transformative Research and Action Agenda for the New Century* (Mahwah, N.J.: Lawrence Erlbaum Associates, 2005).

33. Howard University, *The Journal of Negro Education*, P.O. Box 311, Howard University, Washington, D.C. 20059, http://www.journalnegroed.org/ (26 June 2006).

34. *The Journal of Blacks in Higher Education*, 200 W. 57th St., 15th Floor, New York, N.Y. 10019, http://www.jbhe.com/ (26 June 2006).

35. *Black Issues in Higher Education*, 10520 Warwick Ave, Suite B-8, Fairfax, Va. 22030-3136, http://www.blackissues.com/, to be replaced and continued by *Diversity—Issues in Higher Education*, http://www.diverseeducation.com/ (26 June 2006).

36. *The Black Collegian*, 909 Poydras St., 34th Floor, New Orleans, La. 70112, http://www.blackcollegian.com/ (26 June 2006).

37. Claire Gatrell Stephens, *Coretta Scott King Award Books: Using Great Literature with Children and Young Adults* (Englewood, Colo.: Libraries Unlimited, 2000).

38. Nancy J. Polette, *Celebrating the Coretta Scott King Awards: 101 Ideas and Activities* (Fort Atkinson, Wisc.: Upstart Books, 2000).

39. John Hope Franklin and Alfred A. Moss Jr., *From Slavery to Freedom: A History of African Americans*, eighth edition (New York: Knopf, 2000).

40. Lerone Bennett, *Before the Mayflower: A History of Black America* (Chicago: Johnson Publishing Company, 2003).

41. Robin D. G. Kelley and Earl Lewis, eds., *To Make Our World Anew: The History of African Americans* (New York: Oxford University Press, 2000).

42. Nell Irvin Painter, *Creating Black Americans: African-American History and Its Meanings, 1619 to the Present* (New York: Oxford University Press, 2006).

43. John Langston Gwaltney, *Drylongso: A Self-Portrait of Black America* (New York: Vintage, 1981).

44. Randall Kenan, *Walking on Water: Black American Lives at the Turn of the Twenty-First Century* (New York: Knopf, 1999).

45. David J. Dent, *In Search of Black America: Discovering the African-American Dream* (New York: Simon and Schuster, 2001).

46. Emily Rovetch, ed., *Like It Is: Arthur E. Thomas Interviews Leaders on Black America* (New York: Dutton, 1981).

47. Walter Mosley, Manthia Diawara, Clyde Taylor, and Regina Austin, eds., *Black Genius: African American Solutions to African American Problems* (New York: Norton, 1999).

48. Tavis Smiley, ed. and comp., *How to Make Black America Better: Leading African Americans Speak Out* (New York: Doubleday, 2001).

49. *The Covenant with Black America* (Chicago: Third World Press, 2006).

50. "African American Web Connection," http://www.aawc.com/aawc.html (26 June 2006).

51. "Black History Quest: African American Resources," http://www.blackquest.com/link.htm (26 June 2006).

52. Sylvia Curtis, "Help by Subject—Resources in Black Studies," http://www.library.ucsb.edu/subject/blackstudies/black.html (26 June 2006).

53. *Ebony,* Johnson Publishing Company, 820 S. Michigan Ave., Chicago, Ill. 60605.

54. *Jet,* Johnson Publishing Company, 820 S. Michigan Ave, Chicago, Ill. 60605.

55. *American Legacy: Celebrating African American History and Culture,* American Heritage, 28 W. 23rd St., New York, N.Y. 10010.

56. *Black History Bulletin,* Association for the Study of African-American Life and History, Inc., 7961 Eastern Ave., Suite 301, Silver Spring, Md. 20910.

57. *The Crisis,* Crisis Publishing Company, 4805 Mt. Hope Dr., Baltimore, Md. 21215.

58. *Black Scholar: Journal of Black Studies and Research,* Black World Foundation, P.O. Box 2869, Oakland, Calif. 94609.

59. *Callaloo: A Journal of African-American and African Arts and Letters,* The Johns Hopkins University Press, Journals Publishing Division, 2715 N. Charles St., Baltimore, Md. 21218-4363.

60. *Obsidian III: Literature in the African Diaspora,* North Carolina State University, English Department, P.O. Box 8105, Raleigh, N.C. 27695-8105.

61. *The Western Journal of Black Studies,* Washington State University Press, P.O. Box 645910, Pullman, Wash. 99164-5910.

62. William M. Banks, *Black Intellectuals: Race and Responsibility in American Life* (New York: Norton, 1996).

63. William D. Wright, *Black Intellectuals, Black Cognition, and a Black Aesthetic* (Westport, Conn.: Praeger, 1997).

64. Perry A. Hall, *In the Vineyard: Working in African American Studies* (Knoxville, Tenn.: University of Tennessee Press, 1999).

65. James L. Conyers Jr., ed., *Africana Studies: A Disciplinary Quest for Both Theory and Method* (Jefferson, N.C.: McFarland, 1997).

66. Molefi Kete Asante, *The Afrocentric Idea* (Philadelphia: Temple University Press, 1998).

67. Molefi Kete Asante, *Afrocentricity: The Theory of Social Change* (Chicago: African American Images, 2003).

68. Leonard Harris, ed., *Philosophy Born of Struggle: Anthology of African American Philosophy* (Dubuque, Iowa: Kendall Hunt Publishing Company, 2000).

69. P. Eisenstadt, *Black Conservatism* (New York: Garland, 1998).

70. Stan Faryna, *Black and Right* (New York: Praeger, 1997).

71. John McWhorter, *Authentically Black* (New York: Gotham, 2004).

72. Joy James, *The Black Feminist Reader* (Malden, Mass.: Blackwell, 2000).

73. Gloria T. Hull, Patricia Bell Scott, and Barbara Smith, *All the Women Are White, All the Blacks Are Men, But Some of Us Are Brave: Black Women's Studies* (New York: The Feminist Press at the City University of New York, 1982).

74. Bell Hooks, *Ain't I a Woman: Black Women and Feminism* (Boston, Mass.: South End Press, 1999).

75. Patricia Hill Collins, *Black Feminist Thought: Knowledge, Consciousness, and the Politics of Empowerment,* second edition (New York: Routledge, 2000).

76. Katie Geneva Cannon, *Katie's Canon: Womanism and the Soul of the Black Community* (Chicago: Continuum International Publishing Group, 1997).

77. Stephanie Y. Mitchem, *Introducing Womanist Theology* (Maryknoll, N.Y.: Orbis Books, 2002).

78. Dwight Hopkins, *Introducing Black Theology of Liberation* (Maryknoll, N.Y.: Orbis Books, 1999).

79. Gayraud Wilmore and James H. Cone, *Black Theology: A Documentary History, 1966–1979* (Maryknoll, N.Y.: Orbis Books, 1979); James H. Cone and Gayraud S. Wilmore, *Black Theology: A Documentary History, 1980–1992* (Maryknoll, N.Y.: Orbis, 1993).

80. Donna L. Gilton, "Black Theology: Schools of Thought," *A.M.E. Church Review* 104, no. 34 (Apr.–June 1989): 25–38.

81. Blyden Jackson, *A History of Afro-American Literature,* vol. 1, *The Long Beginning, 1746–1895* (Baton Rouge: Louisiana State University Press, 1989).

82. William L. Andrews, Frances Smith Foster, and Trudier Harris, eds., *The Oxford Companion to African American Literature* (New York: Oxford University Press, 1997).

83. Frank N. Magill, ed., *Masterpieces of African-American Literature: Descriptions, Analyses, Characters, Plots, Themes, Critical Evaluations, and Significance of Major Works of Fiction, Nonfiction, Drama, and Poetry* (New York: Harper Collins, 1992).

84. Nancy Schmidt, *Children's Books on Africa and Their Authors: An Annotated Bibliography* (New York: Africana, 1975); Schmidt, *Supplement to Children's Books on Africa and Their Authors* (New York: Africana, 1979).

85. Osayimwense Osa, *African Children's and Youth Literature* (Detroit: Twayne Publishers, 1995).

86. Meena Khorana, ed., *Critical Perspectives on Postcolonial African Children's and Young Adult Literature* (Westport, Conn.: Greenwood, 1998); Khorana, *Africa in Literature for Children and Young Adults: An Annotated Bibliography of English-Language Books* (Westport, Conn.: Greenwood, 1994).

87. Raoul Granqvist and Jurgen Martini, *Preserving the Landscape of Imagination: Children's Literature in Africa* (Atlanta, Ga.: Rodopi, 1997).

88. Yulisa Amadu Maddy and Donnarae MacCann, *African Images in Juvenile Literature: Commentaries on Neocolonialist Fiction* (Jefferson, N.C.: McFarland, 1996).

89. Cecile Lebon, "The French-Language African Novel for Young People," *Bookbird* 42, no. 3 (2004): 10–18.

90. Vivian Yenika-Agbaw, "Images of West Africa in Children's Books: Replacing Old Stereotypes with New Ones?" in *Stories Matter: The Complexity of Cultural Authenticity in Children's Literature,* ed. Dana L. Fox and Kathy G. Short (Urbana, Ill.: National Council of Teachers of English, 2003), 231–46.

91. Jeffrey Garrett, "Islam and Other Belief Systems in West African Children's Books," *Bookbird* 35, no. 3 (Fall 1997): 21–25.

92. Carol Littlejohn, "Journey to J'Burg," *Voice of Youth Advocates (VOYA)* 19 (October 1996): 199–200.

93. Yulisa Amadu Maddy, "Ambivalent Signals in South African Young Adult Novels," *Bookbird* 36, no. 1 (Spring 1998): 27–32; Donnarae MacCann and Yulisa Amadu Maddy, *Apartheid and Racism in South African Children's Literature, 1985–1995* (New York: Routledge, 2001).

94. University of South Africa, Children's Literature Research Unit, "South African Children's Literature," http://www.childlit.org.za/SAChildLit.html (26 June 2006).

95. Michael Daniel Ambatchew, "Political Protest in Shitaye," *Bookbird* 43, no. 2 (2005): 23–29.

96. DownHomeBooks.com, "Ethiopian Books for Children," http://www .downhomebooks.com/featured.htm (26 June 2006); Ethiopian Books for Children and Educational Foundation, P.O. Box 2677, Addis Ababa, Ethiopia, http://www .ethiopiareads.org/index.html (26 June 2006).

97. Elizabeth Laird, "Stories from the Source of the Nile: Collecting Stories in Ethiopia," *Bookbird* 43, no. 1 (2005): 21–27.

98. Yahaya Bello, "Caribbean American Children's Literature," in *Teaching Multicultural Literature in Grades K–8,* ed. Violet J. Harris (Norwood, Mass.: Christopher-Gordon, 1993), 243–65.

99. Annette Wallace, "Caribbean Children's Literature: A Select Annotated Bibliography," http://www.nalis.gov.tt/Education/BIBLIOGR.htm (26 June 2006).

100. Macmillan Caribbean, "Books—General Interest—Children's Books," http:// www.macmillan-caribbean.com/books/General/childrenpic.htm (26 June 2006).

101. Isabel Schon, *Basic Collection of Children's Books in Spanish* (Metuchen, N.J.: Scarecrow, 1986); Schon, *Books in Spanish for Children and Young Adults: An Annotated Guide,* series I–VI (Metuchen, N.J.: Scarecrow, 1978–1993); Schon, *A Hispanic Heritage: A Guide to Juvenile Books about Hispanic People and Cultures*, series I–IV (Metuchen, N.J.: Scarecrow, 1980–1991); Schon, *Recommended Books in Spanish for Children and Young Adults* (Lanham, Md.: Scarecrow, 2000); Schon, *The Best of Latino Heritage 1996–2002: A Guide to the Best Juvenile Books about Latino People and Cultures* (Lanham, Md.: Scarecrow, 2003); Schon, *A Bicultural Heritage: Themes for the Exploration of Mexican and Mexican-American Culture in Books for Children and Adolescents* (Metuchen, N.J.: Scarecrow, 1978).

102. Barahona Center for the Study of Books in Spanish for Children and Adolescents/Centro Barahona para el Estudio de Libros Infantiles y Juveniles en Español, California State University, San Marcos, Kellogg Library, Fifth Floor, 333 S. Twin Oaks Valley Rd., San Marcos, Calif. 92096-0001, http://www.csusm.edu/csb (26 June 2006).

103. *Criticas,* 369 Park Ave. South, New York, N.Y. 10010, http://www .criticasmagazine.com/ (26 June 2006).

104. Patricia Beilke and Frank J. Sciara, *Selecting Materials For and About Hispanic and East Asian Children and Young People* (Hamden, Conn.: Library Professional Publications, 1986).

105. Judy A. Leavell, Barbara Hatcher, Jennifer Battle, and Nancy Ramos-Michael, "Exploring Hispanic Culture through Trade Books," *Social Education* 66, no. 4 (May/June 2002): 210–15.

106. Carmen L. Medina and Patricia Encisco, "'Some Words Are Messengers/Hay Palabras Mensajeras': Interpreting Sociopolitical Themes in Latino/a Children's Literature," *The New Advocate* 15, no. 1 (Winter 2002): 35–47.

107. Isabel Schon, *Contemporary Spanish-Speaking Writers and Illustrators for Children and Young Adults* (Westport, Conn.: Greenwood, 1994).

108. Sherry York, *Picture Books by Latino Writers: A Guide for Librarians, Teachers, Parents, and Students* (Worthington, Ohio: Linworth Publishing, 2002); York, *Children's and Young Adult Books by Latino Writers: A Guide for Librarians, Teachers, Parents, and Students* (Worthington, Ohio: Linworth Publishing, 2002).

109. Frances Ann Day, *Latina and Latino Voices in Literature: Lives and Works Updated and Expanded* (Westport, Conn.: Greenwood, 2003).

110. Christine M. Hill, *Ten Hispanic American Authors* (Berkeley Heights, N.J.: Enslow, 2002).

111. Rosalinda B. Barrera, Olga Liguori, and Loretta Salas, "Ideas a Literature Can Grow On: Key Insights for Enriching Children's Literature about the Mexican American Experience," in Harris, *Teaching Multicultural Literature in Grades K–8,* 203–41; Rosalinda B. Barrera and Oralia Garza de Cortes, "Mexican American Children's Literature in the 1990s: Toward Authenticity," in Harris, *Using Multiethnic Literature in the K–8 Classroom*, 129–53; Rosalinda B. Barrera, Ruth E. Quiroa, and Cassiette West-Williams, "Poco a Poco: The Continuing Development of Mexican American Children's Literature in the 1990s," *The New Advocate* 12, no. 4 (Fall 1999): 315–30.

112. Sonia Nieto, "We Have Stories to Tell: A Case Study of Puerto Ricans in Children's Books," in Harris, *Teaching Multicultural Literature in Grades K–8,* 171–202; Nieto, "We Have Stories to Tell: Puerto Ricans in Children's Books," in Harris, *Using Multiethnic Literature in the K 8 Classroom,* 59–93.

113. Susan Freiband and Consuelo Figueras, "Understanding Puerto Rican Culture: Using Puerto Rican Children's Literature," *MultiCultural Review* 11, no. 2 (June 2002): 30–34.

114. Asociacion Mexicana para el Fomento del Libro Infantil y Juvenil A.C. (IBBY Mexico), *Guia de libros recomendados para niños y jovenes 2000 (Guide to Books Recommended for Children and Young People)* (Mexico City: The Association, 2000).

115. Yvonne S. Freeman, "Providing Quality Children's Literature in Spanish," *The New Advocate* 11, no. 1 (Winter 1998): 23–38.

116. Margarita Gonzalez-Jensen, "The Status of Children's Fiction Literature Written in Spanish by U.S. Authors," *Bilingual Research Journal* 21, nos. 2–3 (Spring and Summer 1997).

117. Rosalinda B. Barrera and Ruth E. Quiroa, "The Use of Spanish in Latino Children's Literature in English: What Makes for Cultural Authenticity," in Fox and Short, *Stories Matter*, 247–65.

118. Tatiana de la Terra, "International Book Fairs: La Major Via for Buying Books in Spanish," *REFORMA Newsletter* 23, no. 1 (Fall–Winter 2005): 1.

119. John M. Kibler, "Latino Voices in Children's Literature: Instructional Approaches for Developing Cultural Understanding in the Classroom," in *Children of La Frontera: Binational Efforts to Serve Mexican Migrant and Immigrant Students*, ed. Judith LeBlanc Flores, ERIC Education Resources Information Center, ED 393644, 239–68.

120. Adela Artola Allen, *Library Services for Hispanic Children: A Guide for Public and School Librarians* (Phoenix, Ariz.: Oryx, 1987).

121. Barbara Immroth and Kathleen de la Peña McCook, *Library Services to Youth of Hispanic Heritage* (Jefferson, N.C.: McFarland, 2000).

122. Maria Mena, "Library Outreach to Hispanic Children," http://www.cbcbooks.org/cbcmagazine/perspectives/library_outreach_to_hispanic_c.html (26 June 2006).

123. American Library Association (ALA), Association for Library Services to Children (ALSC), "April 30 is El Dia de los Niños: El Dia de Los Libros: How Will You Celebrate?" http://www.ala.org/ala/alsc/alscresources/eldiadelosnios/eldadelosnios.htm (26 June 2006).

124. Lynn Atkinson Smolen and Victoria Ortiz-Castro, "Dissolving Borders and Broadening Perspectives through Latino Traditional Literature," *The Reading Teacher* 53, no. 7 (Apr. 2000): 566–78.

125. James Jupp, "Beyond the Folkloric and Indigenous in Multicultural Thinking about Latin America," *Multicultural Review* 11, no. 1 (March 2002): 22–29; Jupp, "The Necessity of a Multicultural Teaching Canon and the Mexican American Novel," *MultiCultural Review* 9, no. 4 (Dec. 2000): 38–41.

126. Bess A. Isom and Carolyn P. Casteel, "Hispanic Literature: A Fiesta for Literacy Instruction," *Childhood Education* 74 (Winter 1997–1998): 83–89.

127. Maria A. Perez-Stable and Mary H. Cordier, "Add Salsa to Your Classroom with Young Adult Books about Latinos," *Middle School Journal* 28 (March 1997): 23–27.

128. Carmen Medina, "When Jerry Springer Visits Your Classroom: Teaching Latina Literature in a Contested Ground," *Theory into Practice* 40, no. 3 (Summer 2001): 198–204.

129. Antonia Darder, Rodolfo D. Torres, and Henry Gutiérrez, *Latinos and Education: A Critical Reader* (New York: Routledge, 1997).

130. Eugene E. Garcia, *Hispanic Education in the United States* (Summit, Penn.: Rowman and Littlefield, 2001).

131. JoAnn Crandall, *Teaching the Spanish-Speaking Child: A Practical Guide* (Washington, D.C.: Center for Applied Linguistics, 1989).

132. Stanton Wortham, Enrique G. Murillo Jr., and Edmund T. Hamann, *Education in the New Latin Diaspora: Policy and Politics of Identity* (Westport, Conn.: Ablex, 2002).

133. Victoria-Maria MacDonald, ed., *Latino Education in the United States: A Narrated History from 1513–2000* (New York: Palgrave Macmillan, 2004).

134. *The Hispanic Outlook in Higher Education,* 210 Rt. 4E, Suite 310, Paramus, N.J. 07652, http://www.hispanicoutlook.com (26 June 2006).

135. *Aspira,* http://www.aspira.org/ (26 June 2006).

136. Juan Gonzalez, *Harvest of Empire: A History of Latinos in America* (New York: Penguin, 2001).

137. David Gutiérrez, *The Columbia History of Latinos in the United States since 1960* (New York: Columbia University Press, 2004).

138. Edward James Olmos, Carlos Fuentes, and Lea Ybarra, *Americanos: Latino Life in the United States* (Boston, Mass.: Little, Brown, 1999).

139. Ed Morales, *Living in Spanglish: The Search for Latino Identity in America* (New York: St. Martin's Griffin, 2003).

140. Roberto Suro, *Strangers among Us: Latino Lives in a Changing America* (New York: Vintage, 1999).

141. Ilan Stavans, *Growing Up Latino* (Boston, Mass.: Mariner Books, 1993).

142. Geoffrey Fox, *Hispanic Nation: Culture, Politics, and the Constructing of Identity* (Tucson: University of Arizona Press, 1977).

143. Antonia Darder and Rodolfo D. Torres, *The Latino Studies Reader: Culture, Economy, and Society* (Malden, Mass.: Blackwell Publishers, 1998).

144. Richard Delgado, *The Latino/a Condition: A Critical Reader* (New York: New York University, 1998).

145. Earl Shorris, *Latinos: A Biography of the People* (New York: Norton, 2001).

146. Nicolás Kanellos, *Herencia: The Anthology of Hispanic Literature of the United States* (New York: Oxford University Press, 2003).

147. Nicolás Kanellos and Claudio Esteva-Fabregat, eds., *The Handbook of Hispanic Cultures in the United States* (Houston, Tex.: Arte Publico Press, 1994).

148. Latin American Network Information Center (LANIC), http://www1.lanic.utexas.edu/ (26 June 2006).

149. "Andanzas al Web Latino," http://lib.nmsu.edu/subject/bord/latino.html (26 June 2006).

150. *Hispanic Magazine,* http://www.hispaniconline.com magazine/ (26 June 2006).

151. *HispanicOnline.com,* http://www.hispaniconline.com/ (26 June 2006).

152. *Hispanic: The Magazine For and About Hispanics,* Hispanic Publishing Corporation, 999 Ponce de Leon Ave, Suite 600, Coral Gables, Fla. 33134-3037.

153. *Latino Leaders: The National Magazine of the Successful Hispanic American,* Ferraez Publications of America, Corp. Invierno 16, Merced Gomez, 01600 Mexico.

154. *Contacto: A Magazine for Today's Latino,* 1317 N. San Fernando Blvd., PMB 246, Burbank, Calif. 91504.

155. *Latino(a) Research Review,* State University of New York at Albany, Center for Latino, Latin American, and Caribbean Studies (CECAC), SS247, Albany, N.Y. 12222.

156. *Aztlan: A Journal of Chicano Studies,* University of California at Los Angeles, Chicano Studies Research Center Publications, 193 Haines Hall, Box 951544, Los Angeles, Calif. 90095-1544.

157. David E. Hayes-Bautista, "Chicano Studies and the Academy: Opportunities Missed," *Aztlan* 25, no. 1 (Spring 2000): 183–85; Jose Rivera and Luis Ramon Burrola, "Chicano Studies Programs in Higher Education: Scenarios for Further Research," *Aztlan* 15 (Fall 1984): 277–93.

158. Eduardo C. Fernandez, *La Cosecha: Harvesting Contemporary United States Hispanic Theology* (Collegeville, Minn.: The Liturgical Press, 2000).

159. Justo L. Gonzalez, *Mañana: Christian Theology from a Hispanic Perspective* (Nashville, Tenn.: Abingdon Press, 1990).

160. Debbie Reese, "Native Americans in Children's Literature," in Harris, *Using Multicultural Literature in the K–8 Classroom,* 155–92.

161. Cynthia Leitich Smith, "Native American Themes in Books for Children and Teens," http://www.cynthialeitichsmith.com/lit_resources/diversity/native_am/ NativeThemes_intro.html (26 June 2006, 27 Aug. 2005).

162. Council on Interracial Books for Children, *Unlearning Indian Stereotypes: A Teaching Unit for Elementary Teachers and Children's Librarians* (New York: The Racism and Sexism Resource Center for Educators, 1977).

163. R. W. Stedman, *Shadows of the Indian: Stereotypes in American Culture* (Norman: University of Oklahoma Press, 1982).

164. Elizabeth Noll, "Accuracy and Authenticity in American Indian Children's Literature: The Social Responsibility of Authors and Illustrators," *The New Advocate* 8, no. 1 (Winter 1995): 29–43.

165. Donnarae MacCann, "Native Americans in Books for the Young," in Harris, *Teaching Multicultural Literature in Grades K–8,* 137–69.

166. Debbie Reese, "Authenticity and Sensitivity," *School Library Journal* 45, no. 11 (Nov. 1999): 36–37.

167. Arlene B. Hirschfelder, *American Indian Stereotypes in the World of Children: A Reader and Bibliography* (Metuchen, N.J.: Scarecrow, 1982).

168. Arlene B. Hirschfelder, "Native American Literature for Children and Young Adults," *Library Trends* 41, no. 3 (Winter 1993): 414–36.

169. Naomi Caldwell-Wood and Lisa A. Mitten, "'I' Is Not for Indian: The Portrayal of Native Americans in Books for Young People," *MultiCultural Review* 1, no. 2 (April 1992): 26–35.

170. Naomi Caldwell-Wood, "Native American Images in Children's Books," *School Library Journal* 38 (May 1992): 47–48.

171. Donnarae MacCann and Olga Richard, "Picture Books and Native Americans: An Interview with Naomi Caldwell-Wood," *Wilson Library Journal* 67 (February 1993): 30–34.

172. Nina Lindsay, "'I' Still Isn't for Indian," *School Library Journal* 49, no. 11 (November 2003): 42.

173. Beverly Slapin and Doris Seale, eds., *Books without Bias: Through Indian Eyes* (Berkeley, Calif.: Oyate, 1988).

174. Beverly Slapin and Doris Seale, *How to Tell the Difference: A Guide to Evaluating Children's Books for Anti-Indian Bias* (Berkeley, Calif.: Oyate, 1996).

175. Beverly Slapin and Doris Seale, eds., *Through Indian Eyes: The Native Experience in Books for Children* (Berkeley, Calif.: Oyate, 1998).

176. Beverly Slapin and Doris Seale, eds., *A Broken Flute* (Lanham, Md.: Alta Mira, 2004).

177. Beverly Slapin and Doris Seale, Oyate, 2702 Matthews St., Berkeley, Calif. 94702, http://www.oyate.org/intro.html (26 June 2006).

178. Kay Marie Porterfield and Emory Dean Keoke, "Resources for Selecting Fair and Accurate American Indian Books for Libraries and Home," http://www.kporterfield.com/aicttw/excerpts/antibiasbooks.html (26 June 2006).

179. Joan Berman, "Native American Children's Literature in the Classroom: An Annotated Bibliography," http://library.humboldt.edu/~berman/naclit.htm (26 June 2006).

180. Hirschfelder, "Native American Literature for Children and Young Adults," 414–36.

181. *Akwesasne Notes,* Akwesasne Mohawk Territory, P.O. Box 366, via Rooseveltown, N.Y. 13683-0196.

182. *Wicazo Sa Review: A Journal of Native American Studies,* Indian Studies, MS188, Eastern Washington University, Cheney, Wash. 99004, http://www.upress.umn.edu/journals/wsr/default.html; http://www.upress.umn.edu/journals/wsr/default.html (26 June 2006).

183. *The Independent American Indian Review,* PMB 268, 1840 E. Warner Rd., Suite A105, Tempe, Ariz. 85284, http://www.worldviewsintl.com/iair/ (26 June 2006).

184. The Mashantucket Pequot Children's Library, 110 Pequot Trail, P.O. Box 3180, Mashantucket, Conn. 06339, http://www.pequotmuseum.org/Home/LibrariesArchives/CHILDRENSLIBRARY/AboutTheChildrensLibrary.htm (26 June 2006).

185. Newberry Library, D'Arcy McNickle Center for American Indian History, 60 West Walton St., Chicago, Ill. 60610-3380, http://www.newberry.org/mcnickle/darcyhome.html (26 June 2006).

186. University of California, Berkeley, Ethnic Studies Library, Native American Studies Collection, Department of Ethnic Studies, 30 Stephens Hall, #2360, Berkeley, Calif. 94728-2360, http://eslibrary.berkeley.edu/ (26 June 2006).

187. Cornel Pewewardy, "'I' Is for Indigenous: Renaming Ourselves in Our Own Terms," *MultiCultural Review* 12, no. 2 (June 2003): 30–33.

188. Craig S. Womack, *Red on Red: Native American Literary Separatism* (Minneapolis: University of Minnesota Press, 1999).

189. Alaska Native Knowledge Network, http://www.ankn.uaf.edu/ (26 June 2006).

190. Richard Twiss, *One Church, Many Tribes: Following Jesus the Way God Made You* (Ventura, Calif.: Regal Books, 2000).

191. Craig Stephen Smith, *Whiteman's Gospel: A Native American Examines the Christian Church and Its Ministry among Native Americans* (Winnipeg, Manitoba: Indian Life Books, 1997).

192. Jerry H. Gill, *Native American Worldviews: An Introduction* (Amherst, N.Y.: Humanity Books, 2002).

193. Donald Fixico, *The American Indian in a Linear World* (New York: Routledge, 2003).

194. Vine Deloria, *Custer Died for Your Sins: An Indian Manifesto* (New York: Macmillan, 1969); Deloria, *God Is Red* (New York: Grosset and Dunlap, 1973; updated, 2003); Deloria, *Spirit and Reason: The Vine Deloria Reader* (Golden, Colo.: Fulcrum, 1999).

195. Devon A. Mihesuah, *Natives and Academics: Researching and Writing about American Indians* (Lincoln: University of Nebraska Press, 1998); Mihesuah, *Indigenizing the Academy: Transforming Scholarship and Empowering Communities* (Lincoln, Neb.: Bison Books, 2004); Mihesuah, *So You Want to Write about American Indians? A Guide for Writers, Students, and Scholars* (Lincoln, Neb.: Bison Books, 2005).

196. Linda Tuhiwai Smith, *Decolonizing Methodologies: Research and Indigenous People* (New York: St. Martin's Press, 1999).

197. Cheryl Crazy Bull, "Decolonizing Research: Indigenous Scholars Can Take Over the Research Process," *Tribal College Journal* 16, no. 2 (Winter 2004): 14–15.

198. Susan C. Faircloth and John W. Tippeconnic III, "Utilizing Research Methods that Respect and Empower Indigenous Knowledge," *Tribal College Journal* 16, no. 2 (Winter 2004): 24–27.

199. Mary G. Byler, *American Indian Authors for Young Readers: A Selective Bibliography* (New York: Association of Indian Affairs, 1973).

200. Cynthia Leitich Smith, "Children's and YA Books by Native Authors and Illustrators," http://www.cynthialeitichsmith.com/lit_resources/diversity/native_am/nat_lit_front.html (26 June 2006).

201. Hap Gilliland, *Indian Children's Books* (Billings, Mont.: Montana Council for Indian Education, 1980).

202. Sherry York, *Children's and Young Adult Literature by Native Americans* (Worthington, Ohio: Linworth Publishing, 2003).

203. Cynthia Leitich Smith, "A Different Drum: Native American Writing," *The Horn Book Magazine* 78, no. 4 (July/Aug. 2002): 409–12.

204. Jean Mendoza, "Becoming a Voice: A Conversation with George Littlechild, Illustrator," *The New Advocate* 14, no. 4 (Fall 2001): 321–27.

205. DownHomeBooks.com. "Author Interviews: May 2003: Debbie Reese," http://www.downhomebooks.com/drinterview.htm (26 June 2006).

206. Wordcraft Circle, http://www.wordcraftcircle.org/ (26 June 2006).

207. Native Writers' Circle of the Americas, http://www.ou.edu/cas/nas/writers.html (26 June 2006).

208. Storytelling: Native American Authors Online, http://www.hanksville.org/storytellers/ (26 June 2006).

209. Barbara J. Kuipers, *American Indian Reference Books for Children and Young Adults* (Englewood, Colo.: Libraries Unlimited, 1991).

210. Francis De Usabel, *American Indian Resource Materials for Public Libraries* (Madison: Wisconsin Department of Public Instruction, 1992).

211. Karen D. Harvey, Lisa D. Harjo, and Lynda Welborn, *How to Teach about American Indians: A Guide for the School Library Media Specialist* (Westport, Conn.: Greenwood, 1995).

212. Karen D. Harvey, Lisa D. Harjo, and Jane K. Jackson, *Teaching about Native Americans* (Washington, D.C.: National Council for the Social Studies, 1997).

213. Arlene Hirschfelder and Yvonne Beamer, *Native Americans Today: Resources and Activities for Educators, Grades 4–8* (Englewood, Colo.: Teacher Ideas Press, 2000).

214. Debbie Reese and Jean Mendoza, "Native Americans: A Resource List for Teaching—To and About Native Americans," http://www.scils.rutgers.edu/~kvander/ChildrenLit/nalist.html (26 June 2006).

215. Debbie Reese, "Native American Cultures across the United States," http://edsitement.neh.gov/view_lesson_plan.asp?ID=347 (26 June 2006).

216. Loriene Roy, If I Can Read, I Can Do Anything, School of Information, The University of Texas at Austin, 1 University Station D 7000, Austin, Tex. 78712-0390, http://www.gslis.utexas.edu/~ifican/ (26 June 2006).

217. Buffy Sainte-Marie, The Cradleboard Teaching Project, 1191 Kuhio Highway, Kapaa, Hawaii 96746, http://www.cradleboard.org/ (26 June 2006).

218. *Native Youth Magazine*, http://www.nativeyouthmagazine.com/ (26 June 2006).

219. Council for Indian Education, 1240 Burlington Ave., Billings, Mont. 59102-4224, http://www.cie-mt.org/ (26 June 2006).

220. Hap Gilliland, *Teaching the Native American* (Dubuque, Iowa: Kendall/Hunt, 1992).

221. Jon Reyhner, *Teaching American Indian Students* (Norman: University of Oklahoma Press, 1994).

222. Gregory Cajete, *Look to the Mountain: The Ecology of Indigenous Education* (Durango, Colo.: Kivaki Press, 1994).

223. Marylou Schultz, and Miriam Kroeger, *Teaching and Learning with Native Americans: A Handbook for Non–Native American Adult Educators*, http://literacynet.org/lp/namericans/ (26 June 2006).

224. Vine Deloria, *Power and Place: Indian Education in America* (Golden, Colo.: Fulcrum Publishing, 2001.)

225. Linda Miller Cleary and Thomas D. Peacock, *Collected Wisdom: American Indian Education* (Boston: Pearson Education, 1997).

226. *Journal of American Indian Education*, Center for Indian Education, College of Education, Arizona State University, Box 871311, Tempe, Ariz. 85287, http://jaie.asu.edu/ (26 June 2006).

227. *Tribal College Journal: The Voice and Vision of American Indian Higher Education*, Tribal College, 2509 Montgomery Way, Sacramento, Calif. 95818, http://www.tribalcollegejournal.org/ (26 June 2006).

228. *Canadian Journal of Native Education*, University of Alberta, Educational Policy Studies, 7104 Education Centre, North Edmonton, AB T6G 2G5, Canada.

229. *Winds of Change*, American Indian Science and Engineering Society (AISES), 4450 Arapahoe Ave., Suite 100, Boulder, Colo. 80303, http://www.wocmag.org/ (26 June 2006).

230. Daybreak Star Press, 1945 Yale Pl., Seattle, Wash. 98102.

231. Canyon Records, 3131 W. Clarendon Ave., Phoenix, Ariz. 85017. http://www.canyonrecords.com/ (26 June 2006).

232. Indian Historian Press, American Indian Historical Society, 1493 Masonic Ave., San Francisco, Calif. 94117, http://www.americanindian.ucr.edu/unique_heritage/historian_press/index.html (26 June 2006).

233. Theytus Books, Ltd., Lot 45, Green Mountain Rd., RR2 Site 50, Comp. 8 Penticon, British Columbia V2A 6J7, Canada.

234. Lisa J. Watts, "A History of Tribal Museums," *Cross Paths Museum News* 9, no. 1 (Spring 2006): 4, 10–11, and vol. 9, no. 2 (Summer 2006): 5, 9–10.

235. Lisa Mitten, "Native American Nations," http://www.nativeculture.com/lisamitten/nations.html (26 June 2006).

236. American Indian Library Association (AILA), http://www.nativeculture.com/lisamitten/aila.html (22 Aug. 2005).

237. Mashantucket Pequot Museum and Research Center, 110 Pequot Trail, P.O. Box 3180, Mashantucket, Conn. 06339-3180, http://www.pequotmuseum.org/Home/ (26 June 2006).

238. Alvin M. Josephy, *500 Nations: An Illustrated History of North American Indians* (New York: Gramercy, 2002).

239. Philip Deloria and Neal Salisbury, *A Companion to American Indian History* (Malden, Mass.: Blackwell, 2004).

240. Peter Nabokov, *A Forest of Time: American Indian Ways of History* (New York: Cambridge University Press, 2002).

241. George Russell, *Native American FAQ Handbook* (Phoenix, Ariz.: Russell Publications, 2000).

242. Vine Deloria Jr., *Custer Died for Your Sins: An Indian Manifesto* (Norman: University of Oklahoma Press, 1988).

243. Richard A. Grounds, George E. Tinker, and David E. Wilkins, *Native Voices: American Indian Identity and Resistance* (Lawrence: University Press of Kansas, 2003).

244. Suzanne Evertsen Lundquist, *Native American Literatures: An Introduction* (Chicago: Continuum International Publishing Group, 2004).

245. Joy Porter and Kenneth M. Roemer, *The Cambridge Companion to Native American Literature* (New York: Cambridge University Press, 2005).

246. *American Indian*, National Museum of the American Indian, 4220 Silver Hill Rd., Suitland, Md. 20746, http:www.nmai.si.edu/.

247. *Indian Country Today,* 3059 Seneca Turnpike, Canastota, N.Y. 13032.

248. *Native American Times,* Oklahoma Indian Times, Inc., Box 692050, Tulsa, Okla. 74169.

249. *Native Peoples: Arts and Lifeways,* Media Concepts Group, Inc., 5333 N. Seventh St., Suite C 224, Phoenix, Ariz. 85014.

250. *American Indian Culture and Research Journal,* University of California at Los Angeles, American Indian Studies Center, 322 Campbell Hall, P.O. Box 951548, Los Angeles, Calif. 90095.

251. *American Indian Quarterly,* University of Nebraska Press, 233 N. 8th St., Lincoln, Neb. 68588-0255.

252. *The Canadian Journal of Native Studies,* Brandon University, Native Studies Department, Brandon, MB R7A 6A9, Canada.

253. *Native Americas: Hemispheric Journal of Indigenous Issues,* First Nations Development Institute, 2300 Fall Hill Ave., Suite 412, Fredericksburg, Va. 22401, http://www.firstnations.org (26 June 2006).

254. *Studies in American Indian Literatures,* University of Nebraska Press, 233 N. 8th St., Lincoln, Neb. 68588-0255.

255. *Wicazo Sa Review: A Journal of Native American Studies,* University of Minnesota Press, 111 Third Ave. S., Suite 290, Minneapolis, Minn. 55401-2520.

256. Shu-Hsien Lai Chen, "Asian American Literature in School Libraries," *Journal of Educational Media and Library Services* 39, no. 3 (Mar. 2002): 251–68.

257. Sandra S. Yamate, "Asian Pacific American Children's Literature: Expanding Perceptions about Who Americans Are," in Harris, *Using Multiethnic Literature in the K–8 Classroom,* 95–128.

258. Beilke and Sciara, *Selecting Materials For and About Hispanic and East Asian Children and Young People.*

259. Craig Heller, Bruce Cunningham, Ginny Lee, and Hannah H. Heller, "Selecting Children's Picture Books with Positive Chinese, Japanese, and Other Asian and Asian American Fathers and Father Figures," *MultiCultural Review* 9, no. 4 (Dec. 2000): 22–73.

260. Esther Jenkins and Mary C. Austin, *Literature for Children about Asians and Asian Americans* (Westport, Conn.: Greenwood, 1987).

261. Meena Khorana, *The Indian Subcontinent in Literature for Children and Young Adults: An Annotated Bibliography of English Language Books* (Westport, Conn.: Greenwood, 1991).

262. NYPL, Office of Special Services, Chinese Heritage Booklist Committee, "Chinese Heritage: Chinese American Experience in the United States," *EMIE Bulletin* (Spring 1995): 6.

263. Barbara A. Black, *A Guide to Children's Books about Asian Americans* (Hants, England: Scholar Press, 1999).

264. Zheng Ye Yang, "Children's Books by Chinese American Authors: An Annotated Bibliography," http://www.white-clouds.com/cala/publications/childbks.htm (26 June 2006).

265. Council on Interracial Books for Children, "How Children's Books Distort the Asian American Image," *Interracial Books for Children Bulletin* 7, nos. 2–3 (1976/1977): 3–23.

266. Asian Americans for Fair Media, *The Asian Image in the United States: Stereotypes and Realities,* ERIC Education Resources Information Center, ED 134643.

267. Suzanne Lo and Ginny Lee, "Asian Images in Children's Books: What Stories Do We Tell Our Children?" *Emergency Librarian* 20, no. 6 (May–June 1993): 14–18.

268. Valerie Oaka Pang, Carolyn Colvin, My Luang Tran, and Robertta H. Barba, "Beyond Chopsticks and Dragons: Selecting Asian-American Literature for Children," *The Reading Teacher* 46, no. 3 (Nov. 1992): 216–24.

269. Elaine Aoki, "Turning the Page: Asian Pacific American Children's Literature," in Harris, *Teaching Multicultural Literature in Grades K–8*, 109–36.

270. Mingshui Cai, "Images of Chinese and Chinese Americans Mirrored in Picture Books," *Children's Literature in Education* 25, no. 3 (1994): 169–91.

271. Violet H. Harada, "Issues of Ethnicity, Authenticity, and Quality in Asian-American Picture Books, 1983–93," *Journal of Youth Services in Libraries* 8 (Winter 1995): 135–49.

272. Shao-yi Leu, "Reimagining a Pluralistic Society through Children's Fiction about Asian Pacific Americans," *The New Advocate* 14, no. 2 (Spring 2001): 127–42.

273. Uma Krishnaswami, "Common Errors in American Children's Books with South Asian Characters or Content," http://www.umakrishnaswami.com/common errors.html (26 June 2006).

274. Yamate, "Asian Pacific American Children's Literature," 99–128.

275. Greg Leitich Smith, "Children's and YA Books with Asian American Themes," http://www.cynthialeitichsmith.com/lit_resources/diversity/asian_am/asian_am.html (26 June 2006).

276. Nancy Garhan Attebury, "Bridging the Gap in Children's Literature for Asian American Youngsters," *The Delta Kappa Gamma Bulletin* 67, no. 2 (Winter 2001): 33–39.

277. American Library Association (ALA), Association for Library Services to Children (ALSC), "Sharing Cultures: Asian American Children's Authors: A Selected Bibliography," *EMIE Bulletin* 19, no. 1 (Fall 2001): 10–15. Also http://www.ala.org/ala/alsc/alscresources/booklists/sharingcultures.htm (26 June 2006).

278. Meena G. Khorana, "Break Your Silence: A Call to Asian Indian Children's Writers," *Library Trends* 41, no. 3 (Winter 1993): 393–413.

279. Cheri Jones, "East Asian Indian Children in America," *EMIE Bulletin* 17, no. 3 (Spring 2000): 16–17.

280. Catherine E. Studier Chang, "Yoshiko Uchida," *Language Arts* 61, no. 2 (Feb. 1984): 189–94; Violet H. Harada, "Caught between Two Worlds: Themes of Family, Community, and Ethnic Identity in Yoshiko Uchida's Work for Children," *Children's Literature in Education* 29, no. 1 (March 1998): 19–30.

281. Goldsea, "Asian American Bookview, Kids and Young Adults," http://goldsea.com/Bookview/Kids/kids.html (26 June 2006).

282. Pacific Rim Voices, Kiriyama Pacific Rim Institute, 760 Delancy St., San Francisco, Calif. 92107, PaperTigers.org., http://www.papertigers.org/index.html (27 Aug. 2005).

283. Asian American Curriculum Project (AACP), 414 East Third Ave., San Mateo, Calif. 94401, http://www.asianamericanbooks.com/ (26 June 2006).

284. Uma Krishnaswami, "South Asia in Children's Literature," http://www.umakrishnaswami.com/southasia.html (26 June 2006).

285. Polychrome Publishing Corporation, 4509 North Francisco, Chicago, Ill. 60625, http://www.polychromebooks.com/ (26 June 2006).

286. Asia for Kids, P.O. Box 9096, Cincinnati, Ohio 45209-0096, http://www.afk.com/ (26 June 2006).

287. Bess Press, 3565 Harding Ave., Honolulu, Hawaii 96816, http://www.besspress.com/ (26 June 2006).

288. China Books, 360 Swift Ave. South St., San Francisco, Calif. 94110, http://www.chinabooks.com/cart/home.asp (26 June 2006).

289. Shen's Books and Supplies, 821 S. First Ave., Arcadia, Calif. 91006, http://www.shens.com/ (26 June 2006).

290. South Asian Children's Books and Software, http://www.sawnet.org/kidsbooks (26 June 2006).

291. Japanese American Cultural and Community Center (Shop), http://www.jaccc.org/jaccc/library.html (26 June 2006).

292. Press Pacifica, P.O. Box 47, Kailua, Hawaii 96734.

293. Asian American Booksellers, 37 St. Mark's Place, New York, N.Y. 10003.

294. Multicultural Distribution Center, 800 N. Grand Ave., Covina, Calif. 91724.

295. The Asian American Writers' Workshop, 16 West 32nd St., Suite 10A, New York, N.Y. 10001, http://www.aaww.org/ (26 June 2006).

296. *Riksha Magazine,* 3062 S. Broad St., Chicago, Ill. 60608, http://www.riksha.com/ (26 June 2006).

297. Li-Rong Lilly Cheng, *Struggling to Be Heard: The Unmet Needs of Asian Pacific American Children* (Albany, N.Y.: SUNY Press, 1998).

298. Don T. Nakanishi and Tina Yamano Nishida, eds., *The Asian American Educational Experience: A Sourcebook for Teachers and Students* (New York: Routledge, 1994).

299. Clara C. Park and Marilyn Mei-Ying Chi, eds., *Asian American Education: Prospects and Challenges* (Westport, Conn.: Bergin and Garvey, 1999).

300. Khorana, "Break Your Silence," 393–413.

301. Khorana, "Break Your Silence," 393–413.

302. Uma Krishnaswami, "On the Seashore of Worlds: Selected South Asian Voices from North America and the United Kingdom," *Bookbird* 42, no. 2 (April 2004): 23–37; Krishnaswami, "South Asian Voices with North American Accents," PaperTigers.org, http://www.papertigers.org/personalViews/archiveViews/Ukrishnaswami.html (26 June 2006).

303. Khorana, *The Indian Subcontinent in Literature for Children and Young Adults.*

304. Khorana, "Break Your Silence," 393–413.

305. Uma Krishnaswami, "South Asia in Children's Literature," http://www.umakrishnaswami.com/southasia.html (26 June 2006); Krishnaswami, "Common Errors in American Children's Books with South Asian Characters or Content."

306. Mitali Perkins, "The Fire Escape: Books For and About Young Immigrants," http://www.mitaliperkins.com/ (26 June 2006).

307. *Kahani: A South Asian Literary Magazine for Children,* P.O. Box 590155, Newton Centre, Mass. 02459, http://www.kahani.com (26 June 2006).

308. Jones, "East Asian Indian Children in America," 16–17.

309. South Asian Children's Books and Software, http://sawnet.org/kidsbooks/ (26 June 2006).

310. Ronald Takaki, *Strangers from a Different Shore: A History of Asian Americans* (Boston, Mass.: Back Bay Books, 1998).

311. Gary Y. Okihiro, *The Columbia Guide to Asian American History* (New York: Columbia University Press, 2001).

312. Helen Zia, *Asian American Dreams: The Emergence of an American People* (New York: Farrar, Straus and Giroux, 2001).

313. Frank H. Wu, *Yellow: Race in America beyond Black and White* (Boulder, Colo.: Basic Books, 2003).

314. Vickie Nam, *YELL-Oh Girls: Emerging Voices Explore Culture, Identity and Growing Up Asian American* (New York: Harper Paperbacks, 2001).

315. Arar Han and John Hsu, eds., *Asian American X: An Intersection of Twenty-First Century Asian American Voices* (Ann Arbor, Mich.: University of Michigan Press, 2004).

316. Eric Liu, *The Accidental Asian: Notes of a Native Speaker* (New York: Vintage, 1999).

317. Mia Tuan, *Forever Foreigners or Honorary Whites? The Asian Ethnic Experience Today* (New Brunswick, N.J.: Rutgers University Press, 1999).

318. Paul Tokunaga, *Invitation to Lead: Guidance for Emerging Asian American Leaders* (Downers Grove, Ill.: Intervarsity Press, 2003).

319. Min Zhou and James V. Gatewood, eds., *Contemporary Asian America: A Multidisciplinary Reader* (New York: New York University Press, 2000).

320. Gary Okihiro, *Margins and Mainstreams: Asians in American History and Culture* (Seattle: University of Washington Press, 1994).

321. Jean Yu-Wen Shen Wu and Min Song, eds., *Asian American Studies: A Reader* (New Brunswick, N.J.: Rutgers University Press, 2000).

322. King-Kok Cheung, *An Interethnic Companion to Asian American Literature* (New York: Cambridge University Press, 1996).

323. Sau-ling Cynthia Wong, *Reading Asian American Literature* (Princeton, N.J.: Princeton University Press, 1993).

324. Elaine Kim, *Asian American Literature* (Philadelphia, Penn.: Temple University Press, 1984).

325. Peter C. Phan and Jung Young Lee, eds., *Journeys at the Margin: Toward an Autobiographical Theology in American-Asian Perspective* (Collegeville, Minn.: The Liturgical Press, 1999).

326. Fumitaka Matsuoka and Eleazar S. Fernandez, eds., *Realizing the America of Our Hearts* (St. Louis, Mo.: Chalice Press, 2003).

327. "Asian-Nation: 'The Landscape of Asian America,'" IMDiversity.com, http://www.imdiversity.com/eon/asiannation.asp (26 June 2006).

328. Goldsea, *Asian American Daily*, http://www.goldsea.com/ (26 June 2006).

329. Gerardo Colmenar, "Help by Subject—Asian-American Studies," http://www.library.ucsb.edu/subjects/asianamer/asian-am.html (26 June 2006).

330. Association for Asian American Studies (AAAS), http://www.aaastudies.org/index.tpl (26 June 2006).

331. *YOLK: Generasian Next,* http://www.yolk.com/ (26 June 2006).

332. *Monolid Magazine,* 368 Broadway, Suite 516, New York, N.Y. 10013.

333. *Amerasia Journal,* University of California, Los Angeles, Asian American Studies Center, 3230 Campbell Hall, Los Angeles, Calif. 90095-1546.

334. *Journal of Asian American Studies,* The Johns Hopkins University Press, Journal Publishing Division, 2715 N. Charles St., Baltimore, Md. 21218-4363.

335. *Asian American Movement Ezine,* http://www.aamovement.net/ (26 June 2006).

336. *Asian American Policy Review,* Harvard University, John F. Kennedy School of Government, 79 John F. Kennedy St., Cambridge, Mass. 02138.

337. Don T. Nakanishi, "Crossing Borders: 35 Years of Asian American Studies and the New UCLA Department of Asian American Studies," *Amerasian Journal* 30, no. 3 (2005): iii–vii; Arif Dirlik, "Locating Asian American Studies Today: Origins, Identities, Crises," *Amerasia Journal* 29, no. 2 (2003): 166–69; "Asian American Studies: Origins, Identities, Crises," *Amerasia Journal* 29, no. 2 (2003): 165–228; David Palumbo-Liu, "Reimagining Asian American Studies," *Amerasia Journal* 29, no. 2 (2003): 211–19; Stephen H. Sumida, "The More Things Change: Paradigm Shifts in Asian American Studies," *American Studies International* 38, no. 2 (June 2000): 97–114.

338. Kandice Chuh and Karen Shimakawa, eds., *Orientations: Mapping Studies in the Asian Diaspora* (Durham, N.C.: Duke University Press).

5

Where to Go from Here: Emerging Groups and Issues

Several new groups and issues have emerged since the 1960s. While interracial couples and their families have always been part of the United States, they have become a dynamic and rapidly growing force since the 1967 Supreme Court decision of *Loving v. Virginia*, which declared miscegenation laws to be unconstitutional. Since then, interracial and intercultural families have been developing their own organizations, political activities, and resources, including a small body of children's literature. A major accomplishment of this movement was the decision by the Census Bureau to allow people to check more than one racial category on census and other forms in 2000.

Arab Americans have been in the United States since the turn of the twentieth century, and historically, most of them have been Christians. However, the number and percentage of Muslims from Arab and many other countries have increased dramatically since World War II, and even more so since the Immigration Act of 1965. This Muslim population is in addition to U.S. converts, most of whom are African Americans. Like many other groups described in this book, Arab Americans and Muslim Americans have been organizing their own institutions, support structures, and resources. Their near nonexistence in the mainstream world of children's literature is a major issue, especially since 9/11. Arab American and Muslim groups are likely to become more prominent in the field of children's literature in the future.

Between 1820 and 1960, 82 percent of all immigrants came from Europe.[1] New European immigrants have not been studied nearly as much as their predecessors, and may be a somewhat neglected group with cultural issues of their own. Ethnic Europeans who are third, fourth, and fifth generation may also have some cultural needs and issues.[2]

All of the above groups and their resources will be described in this chapter, which will end in a discussion of emerging issues in this field.

EMERGING GROUPS

Bi- and Multicultural People and Families

Interracial couples and people of mixed race have existed in the United States since colonial times. Laws against interracial marriage date to the 1600s. Virginia passed legislation forbidding interracial marriage in 1661, and Maryland passed a series of similar legislation by 1717. By 1924, interracial marriage was illegal in thirty-eight states.[3]

These laws were originally intended to prevent whites from marrying slaves. By the nineteenth century, children of black slave fathers and white mothers were born free, but children of white fathers and black slave mothers were legally slaves. Between 1850 and 1900, the notion of the "one drop" rule became prevalent. Anyone with any African ancestry at all was classified as African American. Under that criterion, some famous Europeans like Alexander Pushkin and Alexandre Dumas would have been classified as black! In addition, anyone with any discernable ancestry from outside of Europe was no longer considered white. While these laws were initially created to discourage European Americans from marrying African Americans, they were extended to prevent Americans of European descent from marrying people from any other race.

This state of affairs would continue until the case of *Loving v. Virginia* in 1967. Perry Loving, a white man, and Mildred Jeter, an African American and Native American woman, wanted to marry but had to leave their home state of Virginia to do so. They married in Washington, D.C., and returned home only to be arrested. They moved to Washington, D.C., and sued Virginia in a case that made it to the Supreme Court, which then struck down all miscegenation laws in the United States.[4] Census 2000, which enabled people to choose more than one race on census forms, represents the symbolic end of the "one drop" rule.[5]

Since 1970, the number of interracial couples has jumped by 275 percent, compared to a 16-percent increase for couples from the same race.[6] According to the *Multiracial Child Resource Book,* published by the MAVIN Foundation,[7] more multiracial children are now born in the states of California and Washington than children of any single race, aside from whites. In cities such as San Antonio, Texas, Seattle, Washington, and Sacramento, California, one out of six babies is multiracial.[8] Interracial people come from all ethnic groups. One specialized population consists of mixed people of Asian descent who identify as Hapa, a term from Hawaii meaning "of mixed blood." In addition, families who adopt babies from abroad, in particular babies of color, are part of this movement.

Multiracial children, sometimes even those in the same family, differ on how they identify. They may also change their minds on how they identify, and do so more than once as they experience many changes over a lifetime. While older people of mixed ancestry tend to identify with the parent of color, younger people often refuse to identify with only part of their ethnic background. Some, like Tiger Woods, prefer to check off all applicable categories on census and other forms. Others, like Ward Connerly, would like to de-emphasize the issue of race altogether. However young multiracial people may otherwise disagree, they do seem to strongly agree on not wanting to be forced to identify with only one race!

Interracial families face many issues seldom encountered by people of other races. Multiracial children are more likely to be physically and sexually abused than children of any other race, and too many are found in foster care systems and in juvenile court. They also suffer from some unique health issues, such as the lack of compatible bone marrow for victims of leukemia.[9] Several scholars have studied discrimination encountered by mixed-race people—and it comes from people of all races. Heather Dalmage[10] mentions discriminatory incidents and comments related to physicality, language, interactions with members of "out groups," geographies, and cultural capital. *Geographies* include home address, school, choice of classes, choice of leisure activities, and even the choice of tables in the school cafeteria! Cultural capital encompasses taste in music, TV programs, sports, magazines, and so on.

Maria P. P. Root[11] interviewed interracial young people and listed fifty comments made to them by people of other races. The comments relate to roughly six areas—"borders," or being forced to "choose sides"; being seen as ambiguous in appearance by others, for example, being asked questions such as "What *are* you?"; other comments on physical appearance; other blatantly racist comments or incidents; comments about family; and issues and interactions within families.

The biggest issue for many multiracial young people is that they are seen as non-categorizable in a society that demands categorization. They have not been recognized as a separate group with special needs and have not yet been recognized in fields such as multicultural education. However, Matt Kelley of MAVIN concludes that well-raised multiracial children are in the best position to blend into and benefit a truly multicultural society. A study by Francis Wardle of the Center for the Study of Biracial Children[12] has also concluded that multiracial children do as well as their peers from other groups.

Before 2000, several general solutions to the quandary of the race cat-
egories on census forms were proposed. Most traditional civil rights organizations, such as the National Association for the Advancement of Colored
People (NAACP), the Mexican American Legal Defense and Education
Funds, and the National Coalition for an Accurate Count of Asian and Pacific
Americans wanted to maintain the status quo. Charles Byrd of *Interracial
Voice* advocated for one separate category for multiracial people. The Association of MultiEthnic Americans (AMEA) and MAVIN, as well as some
other civil rights groups, were in favor of allowing people to check off all
applicable racial categories on forms. The libertarian *Multiracial Activist* is
in favor of dropping racial categories altogether. All of these approaches reflect the worldviews of their advocates—how they see themselves and others.
Since the census of 2000, Americans have been able to check off all racial
categories that apply.

Over the last forty years and especially since the late 1970s, interracial
and intercultural families have created a variety of national and community
support organizations, mixed-race campus clubs, media and websites, scholarly studies, more popular books on this topic for adults and young adults,
children's literature, and bibliographies.[13]

National organizations include the Association of MultiEthnic Americans
(AMEA),[14] the MAVIN Foundation,[15] SWIRL,[16] and the Center for the Study
of Biracial Children.[17] The oldest local group is the Interracial/Intercultural
Pride (I-Pride) of San Francisco. Other examples of local groups include
MIX (organized by MAVIN in Seattle, Washington) and the Oregon Council
on Multiracial Affairs. College groups include Fusion at Wellesley College,
Half and Half at Bryn Mawr, and Mosaic at Dartmouth. MAVIN has helped
to organize MIXED at the University of Washington and Hybrid at Seattle
University. Many other colleges have similar groups.

Activists and scholars have published several resource books on this
subject for parents, teachers, and others working with children. The most
important may be the *Multiracial Child Resource Book: Living Complex
Identities*,[18] which has been compiled and edited by Matt Kelley, the founder
of MAVIN, and Maria P. P. Root, a major researcher on this topic. This book
gives an overview of interracial families, discusses identity issues at each
stage of growing up, and discusses multiracial people of all backgrounds.
This volume ends with an extensive list of resources.

Another resource is *Tomorrow's Children*,[19] a book for parents published
by the Center for the Study of Biracial Children. MAVIN and AMEA are
currently working together to build a national resource center on multiracial
and multicultural families. In addition, Maria P. P. Root has published several
books of research on this topic.

Websites include MAVIN,[20] *Interracial Voice*,[21] and the *Multiracial Activist*.[22] There are many pages linking to other relevant websites. They include pages from AMEA,[23] SWIRL,[24] *Interracial Voice*,[25] and listings in the *Multiracial Child Resource Book*.[26] There are also several more personal links reflecting the history of interracial families. Examples include "My Interracial Family"[27] by Karen Downing and *Eyes of Glory*[28] by Theresa and Keith Stokes.

Bibliographical articles, pathfinders, and links for adults, young people, and children also exist. *The Interracial Voice*[29] offers book reviews of relevant books for adults. AMEA[30] and the *Multiracial Child Resource Book*[31] list books for people of all ages. The latter source also includes a good list of books about transracial adoption as well as an annotated list of relevant films. There are also several bibliographies that focus more on books for children, including web pages by Cynthia Leitich Smith[32] and Kathleen T. Horning[33] as well as articles by Mary Ann Capan and Cynthia Suarez [34] and Capan.[35] In addition, the Internet Public Library has produced an electronic pathfinder on multiracial and multiethnic Americans.[36]

Children's literature on this topic includes fiction or nonfiction picture books showing and describing interracial families, fiction for older children, and some nonfiction and poetry. Nonfiction books for young children, such as *Living in Two Worlds*[37] by Maxine B. Rosenberg, tend to be photo essays showing daily routines of real families. Some of this literature discusses the joys, concerns, and problems of multiracial families, while others are simply stories about mixed families. There are also a few books on the adoption of children from abroad. Books on transracial adoption within the United States are more rare.

Teenagers can take advantage of several titles specifically for them, as well as many recent best sellers on multiracial people that were written for adults but are also of interest to this age group. At this point, some interracial couples and other adults from diverse backgrounds have written books for young children. The late Virginia Hamilton and Arnold Adoff were an interracial and intercultural couple who wrote books separately, and each dealt with this subject in a different way. Their son, Jaime, has also begun to publish for children, although not directly on this subject. There are also interracial illustrating couples who have produced multicultural books on many subjects, but not necessarily on racially or culturally blended families. They include Leo and Diane Dillon, and Cornelius Van Wright and Ying-Hwa Hu.

The first generation of multiracial children who have come of age since 1967 are beginning to write their memoirs and to produce books of interviews and other research. These materials have been marketed mainly to adults. Authors include Teja Arboleda, Lise Funderburg, James McBride, Barack

Obama, Claudine Chiawei O'Hearn, Paisley Rekdal, Maria P. P. Root, Brian Harris, Pearl Gaskin Fuyo, and Rebecca Walker. Ferai Chideya, a bicultural television journalist, has produced a book of interviews of young people from many backgrounds who reflect new ways of looking at race, not only for multiracial youth but for many of their peers. It will be very interesting to see what kinds of literature these authors develop as more of them decide to write particularly for teenagers or for younger children. It is hoped that some multicultural writers who are currently unpublished will also choose to write for the young. This is one area that should be developed. It appears that multiracial and multicultural children and their families are a wave not only of the future, but of the present! They are definitely beginning to redefine the way Americans perceive issues of race, culture, and ethnicity.

Arab Americans and Muslim Americans

Arabs and Muslims are two distinct groups that nevertheless intersect. Worldwide, most but not all Arabs are Muslims, and the rest are Christians, Druze—and Jewish! A few follow other religions and faith traditions.[38] Until recently, most Arab Americans were Christians, but this may be changing.

Most Muslims in the United States and abroad are *not* Arabs. Instead, they come from many countries in Asia, Africa, and Europe, and also from the United States. Worldwide, only 12 percent of all Muslims are Arabs. There are more Muslims in Indonesia than in all of the Arabic countries combined.[39] Muslims make up one-fifth of the world population,[40] and Islam is becoming the second-largest religion in the United States, with Muslims beginning to surpass Jews in number and in percentage of the population.

Arab Americans initially came to the United States between 1880 and 1925. Most came from what was then Greater Syria, particularly present-day Lebanon, and most were working-class Christians, accompanied by some merchants and intellectuals.[41] This first wave of Arab American immigrants settled in the Midwest, especially Michigan, Illinois, and Ohio. They also went to California, parts of the Northeast, and to other areas.[42] In the United States, they established Eastern-rite Catholic or Orthodox churches, an Arabic-language press, and educational and charitable associations. The descendants of this group of immigrants are now relatively assimilated, and many have contributed to America as a whole. Some prominent Arab Americans include Ralph Nader, Khalil Gibran, Helen Thomas, Casey Kasem, Danny and Marlo Thomas, James Abourezk, James Zogby, John Sununu, and Donna Shalala.[43]

A second wave of Arab immigrants has been coming to the United States since World War II and especially since the Immigration Act of 1965. People in this wave are mostly Muslims and come from approximately twenty countries in North Africa and the Middle East. They have fled the Israeli-Palestinian conflict and other wars. This group of immigrants is largely middle class, well educated, and well skilled, and they have settled all over the United States, especially in major cities such as New York, Los Angeles, Chicago, and Detroit.[44]

Arab Americans tend to identify themselves by country of origin and by religion. Many do not see themselves as white. They view themselves as a minority, and some are asking for minority-group classification from the U.S. government. However, they are not viewed as minorities by either white people or other people of color.[45] All Arabs, regardless of religion, suffer from ignorance and stereotyping from the public and from the fallout from 9/11 and other international incidents. Muslim Arabs also encounter the issues described below.

Some general resources to introduce Arab Americans to a non-Arab audience include research and materials from Ayad Al-Qazzaz,[46] the Detroit Free Press,[47] the Montgomery County Public Schools,[48] and Joseph Haiek's *Arab American Almanac*.[49] Al-Qazzaz's report "Transnational Links between the Arab Community in the U.S. and the Arab World" describes diasporan links between Arabs in the Unitd States and those in the Arab world. It describes waves of immigration, how Arab Americans see themselves, and the links to Arab and Arab American kinship media, organizations, governments, and businesses. The Detroit Free Press has published a pamphlet of one hundred questions and answers about Arab Americans that is electronically available, and the Montgomery County Public Schools have compiled curricular materials to promote Arab American Heritage Month. *The Arab American Almanac* is another important starting place for those who want to know more about these very diverse people. In addition, a new website, "Arab Culture and Civilization,"[50] includes information on Arabs around the world as well as Arab Americans. It was compiled and created by the National Institute for Technology and Liberal Education and funded by the Mellon Foundation in response to 9/11.

The Three Continents Press and Interlink, from the United States, and TSAR Publications, from Canada, publish works in English about Arabs abroad. Dahesh Publication in New York publishes works about Arabs and Arab Americans. Vladimir F. Wertsman[51] has conducted a critical analysis on the treatment of Arab Americans in reference books, and *Book Links*[52] has published a bibliographical article on Arabs and Arab Americans.

Approximately two-thirds of Muslim Americans are immigrants; one-third are from the United States, and most of these are African Americans.[53] Muslim immigrants come from approximately twenty predominantly

Muslim countries and forty other countries with Muslim minorities. How Muslims interpret Islam depends on their countries of origin, cultures, and social class. As with Arab Americans, there have been two to three waves of immigration. The first wave of working-class immigrants was between 1880 and 1925, when some Muslims immigrated from Greater Syria (and the present-day areas of Syria, Jordan, and Palestine). Some also came from Turkey, Albania, India, and a few other countries. People from this wave of immigration are separate both from later immigrants and from American Muslim converts. A second wave arrived from many more countries after World War II. Some immigrants were students who stayed in the United States. A third wave has been coming since 1965. Most of the newer immigrants are educated professionals.[54]

As diverse as Muslims may be in how they interpret their religion, there is agreement on the basic meaning of Islam, the Five Pillars of Islam, and several other values. The word *Islam* means submission to Allah. The Five Pillars of Islam include a declaration of faith, five daily ritual prayers at set times of the day, almsgiving, the observance of Ramadan, and hopefully at least one pilgrimage to Mecca in a lifetime. Ramadan can be compared to the Christian Lent, except that it is more stringent and intense. Muslims fast all day during this period, which lasts a month, and eat at night. This is a very solemn time of introspection and prayer. Other Muslim values include the importance of family, community, modesty, morality, nutrition, and cleanliness.[55]

Muslim Americans have created a network of mosques and community and college organizations to teach their religion to their children, and to teach Arabic, which is essential in order for people to read, learn, and recite the Qur'an, their holy book. Even though translations of the Qur'an do exist, only the Arabic version is viewed as authentic. So Muslim Americans emphasize the teaching of the Qur'an, the Arabic language, and basic Islamic beliefs to their children.[56]

Mosques in the Middle East and in much of the Islamic world exist for worship and to teach the Qur'an. However mosques in the United States also serve as community cultural and social centers. In addition, Muslims have created several organizations to promote Islamic values. They include the Islamic Society of North America (ISNA), the Muslim Students Association (MSA), the Council on Islamic Education (CIE), the Institute of Islamic Information and Education (III&E), and the Islamic Foundation of North America.[57]

The ISNA grew out of the MSA. Their headquarters in Plainfield, Indiana, includes a mosque and a campus on one hundred acres of land. They hold annual conferences in U.S. and Canadian cities every Labor Day weekend. MSAs exist on most major U.S. college and university campuses.[58]

The Council on Islamic Education[59] provides curricular materials to public schools to teach general audiences accurate information about Islam. The Institute of Islamic Information and Education[60] seeks to provide accurate information on Islam to both Muslims and non-Muslims and to integrate new converts into the Muslim community. It may also serve as a missionary outreach to non-Muslims.

The Islamic Foundation of North America[61] focuses more on devout Muslims. Their main purpose is to support the curricula of Muslim parochial day schools, weekend schools, summer schools, and summer camps. This organization does provide a web page oriented to public schools, but the links may not work. They also provide links to book suppliers and teacher resources, a guide for new Muslims, directories to schools and camps, and *Living Islam*, a Muslim newspaper for the general reader. In addition, they review children's literature written by Muslims for Muslims. The subjects that they emphasize are the Qur'an, the Arabic language, and Islamic studies.

All of these resources are necessary both to teach Islam and its values and to counteract the stereotypes, discrimination, and other cultural issues in the broader society. Devon Alisa Abdallah[62] states that Arabs are seen as sheiks, belly dancers, desert dwellers, owners of harems and camels, and criminals and terrorists; and these stereotypes are definitely used against Muslims. Christine Bennett and Salman Al-Ani [63] mention that all Muslims are often viewed as being Arab. Arabs and Muslims are often stereotyped in trade books, magazines, television, movies, and school textbooks. Abdallah[64] mentions biased reporting as a particular problem. Many studies have been conducted on the stereotyping of both groups, such as those by Sufia Sabbagh,[65] Rick Blasing,[66] William J. Griswold,[67] and Gilbert T. Sewall.[68]

Arab Americans and Muslims in particular must contend not only with stereotyping in all aspects of mainstream culture, but also with racist comments, incidents, and profiling, especially since 9/11. General cultural issues include the observance of daily and Friday prayers by Muslims, dress codes (especially for Muslim women), and dating and other issues of etiquette between the sexes. Most painful may be the exclusion of Muslims, who follow a Semitic and Abrahamic faith of the book, from the Judeo-Christian tradition promoted in the United States. Some Arab Americans report feeling like foreigners in the United States. Except for the negative stereotypes, Muslims are ignored by the mainstream and by most multiculturalists alike.[69] However, recent editions of multicultural education texts by Bennett[70] and M. Lee Manning and Leroy G. Baruth[71] include chapters on Arab Americans and Muslim Americans.

Educational activities of Arab Americans and Muslim Americans reflect those of many other groups that are described in chapter 1 of this book.

Even though Muslim Americans have established a network of private paro-chial day schools, most Muslim children learn about their faith in evening, weekend, and summer schools and camps and attend public schools.[72] Their problems parallel the general problems encountered by adults in addition to a few issues specific to children. There is ignorance, stereotyping, and a lack of recognition and acknowledgement of Arab and especially Muslim history and cultures that is reflected both in school curriculum and in the way schools are managed. Muslim students must contend with comments, incidents, preju-dice, and misunderstanding from non-Muslim peers and sometimes from staff! Issues include the treatment of dress, the observance of Muslim and non-Muslim holidays, dating and other etiquette issues between the sexes, dietary needs in the cafeteria, and the issues of gym uniforms and activities and of showering. The observance of Ramadan cuts across several of these issues (holidays, food, school management).[73]

Counseling can also be a very sensitive subject. While seen as acceptable in helping students with academic or career preparation or dealing with school incidents, it can be seen by a student's family as an intrusion of privacy when it deals with family issues. Experts stress the importance of working closely with parents and the entire family.[74] Girls face particular issues such as dress, etiquette with the opposite sex in general and dating in particular, and the expectation of many duties at home.[75] Muslim youth also deal with many of the same second-generation issues encountered by young people from other groups, which are described in chapter 1. So far, most identify more strongly with Islamic values than with those from the West.[76] Curricular issues include a lack of information; erroneous information; stereotypes, especially in text-books; a lack of coverage in the curriculum compared with other religious groups; and the treatment of art, drama, music, and physical education.[77]

While the role of knowledgeable social workers, counselors, librarians, and other school personnel is very important, many of these problems can be resolved as all professionals learn much more about Arab Americans and Muslim Americans by working with parents, community leaders, and other re-sources. The American-Arab Anti-Discrimination Committee[78] has a web page on educational issues, and the Council on Islamic Education[79] has published *Teaching about Islam and Muslims in Public School*. In addition, Yvonne Haddad has published many books and much research on contemporary Mus-lim Americans. There are more articles about counseling children from these groups by Darcy Haag Granello,[80] Daneshpour Manijeh,[81] and others.

The website of the Islamic Foundation of North America[82] has reviews of textbooks and children's literature by Muslims and for Muslims.This source also lists book and video suppliers.[83] In addition, materials for children and parents can be ordered through Astrolabe[84] and other sources on and off the web. Some of these materials can give non-Muslims more insight into the values and perspectives of Muslim families.

There is very little information for a general audience on contemporary Muslim children living in North America, and most materials on the Middle East are written from Western viewpoints. However, several Arab and Muslim authors who write for a general audience are beginning to emerge in North America. Naomi Shihab Nye, a Palestinian poet from San Antonio, Texas, published an article, "Singing the Long Song,"[85] that discussed the need for many more materials relevant to this population. She has written a young-adult novel and a picture book, both based on her own family's experiences in the Middle East, and has compiled at least two anthologies of poetry from that region. She has published on many other topics, as well. Another Palestinian American writer, Sally Bahous, has published *Sitti and the Cats: A Tale of Friendship*,[86] a traditional story from the Middle East. The Muslim writer Suhaib Hamid Ghazi has published two books, *Ramadan*[87] and *The Prophets of Allah*[88] that are available from Amazon.com.

An important Canadian writer, who originally came from Pakistan, is Rukhsana Khan. She writes stories that take place in Pakistan and Afghanistan, both non-Arab Muslim countries. She has a brief bibliography of children's books on Islam and related subjects on her website.[89] Her most important contribution, however, may be her two books *Muslim Child: Understanding Islam through Stories and Poems*[90] and *Dahling, If You Luv Me, Would You Please, Please Smile*.[91] These are some of the first books published for a general audience on contemporary Muslim children who live in the West (or at least in North America). The first book features children from Canada, the United States, Nigeria, and Pakistan. It is an introduction to both Islam and the daily lives and realities of Muslim children. The second book is a young-adult novel about a North American Muslim teenager who applies her faith to successfully cope with the normal problems of adolescence and growing up.

These works are an important contribution because stories about contemporary Arab American or Muslim American children for a general audience are still very rare, especially those by Arab American or Muslim American authors. One book by a non-Muslim, *Magid Fasts for Ramadan*[92] by Mary Matthews, has received mixed reviews from Muslims on Amazon.com, most of them negative. Because there is so much misunderstanding between cultures, it is vital that Arab Americans and Muslim Americans be encouraged to tell their own stories to a wider audience. This will probably be an important new literature to be developed in the immediate future.

It is much easier to find materials about the Middle East than it is to find information on Arabs or Muslims in North America, but almost all of it is nonfiction. Elsa Marston[93] in *Our Family, Our Friends, Our World* and

Mohammed A. Bamyeh[94] in *Global Voices, Global Visions* describe fiction and nonfiction materials related to the Middle East that are published in the United States, and literary works by Middle Eastern writers. In addition, another author, Florence Parry Heide, has written two novels about contemporary children in that part of the world, *Sami and the Time of the Troubles*,[95] about a boy in Lebanon, and *Day of Ahmed's Secret*,[96] about a young boy from Egypt.

In researching and writing this book, I have discovered that scholarly attention has been paid to diasporic connections between Arabs and Arab Americans; to stereotypes, especially in the media; to developments in the Middle East; and to educational issues faced by Arab Americans and especially Muslim Americans. There is a body of children's literature by Muslims for Muslims, and several Arab and Muslim authors who write for general audiences of young people have emerged in North America. Information on the Middle East or Islam created by Muslims and books about contemporary Arab American and Muslim American children are still sorely lacking. I believe that cultural outsiders from all professions need to learn much more about Arab Americans and Muslim Americans and need to apply what they learn. More Arabs and Muslims should be encouraged to write about their group and religion for all children. Potential writers can be recruited from parents and community leaders already in touch with schools, and from organizations such as the Council on Islamic Education, the American-Arab Anti-Discrimination Committee, and possibly the Institute of Islamic Information and Education or the Islamic Foundation of North America. Many people involved with these groups already write, and if they cannot be recruited, they may know of others who also write. Encouraging these writers would avoid much of the negative history that has occurred with other groups.

European Immigrants and White Ethnic Americans

There have been several major waves of European immigrants to the United States throughout its history. The earliest immigrants were from the northwest of Europe (England, Scotland, the Netherlands, Germany, France, and Scandinavian countries); most spoke English or a Germanic language, and most (but not all) were Protestants. The English determined the mainstream culture, establishing English as the dominant language and English common law as the basic law.[97]

Irish immigrants started to arrive in the early nineteenth century and came in force in the 1850s after the Irish potato famine. They were English speaking but were seen as a threat, partly because of their Catholicism. They were met with stereotypes, discriminatory comments and incidents, and sometimes violence.[98]

The European immigrants of 1880–1924 were different from all who came before. They were from eastern and southern Europe, predominantly Catholic or Jewish, and shorter and darker than their predecessors. Most were poor or working class and did not speak English very well upon their arrival. They encountered stereotyping, discrimination, pressures to quickly assimilate, and eventually legislation to restrict immigration. At that time, these immigrants were not considered to be the same race as Europeans from the north or the west, and they were often viewed as "incapable of assimilation."[99] These immigrants and their descendants did indeed assimilate or acculturate, but it took them years to do this. In the meantime, they organized religious and secular institutions, media, and other resources, and in some cases, language and ethnic schools for their children. These schools were usually attended at night or on weekends and if successful, generally lasted a generation or two. Schools lasting longer than that usually changed in their focus over time. (These resources are described in more detail in chapter 1.)

When most people think of European immigrants and compare them to people of color (with the implied question, "The immigrants made it. Why can't people from minority groups?"), this is the group that they are thinking of. This group of immigrants and their descendants were studied intensely by sympathetic and unsympathetic scholars for many years.

Europeans continued to immigrate after 1924. The number of all immigrants was very low during the Depression, but Jewish and other refugees came to the United States during and right after World War II. Some famous examples include the adult Albert Einstein—as well as Henry Kissinger and Madeleine Albright as children! This was a very well-educated group of immigrants who assimilated quickly.

One hundred years ago, 80 percent of all immigrants came from Europe. Since 1965, the proportion of immigrants from Europe has been considerably smaller. This group, like their counterparts from elsewhere around the world, is skilled and well educated. Unlike their counterparts of a century ago, relatively few studies have been done on recent European immigrants, and this group may very well be neglected. Because recent and current European immigrants look like the cultural majority and tend to blend in and be quickly assimilated, they tend to be invisible to others.[100] However, new European immigrants are different from the American mainstream, they may differ from earlier waves of immigrants from their country or culture, and in time, they may also encounter generational differences within families.

Donna S. Richey[101] describes cultural differences between recent European immigrants and the U.S. mainstream, which include differences in learning and teaching styles; nonverbal behavior, including use of personal space, body contact, and eye contact; dress codes; and etiquette. Many Europeans define *family* as extended family, not nuclear family, and some may value interdependence over independence, the present over the future, and attention to people over the fulfillment of tasks. Formal religious practices and beliefs (or lack of them) may also influence their behavior.

If there is an established ethnic community from the new immigrant's country or cultural group available in the area, the newcomer still may not fit in. In some cases, new immigrants find themselves to be different both from earlier immigrants and from their descendants. It also is still not unusual for the children of the most recent immigrants to feel both an internal and an external pressure to assimilate. This can lead to some clashes in values with immigrant parents.

However, like everybody else, new European immigrants need to belong, to be affirmed, and to be accepted as people. They need to be able to avoid being stereotyped, and they need contact with both sensitive and encouraging people from the mainstream and role models from their own cultures.[102] These seem to be universal needs that apply to all groups.

Richey suggests that librarians and teachers use poetry (in particular poetry from Europe), picture books and easy-to-read books to promote the learning of English, books on U.S. folklore, and books with realistic models of students' cultures and of the general experiences of immigrants. Students should be encouraged to read biographies about heroes and heroines, such as Anne Frank. Richey suggests that students be encouraged to stay abreast of developments in their home country and to do school projects connected with their past.[103]

I also suggest using folklore in English and occasionally other languages from students' home countries and acquiring other books from those countries, especially those in English. This can be done by consulting specialized bibliographies and keeping and consulting lists of authors, illustrators, and books nominated for the Hans Christian Andersen Medal and the Mildred Batchelder Award. In addition to the multicultural and international bibliographies mentioned in chapter 3, there are a couple of bibliographies of children's books from around the world, and in particular from Europe.

A relatively recent one is *Children's Books from Other Countries*,[104] which is sponsored by the United States Board on Books for Young People. One can quickly check the index to find books from specific countries listed here, and these are books that have been translated into English. Two new similar titles from Europe are *Cross-Currents: A Guide to Multicultural Books for Young People*[105] from Ireland and *Outside In: Children's Books in Translation*[106] from the United Kingdom. Lyn Miller-Lachmann compiled two bibliographies in the 1990s with extensive chapters on Europe. They are entitled *Our Family, Our Friends, Our World*[107] and *Global Voices, Global Visions*.[108] Both books describe the state of literature in many countries and some authors who have been translated into English. *Our Family, Our Friends, Our World* lists books for young people. *Global Voices, Global Visions* lists materials suited for an adult library collection that can also be read and used by teenagers. This book specifically emphasizes ethnic literature in the chapter on the United Kingdom and multicultural literature in western Europe. The chapter on eastern Europe focuses more on that region's general literature, which is little known in the West, and it emphasizes the relatively recent literature of the 1990s. In addition, there is also a much older bibliography entitled *The Best of the Best*.[109]

The United States Board on Books for Young People is the U.S. branch of the International Board on Books for Young People (IBBY), which publishes *Bookbird*,[110] an excellent scholarly journal on children's literature of the world. IBBY also gives the Hans Christian Andersen Medal every other year to the world's best author and illustrator. This is a lifetime achievement award for authors and illustrators with a substantial body of excellent work who are relatively likely to be translated into English. In even-numbered years in the fall, *Bookbird* publishes special issues describing the lives and work of all nominees for the medal, and the nominees come from around the world and almost every country in Europe. It may be a good idea to find those special issues, see what authors and illustrators come from countries represented in a population of interest, and then check Amazon.com to ascertain whether these authors have been translated into English. Amazon is also a good place to find similar or related books.

Another important award is the Mildred Batchelder Award, given by the Association of Library Services to Children (ALSC) of ALA for the best translations of children's books into English. By consulting lists of those nominees, librarians can find more good materials in English from European and other countries.

Acquiring some ethnic and cultural materials may be helpful to all. For instance, Jewish American literature is fairly extensive and relatively well documented and well supported. Most older books were published by Jewish presses, but most books about Jews are now published by mainstream presses and available to all libraries.[111]

Two organizations play important roles in promoting Jewish children's literature. The Association of Jewish Libraries gives the Sidney Taylor Awards for a book for younger readers, one for older readers, a manuscript, and for notable and Honor books. The organization has a website, "The New Jewish Values Finder: A Guide to Values in Jewish Children's Literature,"[112] a list of notable books from between 1985 and 2000, and an online pamphlet, "Excellence in Jewish Children's Literature: A Guide for Book Selectors, Reviewers and Award Judges."[113]

The Jewish Book Council sponsors conferences and Jewish Book Month. It gives the National Jewish Book Awards and publishes the *Jewish Book Annual* and the *Jewish Book World*, which comes out three times a year.

In addition, specialized Jewish children's book clubs and book fairs and children's bookstores issue catalogs of relevant materials,[114] and older bibliographies by Marcia W. Posner[115] and Enid Davis[116] are useful resources.

Finding books on other cultural and ethnic groups may be more of a challenge. Most groups do have local, regional, and national organizations, as well as electronic and print media and specialized publishers, and they publish some materials. Their media also carry book reviews, and children's literature may be published or reviewed there. Another source is groups that maintain language or ethnic schools and publish textbooks and related materials.

There are useful steps that professionals can take in finding out about resources of groups new to them. They include the following:

- Start with reference books about many ethnic groups to get general information on your particular group, such as *Gale Encyclopedia of Multiethnic America*[117] or *Harvard Encyclopedia of American Ethnic Groups*.[118]
- Look also for more specific encyclopedias, handbooks, almanacs, and other *information* on specific groups.
- Look for general information on your specific group, such as their history in their original country or countries, areas of settlement in the United States, demographic information, locations of related local communities, etc.
- Use ethnic and general directories to find organizations, publishers, and media.
- Be sure to consult library catalogs and bibliographies.
- Compile a list of the following. These should lead to any existing children's literature and to reviews:
  - bookstores, publishers, specialized libraries, museums
  - ethnic media—newspapers, periodicals, television and radio station programs, websites
  - colleges, universities, ethnic studies programs
  - institutions and organizations

By acquiring books and other materials from these sources, libraries can serve the needs of recent European immigrants; ethnic Europeans of the third, fourth, and fifth generations; and their audience in general, enabling others to learn more about these groups as well.

EMERGING ISSUES AND CONCLUSIONS

Michael Kerestesi[119] once wrote a very influential essay on how academic disciplines develop. In the early stages, all people connected with the new field know each other, interact informally, and communicate through telephone calls, conferences, and newsletters (and now e-mail and listservs). As a discipline or field becomes more established, practitioners no longer automatically know each other, and directories become important. Formal organizations and conferences are organized, occasional articles become books, and newsletters give rise to specialized journals. Bibliographies and periodical indexes become necessary to keep track of the field, and glossaries explaining specialized terms may become specialized dictionaries. In short, Kerestesi argues that as a discipline or field grows, so does the organizational and bibliographical apparatuses that support it. He believes that one can tell the stage of a discipline by looking at the state of its corresponding literature.

This may also apply to multicultural and ethnic children's literature, which includes literature strictly or mostly for the audience described, some of which is well known to the general public, and some of which is not.

In the early stages, there are few if any titles, and there is a heavy reliance on traditional stories. If literature about a group is available to the general public, it is often largely written by people from outside the group. The development of supplementary curriculum materials by group members may also mark this stage. Literature on Muslim Americans for the general public may be in this stage.

When a literature is really beginning to develop, authors are beginning to produce enough work to make bibliographies and reading lists necessary. At this time, the bibliographies are in the form of pathfinders and bibliographical articles. However, literature at this stage is definitely growing. Critics are paying attention and may develop prizes, both to encourage new writing and to establish a canon of the literature. Literature on mixed-race families and children's literature reviewed by the Islamic Foundation of North America seem to be at the beginning of this stage, and literature by and about Asian Americans seems to be in the middle of this stage. It appears that literature on Native Americans and on Latino/as is moving to the next stage.

Literature that is relatively developed is extensive enough to demand book-length bibliographies to keep track of it. This stage may also include the development of research and other specialized libraries and specialized review media to document this material. Also, more of the literature is written by members of the group portrayed than in previous stages. The well-known African American literature and the not-so-well-known Jewish American literature seem to have these characteristics. This theory remains to be defined. It will also be interesting to track the development of all of the literatures described in this book.

Multiculturalists in the field of children's literature have done a tremendous amount of work not only to create new literature, but also to support it with alternative activities, institutions, and resources. A lot of information on this is scattered, and in too many cases, difficult to find. It is hoped that this guide has shown the many contributions to this field. Research possibilities in multicultural and ethnic children's literature abound, and researchers are definitely encouraged to develop their own spheres of interest. Listed below are a few questions or problems to get scholars excited and started.

Philosophical Issues

1. How do philosophical issues in multiculturalism as a movement and phenomenon affect multicultural and ethnic children's literature?
2. What line, if any, should multiculturalists draw between relativism and an absolute morality? Are there ultimate values to which all must or should subscribe? If so, what are they?
3. How does one deal with authentic cultural phenomena that are negative?
4. Multiculturalism is a double-edged sword that can be used, either to unite or to divide. How can it be used to promote both self-awareness *and* empathy for others?
5. Can elements of all cultures be used to prevent, ameliorate, or resolve the almost inevitable conflict between groups? This is important to those concerned with multiculturalism, but also a very important question for *everybody*.
6. How do U.S. multicultural philosophy and practices compare with those in Canada, Europe, Africa, India, and other places?

Activities of Diverse People

1. People pass on their cultures through informal education, full-time and part-time formal education, and the development of institutions, media, and literature. How do these developments relate to the eventual development of a literature for children and young people? Why and how may this matter? What conditions, such as prizes, funding, or institutional support, are necessary to encourage the creation and growth of this literature?
2. What are diverse, ethnic people thinking and doing, and why?
3. How do they respond to trends in the general society? What new contributions are they making to this field and to children's literature in general? What are their activities? What new paradigms are they developing?
   a. Emerging themes and worldviews in the literature?

  b. Emerging theories of criticism?
4. How do they interact with similar groups elsewhere (in diaspora) and with other groups in their own countries?

Multiculturalism and the West

1. How can the best of multicultural materials be combined with the best materials from Western culture?
2. In fields like history, can one teach about *both* the convergence or coming together of groups from different continents *and* our evolving political democratic traditions? If so, how can the two be combined?
3. How should ancient non-Western civilizations be presented in classrooms? Which cultures should be taught, how much, and in what ways?

Learning about Everybody

1. Which groups should educators focus on, and how much, in designing their curricula, and what kinds of information should be taught?
2. How can students and others supplement information presented in school?
3. How can individuals find information and materials on groups of people new to them? How should they evaluate and use these materials?

Children's Literature in General

1. What ties exist between children's and young adult literatures and between these and any corresponding adult literature?
2. Why is children's and young adult literature usually treated separately across all categories?
3. Children's literature has been used to entertain and instruct the young and as a reflection of popular culture over time. What are the implications and applications of this for our purposes?

Uncovering and Discovering the History of Multicultural and Ethnic Children's Literature

1. Who were the precursors and pioneers in this field? Who were really the first to (. . .) ?
2. What were the contributions of precursors and pioneers, especially in the context of their times?
3. What were the contributions of precursors and pioneers from diverse groups?

Criteria in Evaluating Materials

1. Where do they come from, how do they compare, and how can they be useful?
2. What kinds of criteria should be used and under what circumstances? How should they be used?
    a. traditional literary criteria
    b. criteria to prevent discrimination in children's literature and to promote cultural understanding
    c. emerging literary criteria from diverse groups
    d. other evolving criteria
3. Backgrounds of authors and illustrators
    a. What general qualifications should anybody have to write about or illustrate any group?
    b. How should authors and illustrators prepare to portray groups of people new to them?
    c. How can diverse authors and illustrators be attracted to this field?

More Applications: What Else to Do on Monday Morning

How can you use theoretical and practical multicultural insights from education, business, psychology, ethnic studies, and other fields to enrich everybody in the workplace?

In conclusion, with the world going global, diverse people and their concerns and the issue of multiculturalism will always be with us. We are all flowers in the garden of life, in all colors, shapes, and sizes, and each group of flowers must be able to bloom in its time. As they bloom, it is necessary to weed the garden from fear, hatred, and selfishness. If the human race is to survive and thrive, we must learn to understand the thinking and to incorporate the wisdom of a wide variety of people. This is turning into one world—and the world is here! To quote Langston Hughes,

> Tomorrow,
> I'll be at the table
> When company comes.
> Nobody'll dare
> Say to me,
> "Eat in the kitchen,"
> Then.

> Besides,
> They'll see how beautiful I am
> And be ashamed—

> I, too, am America.[120]

REFERENCES

1. Christine I. Bennett, *Comprehensive Multicultural Education: Theory and Practice* (Boston, Mass.: Pearson Allyn and Bacon, 2007), 121.

2. Arthur M. Schlesinger Jr., *The Disuniting of America* (New York: Norton, 1998), 46–47.

3. Barbara C. Cruz and Michael J. Berson, "The American Melting Pot? Miscegenation Laws in the United States," *OAH Magazine of History* 15, no. 4 (Summer 2001), http://www.oah.org/pubs/magazine/family/cruz-berson.html (26 June 2006).

4. Cruz and Berson, "The American Melting Pot?"

5. Maria P. P. Root and Matt Kelley, eds., *Multiracial Child Resource Book: Living Complex Identities* (Seattle, Wash.: MAVIN Foundation, 2003), xiv.

6. Cynthia Leitich Smith, "Children's and YA Books with Interracial Family Themes," http://cynthialeitichsmith.com/lit_resources/diversity/multiracial/multi_race_intro.html (26 June 2006).

7. Root and Kelley, *Multiracial Child Resource Book.*

8. Root and Kelley, *Multiracial Child Resource Book,* xiv.

9. Root and Kelley, *Multiracial Child Resource Book,* xv.

10. Heather Dalmage, "Patrolling Racial Borders: Discrimination against Mixed Race People," in Root and Kelley, *Multiracial Child Resource Book,* 19–25.

11. Maria P. P. Root, "Issues and Experiences of Racially Mixed People," in Root and Kelley, *Multiracial Child Resource Book*, 132–34.

12. Francis Wardle, *Tomorrow's Children* (Denver, Colo.: Center for the Study of Biracial Children, 1999).

13. Root and Kelley, *Multiracial Child Resource Book*, xv.

14. Association of MultiEthnic Americans (AMEA), P.O. Box 341304, Los Angeles, Calif. 90034-1304, http://www.ameasite.org (26 June 2006).

15. The MAVIN Foundation, 600 First Ave., Suite 600, Seattle, Wash. 98104, http://www.mavinfoundation.org (26 June 2006).

16. SWIRL Inc., 244 Fifth Ave., Suite J 230, New York, N.Y. 10001-7604, http://www.swirlinc.org/ (26 June 2006).

17. Center for the Study of Biracial Children, 2300 S. Kramaria St., Denver, Colo. 80222.

18. Root and Kelley, *Multiracial Child Resource Book.*

19. Wardle, *Tomorrow's Children.*

20. MAVIN, http://www.mavinfoundation.org/ (26 June 2006).

21. *Interracial Voice,* http://www.webcom.com/~intvoice/ (26 June 2006).

22. *The Multiracial Activist,* http://www.multiracial.com/ (28 Aug. 2005).

23. AMEA, "Useful Links," http://www.ameasite.org/links.asp (26 June 2006).

24. SWIRL, "Links," http://swirlinc.org/links.htm (26 June 2006).

25. *Interracial Voice,* "Additional Sites," http://www.webcom.com/~intvoice/add_site.html (26 June 2006).

26. Root and Kelley, *Multiracial Child Resource Book,* "Web Sites," 246–49.

27. Karen Downing, "My Interracial Family," http://www-personal.umich.edu/~kdown/family.html (26 June 2006).

28. Theresa Stokes and Keith Stokes, *Eyes of Glory,* http://www.eyesofglory.com/ (26 June 2006).

29. *Interracial Voice,* "Book Reviews," http://www.webcom.com/~intvoice/ (26 June 2006).

30. AMEA, "Recommended Readings," http://www.ameasite.org/biblio.asp (26 June 2006).

31. Root and Kelley, "Books," *Multiracial Child Resource Book*, 230–45.

32. Smith, "Children and YA Books with Interracial Family Themes."

33. Kathleen T. Horning, "Recommended Picture Books Featuring Interracial Families," http://www.education.wisc.edu/ccbc/books/detailListBooks.asp?idBookLists=143 (26 June 2006).

34. Mary Ann Capan and Cynthia Suarez, "Biracial/Biethnic Characters in Young Adult and Children's Books," *MultiCultural Review* 2, no. 2 (June 1993): 32–37.

35. Mary Ann Capan, "Exploring Biracial/Biethnic Characters in Young Adult and Children's Books," *MultiCultural Review* 3, no. 4 (Dec. 1994): 14–19.

36. Internet Public Library (IPL), Pathfinder, "Resources For and About Multiracial/Multiethnic Americans," http://www.ipl.org/div/pf/entry/48507 (26 June 2006).

37. Maxine Rosenberg, *Living in Two Worlds: The Story of Biracial Children* (New York: Lothrop, Lee and Shepard, 1986).

38. M. Lee Manning and Leroy G. Baruth, "Understanding Arab American Children and Adolescents," in *Multicultural Education of Children and Adolescents* (Boston: Pearson Allyn and Bacon, 2004), 123; Christine I. Bennett, *Comprehensive Multicultural Education: Theory and Practice,* sixth edition (Boston: Pearson Allyn and Bacon, 2007), 182–83; Vladimir F. Wertsman, "Arab Americans: A Comparative and Critical Analysis of Leading Reference Sources," *MultiCultural Review* 10, no.2 (June 2001): 42.

39. Detroit Free Press, "100 Questions and Answers about Arab Americans: A Journalist's Guide," http://freep.com/legacy/jobspage/arabs.htm (26 June 2006).

40. Christine Bennett and Salman Al-Ani, "Muslims in the United States," in Bennett, *Comprehensive Multicultural Education,* 173–74.

41. Bennett, *Comprehensive Multicultural Education,* 181; Wertsman, "Arab Americans: A Comparative and Critical Analysis of Leading Reference Sources," 43.

42. Wertsman, "Arab Americans: A Comparative and Critical Analysis of Leading Reference Sources," 42; Bennett, *Comprehensive Multicultural Education,* 181.

43. Wertsman, "Arab Americans: A Comparative and Critical Analysis of Leading Reference Sources," 43.

44. Bennett, *Comprehensive Multicultural Education,* 182.

45. Devon Alisa Abdallah, "Multiracial Arab Americans," in Root and Kelley, *Multiracial Child Resource Book*, 208.

46. Ayad Al-Qazzaz, "Transnational Links between the Arab Community in the U.S. and the Arab World," ERIC Education Resources Information Center, ED 174525.

47. Detroit Free Press, "100 Questions and Answers about Arab Americans: A Journalist's Guide."

48. Montgomery County Public Schools, "Arab American Heritage Month," http://www.mcps.k12.md.us/departments/oipd/diversity/arabamatvs.html (26 June 2006).

49. Joseph Haiek, *Arab American Almanac* (Glendale, Calif.: News Circle, 2003).

50. National Institute for Technology and Liberal Education Arab World Project, "Arab Culture and Civilization," http://arabworld.nitle.org/ (26 June 2006).

51. Wertsman, "Arab Americans: A Comparative and Critical Analysis of Leading Reference Sources," 42–47.

52. Kristin Lems, "The Arab World and Arab Americans," *Book Links* 9, no. 2 (Nov. 1999): 31, http://www.ala.org/ala/booklinksbucket/arabworld.htm (26 June 2006).

53. Bennett and Al-Ani, "Muslims in the United States," 173–74.

54. Bennett and Al-Ani, "Muslims in the United States," 174.

55. David R. Hodge, "Working with Muslim Youths: Understanding the Values and Beliefs of Islamic Discourse," *Children and Schools* 24, no. 1 (Jan. 2002): 8–10.

56. Bennett and Al-Ani, "Muslims in the United States," 176.

57. Bennett and Al-Ani, "Muslims in the United States," 175; Hodge, "Working with Muslim Youths," 10, 13.

58. Bennett and Al-Ani, "Muslims in the United States," 175.

59. Council on Islamic Education, 9300 Gardenia St. #B-3, Fountain Valley, Calif. 92708, http://www.cie.org/ (26 June 2006).

60. The Institute of Islamic Information and Education, P.O. Box 410129, Chicago, Ill. 60641, http://www.iiie.net/1/content/view/26/44/ (26 June 2006).

61. The Islamic Foundation of North America, http://www.islamicedfoundation.com/ (26 June 2006).

62. Abdallah, "Multiracial Arab Americans," 208–9.

63. Bennett and Al-Ani, "Muslims in the United States," 180.

64. Abdallah, "Multiracial Arab Americans."

65. Sufia Sabbagh, *Sex, Lies, and Stereotypes: The Image of Arabs in American Popular Fiction,* ERIC Education Resources Information Center, ED 363530.

66. Rick Blasing, "Islam: Stereotypes Still Prevail," *Social Education* 60, no. 2 (Feb. 1996): 107–10.

67. William J. Griswold, *The Image of the Middle East in Secondary School Textbooks*, ERIC Education Resources Information Center, ED 117013.

68. Gilbert T. Sewall, *Islam and the Textbooks: A Report of the American Textbook Council*, ERIC Education Resources Information Center, ED 475822.

69. Bennett and Al-Ani, "Muslims in the United States," 179–80; Abdallah, "Multiracial Arab Americans," 209.

70. Bennett and Al-Ani, "Muslims in the United States," 173–80.

71. Manning and Baruth, "Understanding Arab American Children and Adolescents," 111–32.

72. James Hoot, Tunde Szecsi, and Samina Moosa, "What Teachers of Young Children Should Know about Islam," *Early Childhood Education Journal* 31, no. 2 (Winter 2003): 86.

73. Hodge, "Working with Muslim Youth," 10–12; Richard B. Carter and Amelia E. El-Hindi, "Counseling Muslim Children in School Settings," *Professional School Counseling* 2, no. 3 (Feb. 1999): 183–88.

74. Hodge, "Working with Muslim Youth," 12–17; Carter and El-Hindi, "Counseling Muslim Children in School Settings," 183–88.

75. Awatif Elnour and Khadar Bashir-Ali, "Teaching Muslim Girls in American Schools," *Social Education* 67, no. 2 (Jan./Feb. 2003): 62–64.

76. Hodge, "Working with Muslim Youth," 11.

77. Hodge, "Working with Muslim Youth," 15; Elnour and Bashir-Ali, "Teaching Muslim Girls in American Schools," 62–63; Manning and Baruth, "Understanding Arab American Children and Adolescents,"126.

78. American-Arab Anti-Discrimination Committee, "Arab American Students in Public Schools," http://www.adc.org/index.php?id=246&type=100 (26 June 2006).

79. Council on Islamic Education, *Teaching about Islam and Muslims in Public Schools* (Fountain Valley, Calif.: Council on Islamic Education).

80. Darcy Haag Granello, *The Cultural Heritage of Arab Americans and Implications for Counseling*, ERIC Education Resources Information Center, ED 382904.

81. Daneshpour Manijeh, "Muslim Families and Family Therapy," *Journal of Marital and Family Counseling* 24, no. 3 (July 1998): 355–68.

82. Islamic Foundation of North America, "Book Reviews," http://www.islamicedfoundation.com/bookreviews/book.htm (26 June 2006).

83. Islamic Foundation of North America, "Muslim Book/Video Suppliers," http://www.islamicedfoundation.com/serv03.htm (26 June 2006).

84. Astrolabe, LLC, 720 Plainfield Rd., Suite A, Willowbrook, Ill. 60527, http://www.astrolabe.com/ (26 June 2006).

85. Naomi Shihab Nye, "Singing the Long Song," *New Advocate* 2, no. 2 (Spring 1999): 119–26.

86. Sally Bahous, *Sitti and the Cats: A Tale of Friendship* (Lanham, Md.: Roberts Rinehart Publishers, 1997).

87. Suhaib Hamid Ghazi, *Ramadan* (New York: Holiday House, 1994).

88. Suhaib Hamid Ghazi, *The Prophets of Allah* (Skokie, Ill.: IQRA International Education Foundation, 1995.

89. Rukhsana Khan, Rukhsanakhan.com, "Children's Books with Muslim and Other Themes," http://www.rukhsanakhan.com/muslimbooks.htm (26 June 2006).

90. Rukhsana Khan, *Muslim Child: Understanding Islam through Stories and Poems* (Morton Grove, Ill.: Albert Whitman and Co., 2002).

91. Rukhsana Khan, *Dahling, If You Luv Me, Would You Please, Please Smile* (Toronto and New York: Stoddart Kids, 1999; rebound by Sagebrush, 2001).

92. Mary Matthews, *Magid Fasts for Ramadan* (Boston: Clarion Books, 2000).

93. Elsa Marston, "The Middle East and North Africa," in *Our Family, Our Friends, Our World: An Annotated Guide to Significant Multicultural Books for*

Children and Teenagers, ed. Lyn Miller-Lachmann (New Providence, N.J.: Bowker, 1992), 381–416.

94. Mohammed A. Bamyeh, "The Middle East," in *Global Voices, Global Visions: A Core Collection of Multicultural Books,* by Lyn Miller-Lachmann (New Providence, N.J.: Bowker, 1995), 501–38.

95. Florence Parry Heide, *Sami and the Time of the Troubles* (Boston: Clarion Books, 1995).

96. Florence Parry Heide, *Day of Ahmed's Secret* (Scranton, Penn.: Harper Trophy, 1999).

97. Bennett, *Comprehensive Multicultural Education,* 111; Schlesinger, *The Disuniting of America,* 33–36.

98. Bennett, *Comprehensive Multicultural Education,* 124–26.

99. Bennett, *Comprehensive Multicultural Education,* 122–23, 126–27; Schlesinger, *The Disuniting of America,* 37–38.

100. Donna S. Richey, "Understanding and Appreciating the Unique Needs of European Americans," in *Multicultural Aspects of School Media Programs,* ed. Kathy Howard Latrobe and Mildred Knight Laughlin (Englewood, Colo.: Libraries Unlimited, 1992), 61.

101. Richey, "Understanding and Appreciating the Unique Needs of European Americans," 62–65.

102. Richey, "Understanding and Appreciating the Unique Needs of European Americans," 65.

103. Richey, "Understanding and Appreciating the Unique Needs of European Americans," 66–67.

104. Carl Tomlinson, ed., *Children's Books from Other Countries* (Lanham, Md.: Scarecrow, 1999).

105. Liz Morris and Susanna Coghlan, eds., *Cross-Currents: A Guide to Multicultural Books for Young People* (Dublin: IBBY Ireland, 2005).

106. Deborah Hallford and Edgardo Zaghini, eds., *Outside In: Children's Books in Translation* (London: Milet Publishing, 2005).

107. Lyn Miller-Lachmann, *Our Family, Our Friends, Our World: An Annotated Guide to Significant Multicultural Books for Children and Teenagers* (New Providence, N.J.: Bowker, 1992).

108. Lyn Miller-Lachmann, *Global Voices, Global Visions: A Core Collection of Multicultural Books* (New Providence, N.J.: Bowker, 1995).

109. Walter Scherf, *The Best of the Best: Picture, Children's and Youth Books From 57 Countries or Languages* (New York: Bowker, 1971).

110. *Bookbird,* University of Toronto Press, 5201 Dufferin St., North York, ON, Canada M3H5T8.

111. Marcia W. Posner, "Jewish Children's Literature," in *Jewish-American History and Culture: An Encyclopedia,* ed. Jack Fischel and Sanford Pinsker (New York: Garland, 1992), 294–95.

112. Jewish Library Association, "The New Jewish Value Finder: A Guide to Values in Jewish Children's Books," http://www.ajljewishvalues.org/ (26 June 2006).

113. Jewish Library Association, "Excellence in Jewish Children's Literature: A Guide for Book Selectors, Reviewers and Awards Judges," http://www.jewishlibraries.org/ajlweb/publications/excellence.pdf (26 June 2006).

114. Posner, "Jewish Children's Literature," 295.

115. Marcia W. Posner, *Juvenile Judaica: The Jewish Values Book Finder* (New York: Association of Jewish Libraries, 1985).

116. Enid Davis, *A Comprehensive Guide to Children's Books with Jewish Themes* (New York: Schocken, 1982).

117. *Gale Encyclopedia of Multicultural America* (Detroit: Gale Group, 2000).

118. *Harvard Encyclopedia of American Ethnic Groups* (Cambridge, Mass.: Belknap Press of Harvard University, 1980).

119. Michael Kerestesi, "The Science of Bibliography: Theoretical Implications for Bibliographic Instruction," in *Theories of Bibliographic Education*, ed. Cerise Oberman and Katina Strauch (New York: Bowker, 1982), 1–26.

120. Langston Hughes, "I, Too, Sing America," in *American Negro Poetry*, edited by Arna Bontemps (New York: Hill and Wang, 1963), 64.

Bibliography

Abdallah, Devon Alisa. "Multiracial Arab Americans." In *Multiracial Child Resource Book*, edited by Maria P. P. Root and Matt Kelley. Seattle, Wash.: MAVIN Foundation, 2003.

"African American Web Connection." http://www.aawc.com/ (16 Nov. 2006).

Akwesasne Notes. Akwesasne Mohawk Territory, P.O. Box 366, via Rooseveltown, NY 13683-0196.

Alaska Native Knowledge Network. http://www.ankn.uaf.edu/ (16 Nov. 2006).

Allen, Adela Artola. *Library Services for Hispanic Children: A Guide for Public and School Librarians*. Phoenix, Ariz.: Oryx, 1987.

Allen, Paula Gunn. "Who Is Your Mother? Red Roots of White Feminism." In *The Graywolf Annual Five: Multicultural Literacy—Opening the American Mind*, edited by Rick Simonson and Scott Walker. St. Paul, Minn.: Graywolf Press, 1988.

Al-Qazzaz, Ayad. "Transnational Links between the Arab Community in the U.S. and the Arab World." ERIC Education Resources Information Center, ED 174525.

Alvarez, Julia. *How the Garcia Girls Lost Their Accents*. New York: Penguin, 1992.

Ambatchew, Michael Daniel. "Political Protest in Shitaye." *Bookbird* 43, no. 2 (2005): 23–29.

AMEA. "Recommended Readings." http://www.ameasite.org/biblio.asp (16 Nov. 2006).

———. "Useful Links." http://www.ameasite.org/links.asp (16 Nov. 2006).

Amerasia Journal. University of California, Los Angeles: Asian American Studies Center 1971.

American-Arab Anti-Discrimination Committee. "Arab American Students in Public Schools." http://www.adc.org/index.php?id=246&type=100 (16 Nov. 2006).

American Indian. Silver Spring, Md.: National Museum of the American Indian. http://www.nmai.si.edu/ (16 Nov. 2006).

American Indian Culture and Research Journal. University of California at Los Angeles, American Indian Studies Center, 322 Campbell Hall, P.O. Box 951548, Los Angeles, Calif. 90095.

American Indian Library Association (AILA). http://www.nativeculture.com/ lisamitten/aila.html (16 Nov. 2006).

American Indian Quarterly. University of Nebraska Press, 233 N. 8th St., Lincoln, Neb. 68588-0255.

American Legacy: Celebrating African American History and Culture. American Heritage, 28 W. 23rd St., New York, N.Y. 10010.

American Library Association (ALA). Ethnic Materials and Information Exchange Round Table (EMIERT). http://www.ala.org/template.cfm?section=emiert (16 Nov. 2006).

———. Ethnic Materials and Information Exchange Round Table (EMIERT). *EMIE Bulletin.* Now an insert in the *MultiCultural Review.*

American Library Association (ALA), Association for Library Services to Children (ALSC). "April 30 Is El Dia de los Niños: El Dia de Los Libros: How Will You Celebrate?" http://www.ala.org/ala/alsc/diadelosninos/diadelosninos.htm (27 Aug. 2005).

———. "Sharing Cultures: Asian American Children's Authors: A Selected Bibliography." *EMIE Bulletin* 19, no. 1 (Fall 2001): 10–15. Also http://www.ala.org/ala/ alsc/alscresources/booklists/sharingcultures.htm (16 Nov. 2006).

Andrews, William, Frances Smith Foster, and Trudier Harris, eds. *The Oxford Companion to African American Literature.* New York: Oxford University Press, 1997.

Aoki, Elaine. "Turning the Page: Asian Pacific American Children's Literature." In *Teaching Multicultural Literature in Grades K–8,* edited by Violet J. Harris, 109–36. Norwood, Mass.: Christopher-Gordon, 1993.

Appiah, Kwame Anthony, and Henry Louis Gates Jr., eds. *The Dictionary of Global Culture.* New York: Knopf, 1997.

Aronson, Marc. "A Mess of Stories." In *Stories Matter: The Complexity of Cultural Authenticity in Children's Literature,* edited by Dana L. Fox and Kathy G. Short, 78–83. Urbana, Ill.: National Council of Teachers of English, 2003.

Asante, Molefi Kete. *The Afrocentric Idea.* Philadelphia: Temple University Press, 1998.

———. *Afrocentricity: the Theory of Social Change.* (Chicago: African American Images, 2003).

Asia for Kids. P.O. Box 9096, Cincinnati, Ohio 45209-0096. http://www.afk.com/ (16 Nov. 2006).

Asian American Booksellers. 37 St. Mark's Place, New York, N.Y. 10003.

Asian American Curriculum Project (AACP). 414 East Third Ave., San Mateo, Calif. 94401. http://www.asianamericanbooks.com/ (16 Nov. 2005).

Asian American Movement Ezine. http://www.aamovement.net/ (16 Nov. 2006).

Asian American Policy Review. Harvard University, John F. Kennedy School of Government, 79 John F. Kennedy St., Cambridge, Mass. 02138.

"Asian American Studies: Origins, Identities, Crises." *Amerasia Journal* 29, no. 2 (2003): 165–228.

The Asian American Writers' Workshop. 16 West 32nd St., Suite 10A, New York, N.Y. 10001. http://www.aaww.org/ (16 Nov. 2006).

Asian Americans for Fair Media. *The Asian Image in the United States: Stereotypes and Realities.* ERIC Education Resources Information Center, ED 134643.

"Asian-Nation: 'The Landscape of Asian America.'" IMDiversity.com. http://www.imdiversity.com/eon/asiannation.asp (16 Nov. 2007).

Asociacion Mexicana para el Fomento del Libro Infantil y Juvenil A.C. (IBBY Mexico). *Guia de libros recomendados para niños y jovenes 2000 (Guide to Books Recommended for Children and Young People).* Mexico City: The Association, 2000.

Aspira. http://www.aspira.org / (16 Nov. 2006).

Association for Asian American Studies (AAAS). http://www.aaastudies.org/index.tpl (16 Nov 2006).

Association of MultiEthnic Americans (AMEA). P.O. Box 341304, Los Angeles, Calif. 90034-1304. http://www.ameasite.org (16 Nov. 2006).

———. "Recommended Readings." http://www.ameasite.org/biblio.asp (16 Nov. 2006).

———. "Useful Links." http://www.ameasite.org/links.asp (16 June 2006).

Astrolabe, LLC. 720 Plainfield Rd., Suite A, Willowbrook, Ill. 60527. http://www.astrolabe.com/ (16 Nov. 2006)

Atleo, Marlene, et al. "My Heart Is on the Ground and the Indian Boarding School Experience." *MultiCultural Review* 7, no. 1 (Sept. 1999): 34–43. Also in *Alternative Library Literature, 1998/1999*, 205–10. Jefferson, N.C.: McFarland, 2001.

Attebury, Nancy Garhan. "Bridging the Gap in Children's Literature for Asian American Youngsters." *The Delta Kappa Gamma Bulletin* 67, no. 2 (Winter 2001): 33–39.

"The Augusta Baker Collection of African American Children's Literature and Folklore." http://www.sc.edu/library/spcoll/kidlit/baker.html (16 Nov. 2006).

Aztlan: A Journal of Chicano Studies. University of California at Los Angeles, Chicano Studies Research Center Publications, 193 Haines Hall, Box 951544, Los Angeles, Calif. 90095-1544.

Bader, Barbara. "How the Little House Gave Ground: The Beginnings of Multiculturalism in a New Black Children's Literature." *The Horn Book Magazine* 78 (Nov./Dec. 2002): 657–73.

———. "Multiculturalism in the Mainstream." *The Horn Book Magazine* 79 (May/June 2003): 283–84.

———. "Multiculturalism Takes Root." *The Horn Book Magazine* 79 (Mar./Apr. 2003): 143–62, 284.

Badt, Karin. *Charles Eastman: Sioux Physician and Author.* New York: Chelsea House, 1995.

Bahous, Sally. *Sitti and the Cats: A Tale of Friendship.* Lanham, Md.: Roberts Rinehart Publishers, 1997.

Baker, Augusta. *The Black Experience in Children's Books.* New York: New York Public Library, 1971.

———. *Books about Negro Life for Children.* New York: New York Public Library, 1963.

———. "The Negro in Literature." *Child Study* 22 (Winter 1944–1945): 58, 63.

Bamyeh, Mohammed A. "The Middle East." In *Global Voices, Global Visions: A Core Collection of Multicultural Books,* by Lyn Miller-Lachmann, 501–38. New Providence, N.J.: Bowker, 1995.

Banfield, Beryl. "Commitment to Change: The Council on Interracial Books for Children and the World of Children's Books." *African American Review* 32, no. 1 (1998): 7–22.

Banks, James. *Cultural Diversity and Education: Foundations, Curriculum, and Teaching.* Boston: Pearson Allyn and Bacon, 2005.

———. *Multicultural Education: Issues and Perspectives.* New York: Wiley, 2002.

Banks, William M. *Black Intellectuals: Race and Responsibility in American Life.* New York: Norton, 1996.

Barahona Center for the Study of Books in Spanish for Children and Adolescents/ Centro Barahona para el Estudio de Libros Infantiles y Juveniles en Español. California State University, San Marcos, Kellogg Library, Fifth Floor, 333 S. Twin Oaks Valley Rd., San Marcos, Calif. 92096-0001. http://www.csusm.edu/csb (16 Nov. 2006).

Barrera, Rosalinda B., and Oralia Garza de Cortes. "Mexican American Children's Literature in the 1990s: Toward Authenticity." In *Using Multiethnic Literature in the K–8 Classroom,* edited by Violet J. Harris, 129–53. Norwood, Mass.: Christopher-Gordon, 1997.

Barrera, Rosalinda B., Olga Liguori, and Loretta Salas. "Ideas a Literature Can Grow On: Key Insights for Enriching Children's Literature about the Mexican American Experience." In Harris, *Teaching Multicultural Literature in Grades K–8,* 203–41.

Barrera, Rosalinda B., and Ruth E. Quiroa. "The Use of Spanish in Latino Children's Literature in English: What Makes for Cultural Authenticity." In Fox and Short, *Stories Matter,* 247–65.

Barrera, Rosalinda B., Ruth E. Quiroa, and Cassiette West-Williams. "Poco a Poco: The Continuing Development of Mexican American Children's Literature in the 1990s." *The New Advocate* 12, no. 4 (Fall 1999): 315–30.

Beilke, Patricia, and Frank J. Sciara. *Selecting Materials For and About Hispanic and East Asian Children and Young People.* Hamden, Conn.: Library Professional Publications, 1986.

Bell, Derrick. *And We Are Not Saved: The Elusive Quest for Racial Justice.* New York: Basic Books, 1992.

———. *Faces at the Bottom of the Well: The Permanence of Racism.* New York: Basic Books, 1989.

Bello, Yahaya. "Caribbean American Children's Literature." In Harris, *Teaching Multicultural Literature in Grades K–8,* 243–65.

Bennett, Christine. *Comprehensive Multicultural Education: Theory and Practice.* Boston: Pearson Allyn and Bacon, 2007.

Bennett, Christine, and Salman Al-Ani. "Muslims in the United States." In *Comprehensive Multicultural Education: Theory and Practice*, by Christine I. Bennett, 173–80. Boston: Pearson Allyn and Bacon, 2007.

Bennett, Lerone. *Before the Mayflower: A History of Black America.* Chicago: Johnson Publishing Company, 2003.

Berman, Joan. "Native American Children's Literature in the Classroom: An Annotated Bibliography." http://library.humboldt.edu/~berman/naclit.htm (16 Nov. 2006).

Berry, Wendell. "People, Land, and Community." In *The Graywolf Annual Five: Multicultural Literacy—Opening the American Mind,* eds. Rick Simonson and Scott Walker, 41–56. St. Paul, Minn.: Graywolf Press, 1988.

Bess Press. 3565 Harding Ave., Honolulu, Hawaii 96816. http://www.besspress.com/ (16 Nov. 2006).

Bhatnagar, Joti. *Educating Immigrants.* New York: St. Martin's Press, 1981.

Biagi, Shirley, and Marilyn Kern-Foxworth, eds. *Facing Difference: Race, Gender, and Mass Media.* Thousand Oaks, Calif.: Pine Forge Press, 1997.

Bishop, Rudine Sims. "Books from Parallel Cultures: New African American Voices." *The Horn Book Magazine* 68 (Sept./Oct. 1992): 616–20.

———. "Books from Parallel Cultures: What's Happening?" *The Horn Book Magazine* 70 (Jan./Feb.1994): 105–9.

———. "Evaluating Books By and About African Americans." In *The Multicolored Mirror: Cultural Substance in Literature for Children and Young Adults,* edited by Merri Lindgren, 31–34. Fort Atkinson, Wis.: Highsmith, 1991.

———. *Kaleidoscope: A Multicultural Booklist for Grades K–8.* Urbana, Ill.: National Council of Teachers of English, 1994, 1997, 2001, 2003.

———. "Retraining the Debate about Cultural Authenticity." In Fox and Short, *Stories Matter,* 25–37.

———. "Walk Tall in the World: African American Literature for Today's Children." *Journal of Negro Education* 59, no. 4 (1990): 556–65.

———. *See also* Sims (Bishop), Rudine.

Bishop, Rudine Sims, and Jonda McNair. "A Centennial Salute to Arna Bontemps, Langston Hughes and Lorenz Graham." *The New Advocate* 15, no. 2 (Spring 2002): 109–19.

Black, Barbara. *A Guide to Children's Books about Asian Americans.* Hants, England: Scholar Press, 1999.

Black Books Galore. 65 High Ridge Rd. #407, Stamford, Conn. 06905. http://www.blackbooksgalore.com/ (16 Nov. 2006).

The Black Collegian. 909 Poydras St., 34th Floor, New Orleans, La. 70112. http://www.blackcollegian.com/ (16 Nov. 2006).

Black History Bulletin. Association for the Study of African-American Life and History, Inc., 7961 Eastern Ave., Suite 301, Silver Spring, Md. 20910.

"Black History Quest: African American Resources." http://www.blackquest.com/ link.htm (16 Nov. 2006).

Black Issues Book Review. Cox, Matthews and Associates, 10520 Warwick Ave., Suite B-8, Fairfax, Va. 22030-3136. http://www.bibookreview.com/ (16 Nov. 2006).

Black Issues in Higher Education. 10520 Warwick Ave., Suite B-8, Fairfax, Va. 22030-3136. http://www.blackissues.com/. Replaced by *Diverse Issues in Higher Education.* http://www.diverseeducation.com/ (16 Nov. 2006).

Black Scholar: Journal of Black Studies and Research. Black World Foundation, P.O. Box 2869, Oakland, Calif. 94609.

Blasing, Rick. "Islam: Stereotypes Still Prevail." *Social Education* 60, no. 2 (Feb. 1996): 107–10.

Bloom, Allan. *The Closing of the American Mind: How Higher Education Has Failed Democracy and Impoverished the Souls of Today's Students.* New York: Simon and Schuster, 1987.

Bogle, Donald. *Toms, Coons, Mulattoes, Mammies, and Bucks: An Interpretive History of Blacks in American Films.* Third edition. New York: Continuum, 1994.

Bookbird. University of Toronto Press, 5201 Dufferin St., North York, ON, Canada M3H5T8.

Bradunas, Elena, developer, and Brett Topping, compiler and editor. *Ethnic Heritage and Language Schools in America.* Washington, D.C.: Library of Congress, The American Folklife Center, 1988.

Broderick, Dorothy. *Image of the Black in Children's Fiction.* New York: Bowker, 1973.

Brodie, Fawn. *Thomas Jefferson: An Intimate History.* New York: Norton, 1974.

Bruchac, Joseph. "All Our Relations: Native-American Multicultural Understanding." *The Horn Book Magazine* 71 (March/April 1995): 158–62.

Byler, Mary G. *American Indian Authors for Young Readers: A Selective Bibliography.* New York: Association of Indian Affairs, 1973.

Cai, Mingshui. "Can We Fly across Cultural Gaps on the Wings of Imagination?" *The New Advocate* 8, no. 1 (Winter 1995): 1–16. Revised and updated in Fox and Short, *Stories Matter,* 167–81.

———. "Images of Chinese and Chinese Americans Mirrored in Picture Books." *Children's Literature in Education* 25, no. 3 (1994): 169–91.

———. "Multiple Definitions of Multicultural Literature: Is the Debate Really Just 'Ivory Tower' Bickering?" *The New Advocate* 11, no. 4 (Fall 1998): 312. Revised and updated in Fox and Short, *Stories Matter,* 269–83.

Cajete, Gregory. *Look to the Mountain: An Ecology of Indigenous Education.* Durango, Colo.: Kivaki Press, 1994.

Caldwell-Wood, Naomi. "Native American Images in Children's Books." *School Library Journal* 38 (May 1992): 47–48.

Caldwell-Wood, Naomi, and Lisa A. Mitten. "'I' Is Not for Indian: The Portrayal of Native Americans in Books for Young People." *MultiCultural Review* 1, no. 2 (Apr. 1992): 26–35.

Callaloo: A Journal of African-American and African Arts and Letters. The Johns Hopkins University Press, Journals Publishing Division, 2715 N. Charles St., Baltimore, Md. 21218-4363.

Campbell, Patty. "The Sand in the Oyster." *The Horn Book Magazine* 70 (July–August 1994): 491–96.

Canadian Journal of Native Education. University of Alberta, Educational Policy Studies, 7-104 Education Centre, North Edmonton, AB T6G 2G5, Canada.

The Canadian Journal of Native Studies. Brandon University, Native Studies Department, Brandon, MB R7A 6A9, Canada.

Cannon, Katie Geneva. *Katie's Canon: Womanism and the Soul of the Black Community.* Chicago: Continuum International Publishing Group, 1997.

Canyon Records. 3131 W. Clarendon Ave., Phoenix, Ariz. 85017. http://www.canyonrecords.com/ (16 Nov. 2006).

Capan, Mary Ann. "Exploring Biracial/Biethnic Characters in Young Adult and Children's Books." *MultiCultural Review* 3, no. 4 (Dec. 1994): 14–19.

Capan, Mary Ann, and Cynthia Suarez. "Biracial/Biethnic Characters in Young Adult and Children's Books." *MultiCultural Review* 2, no. 2 (June 1993): 32–37.

Carger, Chris Liska. "Harriet Rohmer on New Voices and Visions in Multicultural Literature." *The New Advocate* 14, no. 2 (Spring 2001): 119–26.

Carter, Richard B., and Amelia E. El-Hindi. "Counseling Muslim Children in School Settings." *Professional School Counseling* 2, no. 3 (Feb. 1999): 183–88.

Center for Children's Books. "Gone but Not Forgotten: Augusta Braxton Baker." *The Bulletin of the Center for Children's Books.* http://alexia.lis.uiuc.edu/puboff/bccb/1000gone.html (16 Nov. 2006).

Center for the Study of Biracial Children. 2300 S. Kramaria St., Denver, Colo. 80222. http://www.csbchome.org/ (16 Nov. 2006).

Centro de Estudios Puertorriqueños at Hunter College City University of New York. *Guide to the Pura Belpré Papers.* http://centropr.org/lib-arc/faids/belpreb.html (16 Nov. 2006).

Challener, Daniel D. *Stories of Resilience in Childhood: The Narratives of Maya Angelou, Maxine Hong Kingston, Richard Rodriguez, John Edgar Wideman, and Tobias Wolff.* New York: Garland, 1997.

Champagne, Duane. "Education." In *The Native North American Almanac,* edited by Cynthia Rose and Duane Champagne, 991–1061. Second edition. Detroit: Gale, 2001.

Chang, Catherine E. Studier. "Yoshiko Uchida." *Language Arts* 61, no. 2 (Feb. 1984): 189–94.

Chang, Iris. *The Chinese in America: A Narrative History.* New York: Viking, 2003.

Chen, Shu-Hsien Lai. "Asian American Literature in School Libraries." *Journal of Educational Media and Library Services* 39, no. 3 (Mar. 2002): 251–68.

Cheng, Li-Rong Lilly. *Struggling to Be Heard: The Unmet Needs of Asian Pacific American Children.* Albany, N.Y.: SUNY Press, 1998.

Cheung, King-Kok. *An Interethnic Companion to Asian American Literature.* New York: Cambridge University Press, 1996.

Chideya, Farai. *The Color of Our Future.* New York: Morrow, 1999.

Children's Book Press. 2211 Mission St., San Francisco, Calif. 94110. http://www.childrensbookpress.org/ (16 Nov. 2006).

"Children's Books By and About People of Color Published in the United States: Statistics Gathered by the Cooperative Children's Book Center." http://www .education.wisc.edu/ccbc/books/pcstats.htm (16 Nov.2006).

China Books. 360 Swift Ave., South San Francisco, Calif. 94080. http://www.china-books.com/cart/home.php (16 Nov. 2006)

Chuh, Kandice, and Karen Shimakawa, eds. *Orientations: Mapping Studies in the Asian Diaspora*. Durham, N.C.: Duke University Press, 2001.

Cleary, Linda Miller, and Thomas D. Peacock. *Collected Wisdom: American Indian Education*. Boston: Pearson Education, 1997.

Collins, Patricia Hill. *Black Feminist Thought: Knowledge, Consciousness, and the Politics of Empowerment*. Second edition. New York: Routledge, 2000.

Colmenar, Gerardo. "Help by Subject—Asian-American Studies." http://www .library.ucsb.edu/subjects/asianamer/asian-am.html (16 Nov. 2006).

Colorline Magazine. Department W-100, 4096 Piedmont Ave., PMB 319, Oakland, Calif. 94611. http://www.arc.org/C_Lines/subscribe.html (16 Nov. 2006).

Cone, James H., and Gayraud S. Wilmore. *Black Theology: A Documentary History, 1980–1992*. Maryknoll, N.Y.: Orbis, 1993.

Consortium of Latin American Studies Programs (CLASP). "2005 Americas Award for Children and Young Adult Literature." http://www.uwm.edu/Dept/CLACS/pdf/ aa05.pdf (16 Nov. 2006)

Contacto: A Magazine for Today's Latino. 1317 N. San Fernando Blvd., PMB 246 Burbank, Calif. 91504.

Conyers, James L. Jr., ed. *Africana Studies: A Disciplinary Quest for Both Theory and Method*. Jefferson, N.C.: McFarland, 1997.

Cooperative Children's Book Center, School of Education, University of Wisconsin-Madison. "Small Presses Owned and Operated by People of Color: Publishers of Children's Books." http://www.education.wisc.edu/ccbc/books/pclist.htm (16 Nov. 2006).

Correspondents of the *New York Times. How Race Is Lived in America: Pulling Together, Pulling Apart*. New York: Henry Holt, 2003.

Council for Basic Education. *History in the Making: An Independent Review of the Voluntary National History Standard*. Washington, D.C.: The Council, 1996.

Council for Indian Education. 1240 Burlington Ave., Billings, Mont. 59102-4224. http://www.cie-mt.org/ (16 Nov. 2006).

The Council on Interracial Books for Children. 1841 Broadway, New York, N.Y. 10023.

———. "10 Quick Ways to Analyze Children's Books for Racism and Sexism." In *The New Press Guide to Multicultural Resources for Young Readers,* edited by Daphne Muse, 17–19. New York: The New Press, 1997. Also http://www .birchlane.davis.ca.us/library/10quick.htm (16 Nov. 2006).

———. "How Children's Books Distort the Asian American Image." *Interracial Books for Children Bulletin* 7, nos. 2–3 (1976/1977): 3–23.

———. *Human and Anti-Human Values in Children's Books*. New York: Racism and Sexism Resource Center For Educators, 1976.

———. *Stereotypes, Distortions and Omissions in U.S. History Textbooks: A Content Analysis Instrument for Detecting Racism and Sexism, Supplemental Information on Asian American, Black, Chicano, Native Americans, Puerto Rican, and Women's History.* New York: Racism and Sexism Resource Center for Educators, 1977.

———. *Teaching about Islam and Muslims in Public Schools.* Fountain Valley, Calif.: Council on Islamic Education.

———. *Unlearning Asian Stereotypes.* New York: Racism and Sexism Resource Center for Educators.

———. *Unlearning Indian Stereotypes: A Teaching Unit for Elementary Teachers and Children's Librarians.* New York: The Racism and Sexism Resource Center for Educators, 1977.

Council on Islamic Education. 9300 Gardenia St. #B-3, Fountain Valley, Calif. 92708. http://www.cie.org/ (16 Nov. 2006).

The Covenant with Black America. Chicago: Third World Press, 2006.

Crabtree, Charlotte A., National Council for History Standards, and National Center for History in the Schools. *Lessons from History: Understandings and Historical Perspectives Students Should Acquire.* Los Angeles, Calif.: UCLA, National Center for History in the Schools, 1992.

Crandall, JoAnn. *Teaching the Spanish-Speaking Child: A Practical Guide.* Washington, D.C.: Center for Applied Linguistics, 1989.

Craver, Kathleen W. "Bridging the Gap: Library Services for Immigrant Populations—Newly Arrived, Second and Third Generations, Guest Workers and Refugees." *Journal of Youth Services in Libraries* 4 (Winter 1991): 123–30.

Crazy Bull, Cheryl. "Decolonizing Research: Indigenous Scholars Can Take Over the Research Process." *Tribal College Journal* 16, no. 2 (Winter 2004): 14–15.

Crenshaw, Kimberlé, Neil Gotanda, Gary Peller, and Kendall Thomas, eds. *Critical Race Theory: The Key Writings That Formed the Movement.* New York: New Press, 1996.

The Crisis. Crisis Publishing Company. 4805 Mt. Hope Dr., Baltimore, Md. 21215.

The Critical Thinking Community. "A Brief History of the Idea of Critical Thinking." http://www.criticalthinking.org/aboutCT/briefHistoryCT.shtml (16 Nov. 2006).

Criticas. 369 Park Ave. South, New York, N.Y. 10010. http://www.criticasmagazine.com/ (16 Nov.. 2006).

Cross, William E. *Shades of Black: Diversity in African American Identity.* Philadelphia: Temple University Press, 1991.

Cruz, Barbara C., and Michael J. Berson. "The American Melting Pot? Miscegenation Laws in the United States." *OAH Magazine of History* 15, no 4 (Summer 2001). http://www.oah.org/pubs/magazine/family/cruz-berson.html (16 Nov. 2006).

Curtis, Sylvia. "Help by Subject—Resources in Black Studies." http://www.library.ucsb.edu/subjects/blackstudies/blac.html (16 Nov. 2006).

Dalmage, Heather. "Patrolling Racial Borders: Discrimination against Mixed Race People." In Root and Kelley, *Multiracial Child Resource Book,* 19–25.

Danticat, Edwidge. *Breath, Eyes, Memory.* New York: Vintage, 1998.

Darder, Antonia, and Rodolfo D. Torres. *The Latino Studies Reader: Culture, Economy, and Society.* Malden, Mass.: Blackwell Publishers, 1998.

Darder, Antonia, Rodolfo D. Torres, and Henry Gutiérrez. *Latinos and Education: A Critical Reader.* New York: Routledge, 1997.

Davis, Enid. *A Comprehensive Guide to Children's Books with a Jewish Theme.* New York: Schocken, 1982.

Day, Frances Ann. *Latina and Latino Voices in Literature: Lives and Works Updated and Expanded.* Westport, Conn.: Greenwood, 2003.

———. *Multicultural Voices in Contemporary Literature: A Resource for Teachers.* Portsmouth, N.H.: Heinemann, 1994.

Daybreak Star Press. 1945 Yale Pl., Seattle, Wash. 98102.

De la Terra, Tatiana. "International Book Fairs: La Major Via for Buying Books in Spanish." *REFORMA Newsletter* 23, no. 1 (Fall–Winter 2005): 1.

De León, Arnoldo. *They Called Them Greasers: Anglo Attitudes Toward Mexicans in Texas, 1821–1900.* Austin: University of Texas Press, 1983.

Delgado, Richard. *Critical Race Theory: The Cutting Edge.* Philadelphia: Temple University Press, 1999.

———. *Critical White Studies: Looking behind the Mirror.* Philadelphia: Temple University Press, 1997.

———. *The Latino/a Condition: A Critical Reader.* New York: New York University, 1998.

Deloria, Philip, and Neal Salisbury. *A Companion to American Indian History.* Malden, Mass.: Blackwell, 2004.

Deloria, Vine. *Custer Died for Your Sins: An Indian Manifesto.* New York: Macmillan, 1969.

———. *God Is Red.* New York: Grosset and Dunlap, 1973. Updated, 2003.

———. *Power and Place: Indian Education in America.* Golden, Colo.: Fulcrum Publishing, 2001.

———. *Spirit and Reason: The Vine Deloria Reader.* Golden, Colo.: Fulcrum, 1999.

Delpit, Lisa. *Other People's Children: Cultural Conflict in the Classroom.* New York: New Press, 1995.

Dent, David J. *In Search of Black America: Discovering the African-American Dream.* New York: Simon and Schuster, 2001.

Detroit Free Press. "100 Questions and Answers about Arab Americans: A Journalist's Guide." http://www.allied-media.com/Arab-American/100%20questions%20about%20arab%20americans.htm (16 Nov. 2006).

De Usabel, Francis. *American Indian Resource Materials for Public Libraries.* Madison: Wisconsin Department of Public Instruction, 1992.

"Diaspora." In *The Dictionary of Global Culture,* edited by Kwame Anthony Appiah and Henry Louis Gates Jr. New York: Knopf, 1997.

Dinnerstein, Leonard, Roger L. Nichols, and David M. Reimers, eds. *Natives and Strangers: A Multicultural History of Americans.* New York: Oxford University Press, 2003.

Dirlik, Arif. "Locating Asian American Studies Today: Origins, Identities, Crises." *Amerasia Journal* 29, no. 2 (2003): 166–69.

Diverse Issues in Higher Education. http://www.diverseeducation.com/ (16 Nov. 2006).

DownHomeBooks.com. "Ethiopian Books for Children." http://www.downhomebooks.com/featured.htm (16 Nov. 2006).

————. "Author Interviews: May 2003: Debbie Reese." http://www.downhomebooks.com/drinterview.htm (16 Nov. 2006).

Downing, Karen. "My Interracial Family." http://www-personal.umich.edu/~kdown/family.html (16 Nov. 2006).

DuBois, W. E. B. *The Souls of Black Folk.* Greenwich, Conn.: Fawcett, 1961.

Ebony. Johnson Publishing Company. 820 S. Michigan Ave., Chicago, Ill. 60605.

Eisenstadt, Peter. *Black Conservatism.* New York: Garland, 1998.

Elnour, Awatif, and Khadar Bashir-Ali. "Teaching Muslim Girls in American Schools." *Social Education* 67, no. 2 (Jan./Feb. 2003): 62–64.

Emerson, Gloria. "Foreword." In *Native American Picture Books of Change: The Art of Historic Children's Editions*, by Rebecca C. Benes, ix–xiv. Santa Fe: Museum of New Mexico Press, 2004.

Ethiopian Books for Children and Educational Foundation. P.O. Box 2677, Addis Ababa, Ethiopia. http://www.janekurtz.com/ebcef.html (16 Nov. 2006).

Evans, Eva Knox. "The Negro in Children's Fiction." *Publishers Weekly* 140 (August 30, 1941): 650–53.

Faces: The Magazine about People. Cobblestone Publishing, Carus Publishing Company, 30 Grove St., Suite C, Peterborough, N.H. 03458. http://www.cobblestonepub.com/magazine/FAC/ (16 Nov. 2006).

Facing History and Ourselves. National Foundation, 25 Kennard Rd., Brookline, Mass. 02146. http://facinghistory.org/ (16 Nov. 2006).

Faircloth, Susan C., and John W. Tippeconnic III. "Utilizing Research Methods that Respect and Empower Indigenous Knowledge." *Tribal College Journal* 16, no. 2 (Winter 2004): 24–27.

Fang, Zhihui, Danling Fu, and Linda L. Lamme. "Rethinking the Role of Multicultural Literature in Literacy Instruction: Problems, Paradox, Possibilities." *The New Advocate* 12, no. 3 (Summer 1999): 259–76. Revised and updated as "The Trivialization and Misuse of Multicultural Literature: Issues of Representation and Communication," in Fox and Short, *Stories Matter*, 284–303.

Faryna, Stan. *Black and Right.* New York: Praeger, 1997.

Fernández, Eduardo C. *La Cosecha: Harvesting Contemporary United States Hispanic Theology, 1972–1998.* Collegeville, Minn.: The Liturgical Press, 2000.

Fernandez, John. *The Diversity Advantage: How American Business Can Outperform Japanese and European Companies in the Global Marketplace.* New York: Lexington, 1993.

————. *Managing a Diverse Work Force: Regaining the Competitive Edge.* Lexington, Mass.: Lexington Books, 1971.

————. *Race, Gender and Rhetoric: The True State of Race and Gender Relations in Corporate America.* New York: McGraw-Hill, 1999.

Fine, Michelle. *Off White: Readings on Power, Privilege, and Resistance.* New York: Routledge, 2004.

Finkelman, Paul. "Jefferson and Slavery: Treason against the Hope of the World." In *Jeffersonian Legacies,* edited by Peter S. Onuf, 185–86. Charlottesville: University Press of Virginia, 1993.

Fishman, A. R. "Finding Ways in Redefining Multicultural Literature." *English Journal* 84, no. 6 (October 1995): 73–79.

Fixico, Donald. *The American Indian Mind in a Linear World.* New York: Routledge, 2003.

Foster, Michele. *Black Teachers on Teaching.* New York: New Press, 1997.

Fox, Dana L., and Kathy G. Short. "The Complexity of Cultural Authenticity in Children's Literature: Why the Debates Really Matter." In Fox and Short, *Stories Matter,* 3–24..

Fox, Dana L., and Kathy G. Short., eds. *Stories Matter: The Complexity of Cultural Authenticity in Children's Literature.* Urbana, Ill.: National Council of Teachers of English, 2003.

Fox, Geoffrey. *Hispanic Nation: Culture, Politics, and the Constructing of Identity.* Tucson: University of Arizona Press, 1977.

Franklin, John Hope. *Mirror to America: The Autobiography of John Hope Franklin.* New York: Farrar, Strauss, and Giroux, 2005.

Franklin, John Hope, and Alfred A. Moss Jr. *From Slavery to Freedom: A History of African Americans.* Eighth edition. New York: Knopf, 2000.

Frederickson, George M. *The Black Image in the White Mind: The Debate on Afro-American Character and Destiny, 1817–1914.* Hanover, N.H.: Wesleyan University Press, 1971.

Freeman, Evelyn B., and Barbara A. Lehman. *Global Perspectives in Children's Literature.* Boston: Allyn and Bacon, 2001.

Freeman, Yvonne S. "Providing Quality Children's Literature in Spanish." *The New Advocate* 11, no. 1 (Winter 1998): 23–38.

Freiband, Susan, and Consuelo Figueras. "Understanding Puerto Rican Culture: Using Puerto Rican Children's Literature." *MultiCultural Review* 11, no. 2 (June 2002): 30–34.

Galeano, Eduardo. "In Defense of the Word: Leaving Buenos Aires, June, 1976." In Simonson and Walker, *The Graywolf Annual Five,* 113–25. .

Gale Encyclopedia of Multicultural America. Detroit: Gale Group, 2000.

Garcia, Cristina. *Dreaming in Cuban.* New York: Ballantine Books, 1993.

Garcia, Eugene E. *Hispanic Education in the United States.* Summit, Penn.: Rowman and Littlefield, 2001.

Garrett, Jeffrey. "Islam and Other Belief Systems in West African Children's Books." *Bookbird* 35, no. 3 (Fall 1997): 21–25.

Gates, Henry. "'Authenticity,' or the Lesson of Little Tree." In Fox and Short, *Stories Matter,* 135–42.

Gates, Henry Louis Jr. *Loose Canons: Notes on the Culture Wars*. New York: Oxford University Press, 1992.

Gayle, Addison. *The Black Aesthetic*. Garden City, N.Y.: Doubleday, 1971.

Ghazi, Suhaib Hamid. *The Prophets of Allah*. Skokie, Ill.: IQRA International Education Foundation, 1995.

————. *Ramadan*. New York: Holiday House, 1994.

Gill, Jerry H. *Native American Worldviews: An Introduction*. Amherst, N.Y.: Humanity Books, 2002.

Gilliland, Hap. *Indian Children's Books*. Billings, Mont.: Montana Council for Indian Education, 1980.

————. *Teaching the Native American*. Dubuque, Iowa: Kendall/Hunt, 1992.

Gilton, Donna L. "Black Theology: Schools of Thought." *A.M.E. Church Review* 104, no. 34 (Apr.–June 1989): 25–38.

Glazer, Nathan. *Ethnic Dilemmas: 1964–1982*. Cambridge, Mass.: Harvard University Press, 1983.

————. *We Are All Multiculturalists Now*. Cambridge, Mass.: Harvard University Press, 1997.

Goldsea. "Asian American Bookview. Kids and Young Adults." http://goldsea.com/Bookview/Kids/kids.html (16 Nov. 2006).

————. *Asian American Daily*. http://www.goldsea.com/ (16 Nov. 2006).

Gomez-Pena, Guillermo. "Documented/Undocumented." In Simonson and Walker, *The Graywolf Annual Five*, 127–34.

Gonzalez, Juan. *Harvest of Empire: A History of Latinos in America*. New York: Penguin, 2001.

Gonzalez, Justo L. *Mañana: Christian Theology from a Hispanic Perspective*. Nashville, Tenn.: Abingdon Press, 1990.

Gonzalez-Jensen, Margarita. "The Status of Children's Fiction Literature Written in Spanish by U.S. Authors." *Bilingual Research Journal* 21, nos. 2–3 (Spring and Summer 1997): 203–12.

Gordon-Reed, Annette. *Thomas Jefferson and Sally Hemings: An American Controversy*. Charlottesville: University Press of Virginia, 1998.

Gorski, Paul. *Multicultural Education and the Internet*. McGraw-Hill, 2005. http://www.mhhe.com/socscience/education/multi_new/ (16 Nov. 2006).

Granello, Darcy Haag. *The Cultural Heritage of Arab Americans and Implications for Counseling*. ERIC Education Resources Information Center, ED 382904.

Granqvist, Raoul, and Jürgen Martini. *Preserving the Landscape of Imagination: Children's Literature in Africa*. Atlanta, Ga.: Rodopi, 1997.

Greenfield Review. 2 Middle Grove Rd., Greenfield Center, N.Y. 12833. http://www.nativeweb.org/pages/greenfield.html (16 Nov. 2006).

Griswold, William J. *The Image of the Middle East in Secondary School Textbooks*. ERIC Education Resources Information Center, ED 117013.

Grounds, Richard A., George E. Tinker, and David E. Wilkins. *Native Voices: American Indian Identity and Resistance*. Lawrence: University Press of Kansas, 2003.

Groundwood Books. 720 Bathurst St., Suite 500, Toronto, Ontario M5S 2R4, Canada. http://www.groundwoodbooks.com/ (16 Nov. 2006).

Guinier, Lani, and Gerald Torres. *The Miner's Canary: Enlisting Race, Resisting Power, Transforming Democracy.* Cambridge, Mass.: Harvard University Press, 2002.

Gutek, Gerald L. *Education in the United States: An Historical Perspective.* Englewood Cliffs, N.J.: Prentice-Hall, 1986.

Gutiérrez, David. *The Columbia History of Latinos in the United States since 1960.* New York: Columbia University Press, 2004.

Gwaltney, John Langston. *Drylongso: A Self-Portrait of Black America.* New York: Vintage, 1981.

Haiek, Joseph. *Arab American Almanac.* Glendale, Calif.: News Circle, 2003.

Hakim, Joy. *A History of Us.* 11 vols. New York: Oxford University Press, 2003.

———. *Freedom: A History of Us.* New York: Oxford University Press, 2003.

Hale, Janice E. *Black Children: Their Roots, Culture, and Learning Styles.* Baltimore, Md.: Johns Hopkins University Press, 1982.

———. *Learning While Black: Creating Educational Excellence for African American Children.* Baltimore: Johns Hopkins University Press, 2001.

Hall, Perry A. *In the Vineyard: Working in African American Studies.* Knoxville, Tenn.: University of Tennessee Press, 1999.

Hallford, Deborah, and Edgardo Zaghini, eds. *Outside In: Children's Books in Translation.* London: Milet Publishing, 2005.

Han, Arar, and John Hsu, eds. *Asian American X: An Intersection of Twenty-First Century Asian American Voices.* Ann Arbor: University of Michigan Press, 2004.

Hansen, Joyce. *I Thought My Soul Would Rise and Fly: The Diary of Patsy, a Freed Girl.* New York: Scholastic, 2003.

Harada, Violet H. "Caught between Two Worlds: Themes of Family, Community, and Ethnic Identity in Yoshiko Uchida's Work for Children." *Children's Literature in Education* 29, no. 1 (March 1998): 19–30.

———. "Issues of Ethnicity, Authenticity, and Quality in Asian-American Picture Books, 1983–93." *Journal of Youth Services in Libraries* 8 (Winter 1995): 135–49.

Harris, Angela. *Critical Race Theory: An Introduction.* New York: New York University Press, 2001.

Harris, Leonard, ed. *Philosophy Born of Struggle: Anthology of Afro-American Philosophy from 1917.* Dubuque, Iowa: Kendall Hunt Publishing Company, 2000.

Harris, Violet J. "African American Children's Literature: The First One Hundred Years." *Journal of Negro Education* 59, no. 4 (1990): 540–55.

———. "Children's Literature Depicting Blacks." In Harris, *Using Multiethnic Literature in the K–8 Classroom,* 21–58.

———. "Contemporary Griots: African American Writers of Children's Literature." In Harris, *Teaching Multicultural Literature in Grades K–8,* 55-108.

———, ed. *Teaching Multicultural Literature in Grades K–8.* Norwood, Mass.: Christopher-Gordon, 1993.

————, ed. *Using Multiethnic Literature in the K–8 Classroom.* Norwood, Mass.: Christopher-Gordon, 1997.

Harvard Encyclopedia of American Ethnic Groups. Cambridge, Mass.: Belknap Press of Harvard University, 1980.

Harvey, Karen D., Lisa D. Harjo, and Jane K. Jackson. *Teaching about Native Americans.* Washington, D.C.: National Council for the Social Studies, 1997.

Harvey, Karen D., Lisa D. Harjo, and Lynda Welborn. *How to Teach about American Indians: A Guide for the School Library Media Specialist.* Westport, Conn.: Greenwood, 1995.

Hayes-Bautista, David E. "Chicano Studies and the Academy: Opportunities Missed." *Aztlan* 25, no. 1 (Spring 2000): 183–85.

Heide, Florence Parry. *Day of Ahmed's Secret.* Scranton, Penn.: Harper Trophy, 1999.

————. *Sami and the Time of the Troubles.* Boston: Clarion Books, 1995.

Helbig, Alethea K. *This Land Is Our Land: A Guide to Multicultural Literature for Children and Young Adults.* Westport, Conn.: Greenwood, 1994.

Heller, Craig, Bruce Cunningham, Ginny Lee, and Hannah H. Heller. "Selecting Children's Picture Books with Positive Chinese, Japanese, and Other Asian and Asian American Fathers and Father Figures." *MultiCultural Review* 9, no. 4 (Dec. 2000): 22–73.

Hill, Christine M. *Ten Hispanic American Authors.* Berkeley Heights, N.J.: Enslow, 2002.

Hirsch, E. D., Jr. *Cultural Literacy: What Every American Needs to Know.* New York: Vintage, 1987.

————. *A First Dictionary of Cultural Literacy.* Boston: Houghton Mifflin, 1989.

————. *What Your Fifth Grader Needs to Know: Fundamentals of a Good Fifth-Grade Education.* Garden City, N.Y.: Doubleday, 2005.

————. *What Your First Grader Needs to Know: Fundamentals of a Good First-Grade Education.* Garden City, N.Y.: Doubleday, 1998.

————. *What Your Fourth Grader Needs to Know: Fundamentals of a Good Fourth-Grade Education.* Garden City, N.Y.: Doubleday, 2004.

————. *What Your Second Grader Needs to Know: Fundamentals of a Good Second-Grade Education Revised.* Garden City, N.Y.: Doubleday, 1999.

————. *What Your Sixth Grader Needs to Know: Fundamentals of a Good Sixth-Grade Education.* Garden City, N.Y.: Doubleday, 1995.

————. *What Your Third Grader Needs to Know: Fundamentals of a Good Third-Grade Education.* Garden City, N.Y.: Doubleday, 2002.

Hirsch, E. D., Jr., Joseph F. Kett, and James Trefil. *The Dictionary of Cultural Literacy: What Every American Needs to Know.* Boston: Houghton Mifflin, 1993.

Hirsch, E. D., Jr., Joseph Kett, and James Trefil. "What Literate Americans Know: A Preliminary List." In Hirsch, *Cultural Literacy: What Every American Needs to Know,* 146–215.

Hirschfelder, Arlene B. *American Indian Stereotypes in the World of Children: A Reader and Bibliography.* Metuchen, N.J.: Scarecrow, 1999.

————. "Native American Literature for Children and Young Adults." *Library Trends* 41, no. 3 (Winter 1993): 414–36.

Hirschfelder, Arlene, and Yvonne Beamer. *Native Americans Today: Resources and Activities for Educators: Grades 4–8.* Englewood, Colo.: Teacher Ideas Press, 2000.

Hispanic Magazine. http://www.hispaniconline.com/magazine/ (16 Nov. 2006).

HispanicOnline.com. http://www.hispaniconline.com/ (16 Nov. 2006).

The Hispanic Outlook in Higher Education. 210 Rt. 4E., Suite 310, Paramus, N.J. 07652.

History–Social Science Framework for California Public Schools: Kindergarten through Grade Twelve. Sacramento: California State Board of Education, 1988.

Hodge, David R. "Working with Muslim Youths: Understanding the Values and Beliefs of Islamic Discourse." *Children and Schools* 24, no. 1 (Jan. 2002): 6–20.

Holloway, Joseph E., ed. *Africanisms in American Culture.* Bloomington, Ind.: Indiana University Press, 1990.

Hooks, Bell. *Ain't I a Woman: Black Women and Feminism.* Boston, Mass.: South End Press, 1999.

Hoot, James, Tunde Szecsi, and Samina Moosa. "What Teachers of Young Children Should Know about Islam." *Early Childhood Education Journal* 31, no. 2 (Winter 2003): 85–90.

Hopkins, Dwight. *Introducing Black Theology of Liberation.* Maryknoll, N.Y.: Orbis Books, 1999.

Horning, Kathleen T. *Alternative Press Publishers of Children's Books: A Directory.* Madison, Wis.: Friends of the Cooperative Children's Book Center, 1992.

————. "The Contributions of Alternative Press Publishers to Multicultural Literature for Children." *Library Trends* 41, no. 3 (Winter 1993): 524–40.

————. "Recommended Picture Books Featuring Interracial Families." (26 June 2006). http://www.education.wisc.edu/ccbc/books/detailListBooks.asp?idBookLists=143.

Horning, Kathleen T., Merri V. Lindgren, Hollis Rudiger, Megan Schliesman, with Tana Elias. *CCBC Choices 2006.* Madison, Wis.: Cooperative Children's Book Center, School of Education, University of Wisconsin, 2006.

Howard, Gary R. *We Can't Teach What We Don't Know: White Teachers, Multiracial Schools.* Second edition. New York: Teachers College Press, 2006.

Hughes, Langston. *The Collected Works of Langston Hughes—Works for Children and Young Adults: Poetry, Fiction and Other Writing.* Columbia: University of Missouri, 2003.

————. *The Collected Works of Langston Hughes—Works for Children and Young Adults: Biographies.* Columbia: University of Missouri, 2001.

————. "I, Too, Sing America." In *American Negro Poetry*, edited by Arna Bontemps. New York: Hill and Wang, 1963.

Hull, Gloria T., Patricia Bell Scott, and Barbara Smith, *All the Women Are White, All the Blacks Are Men, But Some of Us Are Brave: Black Women's Studies.* New York: The Feminist Press at the City University of New York, 1982.

Hurh, Win Moo. *The Korean Americans.* Westport, Conn.: Greenwood, 1998.

Hyperion Books for Children. "Jump at the Sun." 114 Fifth Ave., New York, N.Y. 10011. http://www.hyperionbooksforchildren.com/jump/moreabout.asp (16 Nov. 2006).

"Immigration Act of 1965." http://en.wikipedia.org/wiki/Immigration_Act_of_1965 (16 Nov. 2006).

Immroth, Barbara, and Kathleen de la Peña McCook. *Library Services to Youth of Hispanic Heritage*. Jefferson, N.C.: McFarland, 2000.

The Independent American Indian Review. PMB 268, 1840 E. Warner Rd., Suite A105 Tempe, Ariz. 85284. http://www.worldviewsintl.com/iair/ (16 Nov. 2006).

Indian Country Today. 3059 Seneca Turnpike, Canastota, N.Y. 13032.

Indian Historian Press. American Indian Historical Society. 1493 Masonic Ave., San Francisco, Calif. 94117. http://www.americanindian.ucr.edu/unique_heritage/historian_press/index.html (16 Nov. 2006).

The Institute of Islamic Information and Education. P.O. Box 410129, Chicago, Ill. 60641. http://www.iiie.net/Home/tabid/36/Default.aspx (16 Nov. 2006).

International Board on Books for Young People (IBBY). Nonnenweg 12, Postfach, CH-4003, Basel, Switzerland. http://www.ibby.org/ (16 Nov. 2006).

————. *Bookbird,* Anne Marie Corrigan, Bookbird Subscriptions, University of Toronto Press, 5201 Dufferin St., North York, ONT M3H 5T8, Canada. http://www.ibby.org/index.php?id=276 (16 Nov. 2006).

"The International Indigenous Librarians' Forum." http://www.5iilf.org/ (26 June 2006).

Internet Public Library (IPL). Pathfinder. "Resources For and About Multiracial/Multiethnic Americans." http://www.ipl.org/div/pf/entry/48507 (16 Nov. 2006).

Interracial Voice. http://www.webcom.com/~intvoice/ (16 Nov. 2006).

————. "Book Reviews http://www.interracialvoice.com/ (26 Mar. 2007).

The Islamic Foundation of North America. http://www.islamicedfoundation.com/ (16 Nov. 2006).

————. "Book Reviews." http://www.islamicedfoundation.com/bookreviews/book.htm (23 Aug. 2005).

————. "Muslim Book/Video Suppliers," http://www.islamicedfoundation.com/serv03.htm (23 Aug. 2005).

Isom, Bess A., and Carolyn P. Casteel. "Hispanic Literature: A Fiesta for Literacy Instruction." *Childhood Education* 74 (Winter 1997–1998): 83–89.

Jackson, Blyden. *A History of Afro-American Literature,* v. 1, *The Long Beginning, 1746–1895*. Baton Rouge: Louisiana State University Press, 1989.

James, Joy. *The Black Feminist Reader*. Malden, Mass.: Blackwell, 2000.

Japanese American Cultural and Community Center. http://www.jaccc.org/jaccc/library.html (22 Aug. 2005).

Jefferson, Thomas. *Notes on the State of Virginia*. Chapel Hill: University of North Carolina Press, 1995.

Jenkins, Esther, and Mary C. Austin. *Literature for Children about Asians and Asian Americans*. Westport, Conn.: Greenwood, 1987.

Jensen, Robert. *The Heart of Whiteness: Confronting Race, Racism, and White Privilege*. San Francisco: City Lights Publisher, 2005.

Jet. Johnson Publishing Company, 820 S. Michigan Ave., Chicago, Ill. 60605.

Jewish Library Association. "Excellence in Jewish Children's Literature: A Guide for Book Selectors, Reviewers and Awards Judges." http://www.jewishlibraries.org/ajlweb/publications/excellence.pdf (16 Nov. 2006)

————. "The New Jewish Value Finder: A Guide to Values in Jewish Children's Books." http://www.ajljewishvalues.org/ (22 Aug. 2005).

Johnson, Dianne. "The Langston Hughes, Arna Bontemps Legacy: Historical Fiction, Realistic Fiction and the American Dream." In *Telling Tales: The Pedagogy and Promise of African American Literature for Youth*, by Johnson, 39–79. New York: Greenwood, 1990.

————. *Telling Tales: The Pedagogy and Promise of African American Literature for Youth*. New York: Greenwood, 1990.

Johnson-Feelings, Dianne. "Children's and Young Adult Literature." In *The Oxford Companion to African American Literature*, edited by William L. Andrews, Frances Smith Foster, and Trudier Harris, 133–40. New York: Oxford University Press, 1997.

Jones, Cherri. "East Asian Indian Children in America." *EMIE Bulletin* 17, no. 3 (Spring 2000): 16–17.

Jones, Eugene H.. *Native Americans as Shown on the Stage: 1753–1916*. Metuchen, N.J.: Scarecrow Press, 1988.

Jordan, Winthrop. *The White Man's Burden: Historical Origins of Racism in the United States*. Chapel Hill: University of North Carolina Press, 1995.

————. *White Over Black: American Attitudes towards the Negro, 1550–1812*. Chapel Hill: University of North Carolina Press, 1995.

Josephy, Alvin M. *500 Nations: An Illustrated History of North American Indians*. New York: Gramercy, 2002.

Journal of American Indian Education. Center for Indian Education, College of Education, Arizona State University, Box 871311, Tempe, Ariz. 85287. http://jaie.asu.edu/ (22 Aug. 2005).

Journal of Asian American Studies. The Johns Hopkins University Press, Journal Publishing Division, 2715 N. Charles St., Baltimore, Md. 21218-4363.

The Journal of Blacks in Higher Education. 200 W. 57th St., 15th Floor, New York, N.Y. 10019. http://www.jbhe.com/ (16 Nov. 2006).

The Journal of Negro Education. P.O. Box 311, Howard University, Washington, D.C. 20059. http://www.journalnegroed.org/ (16 Nov. 2006).

Jupp, James. "Beyond the Folkloric and Indigenous in Multicultural Thinking about Latin America." *MultiCultural Review* 11, no. 1 (March 2002): 22–29.

————. "The Necessity of a Multicultural Teaching Canon and the Mexican American Novel." *MultiCultural Review* 9, no. 4 (Dec. 2000): 38–41.

Just Us Books. 356 Glenwood Ave., East Orange, N.J. 07017. http://www.justusbooks.com/ (22 Aug. 2005).

Kahani: A South Asian Literary Magazine for Children. P.O. Box 590155, Newton Centre, Mass. 02459. http://www.kahani.com (23 Aug. 05).

Kallen, Horace. *Culture and Democracy in the United States*. New York: Boni and Liveright, 1924.

Kanellos, Nicolás. *Herencia: The Anthology of Hispanic Literature of the United States*. New York: Oxford University Press, 2003.

Kanellos, Nicolás, and Claudio Esteva-Fabregat, eds. *The Handbook of Hispanic Cultures in the United States*. Houston, Tex.: Arte Publico Press, 1994.

Katz, Ilan. *The Construction of Racial Identity in Children of Mixed Parentage: Mixed Metaphors*. London: Jessica Kingsley Publishers, 1996.

Kelley, Robin D. G., and Earl Lewis, eds. *To Make Our World Anew: The History of African Americans*. New York: Oxford University Press, 2000.

Kenan, Randall. *Walking on Water: Black American Lives at the Turn of the Twenty-First Century*. New York: Knopf, 1999.

Kendall, Frances E.. *Understanding White Privilege: Creating Pathways to Authentic Relationships across Race*. New York: Routledge, 2002.

Kerestesi, Michael. "The Science of Bibliography: Theoretical Implications for Bibliographic Instruction." In *Theories of Bibliographic Education,* edited by Cerise Oberman and Katina Strauch, 1–26. New York: Bowker, 1982.

Khan, Rukhsana. *Dahling, If You Luv Me, Would You Please, Please Smile*. Toronto and New York: Stoddart Kids, 1999. Rebound by Sagebrush, 2001.

———. *Muslim Child: Understanding Islam through Stories and Poems*. Morton Grove, Ill.: Albert Whitman and Co., 2002.

———. "Children's Books with Muslim and Other Themes." Rukhsanakhan.com. http://www.rukhsanakhan.com/muslimbooks.htm (28 Aug. 2005).

Khorana, Meena. *Africa in Literature for Children and Young Adults: An Annotated Bibliography of English-Language Books*. Westport, Conn.: Greenwood, 1994.

———. "Break Your Silence: A Call to Asian Indian Children's Writers." *Library Trends* 41, no. 3 (Winter 1993): 393–413.

———. *The Indian Subcontinent in Literature for Children and Young Adults: An Annotated Bibliography of English Language Books*. Westport, Conn.: Greenwood, 1991.

Khorana, Meena, ed. *Critical Perspectives on Postcolonial African Children's and Young Adult Literature*. Westport, Conn.: Greenwood, 1998.

Kibler, John M. "Latino Voices in Children's Literature: Instructional Approaches for Developing Cultural Understanding in the Classroom." In *Children of La Frontera: Binational Efforts to Serve Mexican Migrant and Immigrant Students*, edited by Judith LeBlanc Flores, 239–68. ERIC Education Resources Information Center, ED 393644.

Kim, Elaine. *Asian American Literature*. Philadelphia, Penn.: Temple University Press, 1984.

King, Joyce E. *Black Education: A Transformative Research and Action Agenda for the New Century*. Mahwah, N.J.: Lawrence Erlbaum Associates, 2005.

Kohl, Herbert. *The Discipline of Hope: Learning from a Lifetime of Teaching*. New York: New Press, 1998.

Krishnaswami, Uma. "Common Errors in American Children's Books with South Asian Characters or Content." http://www.umakrishnaswami.com/commonerrors.html (16 Nov. 2006).

————. "Interviews with Children's/YA Writers of South Asian Origin." http://www
.umakrishnaswami.com/interviews.html (22 Aug. 2005).

————. "On the Seashore of Worlds: Selected South Asian Voices from North America and the United Kingdom." *Bookbird* 42, no. 2 (April 2004): 23–37.

————. "South Asia in Children's Literature." http://www.umakrishnaswami.com/
southasia.html (16 Nov. 2006).

————. "South Asian Voices with North American Accents." PaperTigers.org. http://
www.papertigers.org/personalViews/archiveViews/UKrishnaswami.html (16 Nov.
2006).

Kruse, Ginny Moore, Kathleen T. Horning, and Megan Schliesman. *Multicultural Lit-
erature for Children and Young Adults: A Selected Listing of Books By and About
People of Color.* Madison, Wis.: Cooperative Children's Book Center, 1991. ERIC
Education Resources Information Center, ED 418710.

Kuipers, Barbara J. *American Indian Reference Books for Children and Young Adults.*
Englewood, Colo.: Libraries Unlimited, 1991.

Kutenplon, Deborah, and Ellen Olmstead. *Young Adult Fiction by African American
Writers, 1968–1993.* New York: Garland, 1996.

Ladson-Billings, Gloria. *Beyond the Big House: African American Educators on
Teacher Education.* New York: Teachers College Press, 2005.

————. *The Dreamkeepers: Successful Teachers of African American Children.* San
Francisco: Jossey Bass, 1994.

Lai, Him Mark. "Retention of the Chinese Heritage, Part II: Chinese Schools in
America, World War II to Present." *Chinese America: History and Perspectives.*
(2001): 1–30.

Laird, Elizabeth. "Stories from the Source of the Nile: Collecting Stories in Ethiopia."
Bookbird 43, no. 1 (2005): 21–27.

Larrick, Nancy. "The All-White World of Children's Books." *Saturday Review* 48
(September 11, 1965): 63–65, 84–85. Also in Muse, *The New Press Guide to Multicultural Resources for Young Readers*, 19–25.

Lasky, Kathryn. "To Stingo with Love: An Author's Perspective on Writing Outside
One's Culture." In Fox and Short, *Stories Matter*, 84–92.

Latin American Network Information Center (LANIC). http://www1.lanic.utexas
.edu/. (26 June 2006).

Latino Leaders: The National Magazine of the Successful Hispanic American.
Ferraez Publications of America, Corp. Invierno 16, Merced Gomez, 01600
Mexico.

Latino(a) Research Review. State University of New York at Albany, Center for
Latino, Latin American, and Caribbean Studies (CELAC), SS247, Albany, N.Y.
12222.

Leavell, Judy A., Barbara Hatcher, Jennifer Battle, and Nancy Ramos-Michael.
"Exploring Hispanic Culture through Trade Books." *Social Education* 66, no. 4
(May/June 2002): 210–15.

Lebon, Cecile. "The French-Language African Novel for Young People." *Bookbird*
42, no. 3 (2004): 10–18.

Lee, Jung Young. *Marginality: The Key to Multicultural Theology.* Minneapolis, Minn.: Augsberg Fortress, 1995.

Lee, Philip. "Multicultural Book Publishing." Children's Book Council. http://www.cbcbooks.org/cbcmagazine/perspectives/multicultural_book_publishing.html (23 Aug. 2005).

Lee and Low Books. 95 Madison Ave., Suite #606, New York, N.Y. 10016. http://www.leeandlow.com/home/index.html (22 Aug. 2005).

Lems, Kristin. "The Arab World and Arab Americans." *Book Links* 9, no. 2 (Nov. 1999): 31. http://www.ala.org/ala/booklinksbucket/arabworld.htm (25 Aug. 2005).

Leu, Shao-yi. "Reimagining a Pluralistic Society through Children's Fiction about Asian Pacific Americans." *The New Advocate* 14, no. 2 (Spring 2001): 127–42.

Lewis, Jan, and Peter Onuf, eds. *Sally Hemings and Thomas Jefferson: History, Memory, and Civic Culture.* Charlottesville: University Press of Virginia, 1999.

Lind, Beth Beutler. *Multicultural Children's Literature: An Annotated Bibliography K–8.* Jefferson, N.C.: McFarland, 1996.

Lindgren, Merri V., ed. *The Multicolored Mirror: Cultural Substance in Literature for Children and Young Adults.* Fort Atkinson, Wis.: Highsmith, 1991.

Lindsay, Nina. "'I' Still Isn't for Indian." *School Library Journal* 49, no. 11 (November 2003): 42–43.

Littlejohn, Carol. "Journey to J'Burg." *Voice of Youth Advocates (VOYA)* 19 (October, 1996): 199–200.

Liu, Eric. *The Accidental Asian: Notes of a Native Speaker.* New York: Vintage, 1999.

Lo, Suzanne, and Ginny Lee. "Asian Images in Children's Books: What Stories Do We Tell Our Children?" *Emergency Librarian* 20 (May–June 1993): 14–18.

Lundquist, Suzanne Evertsen. *Native American Literatures: An Introduction.* Chicago: Continuum International Publishing Group, 2004.

MacCann, Donnarae. "Native Americans in Books for the Young." In Harris, *Teaching Multicultural Literature in Grades K–8*, 137–69.

———. *White Supremacy in Children's Literature: Characterizations of African Americans, 1830–1900.* New York: Routledge, 2000.

MacCann, Donnarae, and Yulisa Amadu Maddy. *Apartheid and Racism in South African Children's Literature, 1985–1995.* New York: Routledge, 2001.

MacCann, Donnarae, and Olga Richard. "Picture Books and Native Americans: An Interview with Naomi Caldwell-Wood." *Wilson Library Journal* 67 (February 1993): 30–34.

MacCann, Donnarae, and Gloria Woodard. *The Black American in Books for Children.* Metuchen, N.J.: Scarecrow, 1972.

MacCann, Donnarae, and Gloria Woodard. *Cultural Conformity in Books for Children: Further Readings in Racism.* Metuchen, N.J.: Scarecrow Press, 1977.

MacDonald, Victoria-Maria, ed. *Latino Education in the United States: A Narrated History from 1513–2000.* New York: Palgrave Macmillan, 2004.

Macmillan Caribbean. "Books, General Interest, Children's Books." http://www.macmillan-caribbean.com/books/General/childrenpic.htm (16 Nov. 2006).

Maddy, Yulisa Amadu. "Ambivalent Signals in South African Young Adult Novels."
    Bookbird 36, no. 1 (Spring 1998): 27–32.
Maddy, Yulisa Amadu, and Donnarae MacCann. *African Images in Juvenile Litera-
    ture: Commentaries on Neocolonialist Fiction*. Jefferson, N.C.: McFarland, 1996.
Magill, Frank N., ed. *Masterpieces of African-American Literature: Descriptions, Anal-
    yses, Characters, Plots, Themes, Critical Evaluations, and Significance of Major
    Works of Fiction, Nonfiction, Drama, and Poetry*. New York: Harper Collins, 1992.
Manijeh, Daneshpour. "Muslim Families and Family Therapy." *Journal of Marital
    and Family Counseling* 24, no. 3 (July 1998): 355–68.
Manning, M. Lee, and Leroy G. Baruth. *Multicultural Education of Children and
    Adolescents*. Boston: Pearson Allyn and Bacon, 2003.
Manning, M. Lee, and Leroy G. Baruth. "Understanding Arab American Children and
    Adolescents." In *Multicultural Education of Children and Adolescents*, by Man-
    ning and Baruth, 111–32. Boston: Pearson Allyn and Bacon, 2004.
Maples, Don, prod. *The Inaugural World Christian Gathering on Indigenous People*.
    The Whole World Network, 1997.
Mar, M. Elaine. *Paper Daughter*. New York: Harper Perennial, 2000.
Marantz, Sylvia, and Kenneth Marantz. *Multicultural Picture Books: Art for Under-
    standing Others*. Worthington, Ohio: Linworth Publishing, 1994.
Marshall, Paule. *Brown Girl, Brownstones*. New York: The Feminist Press at City
    University of New York, 2006.
Marston, Elsa. "The Middle East and North Africa." In *Our Family, Our Friends,
    Our World: An Annotated Guide to Significant Multicultural Books for Children
    and Teenagers*, edited by Lyn Miller-Lachmann, 381–416. New Providence, N.J.:
    Bowker, 1992.
The Mashantucket Pequot Children's Library. 110 Pequot Trail, P.O. Box 3180,
    Mashantucket, Conn. 06339. http://www.pequotmuseum.org/Home/Libraries
    Archives/CHILDRENSLIBRARY/AboutTheChildrensLibrary.htm (16 Nov. 2006).
Mashantucket Pequot Museum and Research Center. http://www.pequotmuseum
    .org/Home/ (26 Mar.. 2006).
Matsuoka, Fumitaka, and Eleazar S. Fernandez, eds. *Realizing the America of Our
    Hearts*. St. Louis, Mo.: Chalice Press, 2003.
Matthews, Mary. *Magid Fasts for Ramadan*. Boston: Clarion Books, 2000.
MAVIN Foundation. 600 First Ave., Suite 600, Seattle, Wash. 98104. http://www
    .mavinfoundation.org (16 Nov. 2006).
Mbiti, John. *African Religions and Philosophy*. Garden City, N.Y.: Doubleday, 1970.
McClain, Margy. "Polish Saturday Schools." In *Ethnic Heritage and Language
    Schools in America*, developed by Elena Bradunas and compiled and edited by
    Brett Topping, 138–55. Washington, D.C.: Library of Congress, The American
    Folklife Center, 1988.
McNair, Jonda. "'He May Mean Good, But He Do So Doggone Poor!': A Critical
    Analysis of Recently Published 'Social Conscience' Children's Literature." *Multi-
    Cultural Review* 12, no. 1 (March 2003): 26–32.
McWhorter, John. *Authentically Black*. New York: Gotham, 2004.

Medina, Carmen. "When Jerry Springer Visits Your Classroom: Teaching Latina Literature in a Contested Ground." *Theory into Practice* 40, no. 3 (Summer 2001): 198–204.

Medina, Carmen L., and Patricia Encisco. "'Some Words Are Messengers/Hay Palabras Mensajeras': Interpreting Sociopolitical Themes in Latino/a Children's Literature." *The New Advocate* 15, no. 1 (Winter 2002): 35–47.

Meier, Deborah. *The Power of Their Ideas: Lessons for America from a Small School in Harlem.* Boston: Beacon Press, 1995.

Mena, Maria. "Library Outreach to Hispanic Children." The Children's Book Council. http://www.cbcbooks.org/cbcmagazine/perspectives/library_outreach_to _hispanic_c.html (16 Nov. 2006).

Mendoza, Jean. "Becoming a Voice: A Conversation with George Littlechild, Illustrator." *The New Advocate* 14, no. 4 (Fall 2001): 321–27.

Mihesuah, Devon A. *Indigenizing the Academy: Transforming Scholarship and Empowering Communities.* Lincoln, Neb.: Bison Books, 2004.

———. *Natives and Academics: Researching and Writing about American Indians.* Lincoln: University of Nebraska Press, 1998.

———. *So You Want to Write about American Indians?: A Guide for Writers, Students, and Scholars.* Lincoln, Neb.: Bison Books, 2005.

Mikkelson, Nina. "Insiders, Outsiders, and the Questions of Authenticity: Who Shall Write for African American Children?" *African American Review* 32, no. 1 (1998): 33–49.

Miller-Lachmann, Lyn. *Global Voices, Global Visions: A Core Collection of Multicultural Books.* New Providence, N.J.: Bowker, 1995.

———. *Our Family, Our Friends, Our World: An Annotated Guide to Significant Multicultural Books for Children and Teenagers.* New Providence, N.J.: Bowker, 1992.

Mitchem, Stephanie Y. *Introducing Womanist Theology.* Maryknoll, N.Y.: Orbis Books, 2002.

Mitten, Lisa. "Native American Nations." http://www.nativeculture.com/lisamitten/nations.html (16 Nov. 2006).

Mo, Weimin, and Wenju Shen. "Accuracy Is Not Enough: The Role of Cultural Values in the Authenticity of Picture Books." In Fox and Short, *Stories Matter*, 198–212.

Molloy, Molly, comp. "Andanzas al Web Latino." http://lib.nmsu.edu/subject/bord/latino.html (16 Nov. 2006).

Monolid Magazine. 368 Broadway, Suite 516, New York, N.Y. 10013.

Montgomery County Public Schools. "Arab American Heritage Month." http://www.mcps.k12.md.us/departments/oipd/diversity/arabamatvs.html (16 Nov. 2006).

Morales, Ed. *Living in Spanglish: The Search for Latino Identity in America.* New York: St. Martin's Griffin, 2003.

Moreillon, Judi. "The Candle and the Mirror: One Author's Journey as an Outsider." *The New Advocate* 12, no. 2 (Spring 1999): 127–40. Revised and updated in Fox and Short, *Stories Matter*, 61–77.

Morris, Liz, and Susanna Coghlan, eds. *Cross-Currents: A Guide to Multicultural Books for Young People*. Dublin: IBBY Ireland, 2005.

Mosley, Walter, Manthia Diawara, Clyde Taylor, and Regina Austin, eds. *Black Genius: African American Solutions to African American Problems*. New York: Norton, 1999.

Multicultural Distribution Center. 800 N. Grand Ave., Covina, Calif. 91724.

Multicultural Education Journal. Alberta Teachers' Association, Multicultural Education, 11010 142nd St., Edmonton, T5N 2R1 Alberta, Canada.

Multicultural Kids. http://www.multiculturalkids.com/ (16 Nov. 2006).

The MultiCultural Review. 14497 N. Dale Mabry Highway, Suite 205N, Tampa, Fla. 33618. http://www.mcreview.com/ (16 Nov. 2006).

The Multiracial Activist. http://www.multiracial.com/ (28 Aug. 2005).

Mura, David. "Strangers in the Village." In Simonson and Walker, *The Graywolf Annual Five*, 135–53.

Murphy, Barbara Thrash. *Black Authors and Illustrators of Books for Children and Young Adults: A Biographical Dictionary*. New York: Garland, 1999.

Muse, Daphne. "Black Children's Literature: The Birth of a Neglected Genre." *The Black Scholar* 7, no. 4 (December 1975): 11–15.

———. "Ebony Voices and Cowrie Shell Dreams: Black American Classics in Fiction and Poetry for Young Readers." In Muse, *The New Press Guide to Multicultural Resources for Young Readers*, 320–26. New York: New Press, 1997.

———. *The New Press Guide to Multicultural Resources for Young Readers*. New York: New Press, 1997.

Myers, Walter Dean. "I Actually Thought We Would Revolutionize the Industry." *New York Times Book Review*, 9 Nov. 1986.

Nabokov, Peter. *A Forest of Time: American Indian Ways of History*. New York: Cambridge University Press, 2002.

Nakanishi, Don T. "Crossing Borders: 35 Years of Asian American Studies and the New UCLA Department of Asian American Studies." *Amerasian Journal* 30, no. 3 (2005): ii–vii.

Nakanishi, Don T., and Tina Yamano Nishida, eds. *The Asian American Educational Experience: A Sourcebook for Teachers and Students*. New York: Routledge, 1994.

Nam, Vickie. *YELL-Oh Girls: Emerging Voices Explore Culture, Identity and Growing Up Asian American*. New York: Harper Paperbacks, 2001.

Nash, Gary B. "American History Reconsidered: Asking New Questions about the Past." In *Learning from the Past: What History Teaches Us about School Reform*, edited by Diane Ravitch and Maris A. Vinovskis, 137–42. Baltimore, Md.: Johns Hopkins University Press, 1995.

National Association for Multicultural Education (NAME). 733 Fifteenth St. NW, Suite 430, Washington, D.C. 20005. http://www.nameorg.org (16 Nov. 2006).

———. *Multicultural Perspectives*. Lawrence Erlbaum Associates, 10 Industrial Ave., Mahwah, N.J. 07430.

National Council of Teachers of English (NCTE). "The Eighteenth National African American Read-In." http://www.ncte.org/prog/readin/107901.htm (16 Nov. 2006).

National Institute for Technology and Liberal Education Arab World Project. "Arab Culture and Civilization." http://arabworld.nitle.org/ (26 June 2006).

Native American Authors Distribution Project. The Greenwood Review Press, 2 Middle Grove Rd., P.O. Box 308, Greenfield Center, N.Y. 12833. http://www.nativeweb.org/pages/greenfield.html (16 Nov. 2006). *See also* North American Native Authors Project.

Native American Times. Oklahoma Indian Times, Inc., Box 692050, Tulsa, Okla. 74169.

Native Americas: Hemispheric Journal of Indigenous Issues. First Nations Development Institute, 2300 Fall Hill Ave., Suite 412, Fredericksburg, Va. 22401. http://www.firstnations.org (16 Nov. 2006).

Native Peoples: Arts and Lifeways. Media Concepts Group, Inc., 5333 N. Seventh St., Suite C 224, Phoenix, Ariz. 85014.

Native Writers' Circle of the Americas. http://www.ou.edu/cas/nas/writers.html (16 Nov. 2006).

Native Youth Magazine. http://www.nativeyouthmagazine.com/ (16 Nov. 2006).

The New Advocate. Christopher-Gordon Publishers, 1502 Providence Highway, Suite 12, Norwood, Mass. 02062.

Newberry Library. D'Arcy McNickle Center for American Indian History, 60 West Walton St., Chicago, Ill. 60610-3380. http://www.newberry.org/mcnickle/darcyhome.html (16 Nov. 2005).

New York Public Library Office of Special Services. Chinese Heritage Booklist Committee. "Chinese Heritage: Chinese American Experience in the United States." *EMIE Bulletin* (Spring 1995): 6.

New York State Social Studies Review and Development Committee. *One Nation, Many Peoples: A Declaration of Cultural Interdependence.* Albany, N.Y.: New York State Education Department, 1991.

Nieto, Sonia. "We Have Stories to Tell: A Case Study of Puerto Ricans in Children's Books." In Harris, *Teaching Multicultural Literature in Grades K–8,* 171–202.

Nieto, Sonia. "We Have Stories to Tell: Puerto Ricans in Children's Books." In Harris, *Using Multiethnic Literature in the K–8 Classroom,* 59–93.

Noll, Elizabeth. "Accuracy and Authenticity in American Indian Children's Literature: The Social Responsibility of Authors and Illustrators." *The New Advocate* 8, no. 1 (Winter 1995): 29–43.

North American Native Authors Project. The Greenfield Review Press, P.O. Box 308, Greenfield Center, N.Y. 12833. http://www.nativeweb.org/pages/greenfield.html (16 Nov. 2006).

Nye, Naomi Shihab. "Singing the Long Song." *New Advocate* 12, no. 2 (Spring 1999): 119–26.

Obsidian III: Literature in the African Diaspora. North Carolina State University, English Department, P.O. Box 8105, Raleigh, N.C. 27695-8105.

Okihiro, Gary Y. *The Columbia Guide to Asian American History*. New York: Columbia University Press, 2001.

———. *Margins and Mainstreams: Asians in American History and Culture*. Seattle: University of Washington Press, 1994.

Olmos, Edward James, Carlos Fuentes, and Lea Ybarra. *Americanos: Latino Life in the United States*. Boston, Mass.: Little, Brown, 1999.

Osa, Osayimwense. *African Children's and Youth Literature*. Detroit: Twayne Publishers, 1995.

———. *The All-White World of Children's Books and African American Children's Literature*. Trenton, N.J.: Africa World Press, 1995.

Oyate. 2702 Matthews St., Berkeley, Calif. 94702. http://www.oyate.org/aboutus.html (16 Nov. 2006).

Pacific Rim Voices. Kiriyama Pacific Rim Institute, 760 Delancy St., San Francisco, Calif. 92107. PaperTigers.org. http://www.papertigers.org/index.html (16 Nov. 2006).

Painter, Nell Irvin. *Creating Black Americans: African-American History and Its Meanings, 1619 to the Present*. New York: Oxford University Press, 2006.

Palumbo-Liu, David. "Reimagining Asian American Studies." *Amerasia Journal* 29, no. 2 (2003): 211–19.

Pang, Valerie Oaka, Carolyn Colvin, My Luang Tran, and Robertta H. Barba. "Beyond Chopsticks and Dragons: Selecting Asian-American Literature for Children." *The Reading Teacher* 46, no. 3 (Nov. 1992): 216–24.

Park, Clara C., and Marilyn Mei-Ying Chi, eds. *Asian American Education: Prospects and Challenges*. Westport, Conn.: Bergin and Garvey, 1999.

Penti, Marsha. "Escola Officializada Portuguesa do Taunton Sports Club." In Bradunas and Topping, *Ethnic Heritage and Language Schools in America*, 68–93.

Perez-Stable, Maria A., and Mary H. Cordier. "Add Salsa to Your Classroom with Young Adult Books about Latinos." *Middle School Journal* 28 (March 1997): 23–27.

Perkins, Mitali. "The Fire Escape: Books for and about Young Immigrants." http://www.mitaliperkins.com/ (16 Nov. 2006).

Perry, Theresa, and James W. Fraser. *Freedom's Plow: Teaching in the Multicultural Classroom*. New York: Routledge, 1993.

Pewewardy, Cornel. "'I' Is for Indigenous: Renaming Ourselves in Our Own Terms." *MultiCultural Review* 12, no. 2 (June 2003): 30–33.

Phan, Peter C., and Jung Young Lee, eds. *Journeys at the Margin: Toward an Autobiographical Theology in American-Asian Perspective*. Collegeville, Minn.: Liturgical Press, 1995.

Pleasant Company Publications. "Meet Authors and Illustrators: Connie Porter." http://www.childrenslit.com/f_connieporter.htm (16 Nov. 2006).

Polette, Nancy J. *Celebrating the Coretta Scott King Awards: 101 Ideas and Activities*. Fort Atkinson, Wisc.: Upstart Books, 2000.

Polychrome Publishing Corporation. 4509 North Francisco, Chicago, Ill. 60625. http://www.polychromebooks.com/ (16 Nov. 2005).

Porter, Joy, and Kenneth M. Roemer. *The Cambridge Companion to Native American Literature*. New York: Cambridge University Press, 2005.

Porter, Rosalie Pedalino. *Forked Tongue: The Politics of Bilingual Education*. New Brunswick, N.J.: Transaction Publishers, 1996.

Porterfield, Kay Marie, and Emory Dean Keoke. "Resources for Selecting Fair and Accurate American Indian Books for Libraries and Home." http://www.kporterfield.com/aicttw/excerpts/antibiasbooks.html (16 Nov. 2005).

Portes, Alejandro, ed. *The New Second Generation*. New York: The Russell Sage Foundation, 1996.

Portes, Alejandro, and Rubén G. Rumbaut. *Legacies: The Story of the Immigrant Second Generation*. Berkeley: University of California Press, 2001.

Posner, Marcia W. "Jewish Children's Literature." In *Jewish-American History and Culture: An Encyclopedia*, edited by Jack Fischel and Sanford Pinsker, 292–301. New York: Garland, 1992.

———. *Juvenile Judaica: The Jewish Values Book Finder*. New York: Association of Jewish Libraries, 1985.

Press Pacifica. P.O. Box 47, Kailua, Hawaii 96734.

Rand, Donna, Toni Trent Parker, and Sheila Foster. *Black Books Galore! Guide to Great African American Children's Books*. Stamford, Conn.: Wiley, 1998.

———. *Black Books Galore! Guide to Great African American Children's Books about Boys*. Stamford, Conn.: Wiley, 2000.

———. *Black Books Galore! Guide to Great African American Children's Books about Girls*. Stamford, Conn.: Wiley, 2000.

———. *Black Books Galore! Guide to More Great African American Children's Books*. Stamford, Conn.: Wiley, 2001.

Rang, Xue Lan, and Judith Preissle. *Educating Immigrant Children: What We Need to Know to Meet the Challenges*. Thousand Oaks, Calif.: Corwin Press, 1997.

Ravitch, Diane. "The Atkinson-Ravitch Sampler of Classic Literature for Home and School." In Ravitch, *The Language Police: How Pressure Groups Restrict What Students Learn*, 203–34.

———. *The Great School Wars: New York City, 1805–1973*. New York: W. W. Norton, 1973.

———. *The Language Police: How Pressure Groups Restrict What Children Learn*. New York: Knopf, 2003.

———. "Literature: Forgetting the Tradition." In Ravitch, *The Language Police: How Pressure Groups Restrict What Students Learn*, 112–32.

———. "Minority Group Education in the United States." In *The Schools We Deserve: Reflections on the Educational Crises of Our Times*, by Ravitch, 190–92. New York: Basic Books, 1985.

Rovetch, Emily, ed. *Like It Is: Arthur E. Thomas Interviews Leaders on Black America*. New York: Dutton, 1981.

Reed, Ishmael. "America: The Multinational Society." In Simonson and Walker, *The Graywolf Annual Five*, 155–60..

Reese, Debbie. "Authenticity and Sensitivity." *School Library Journal* 45, no. 11 (Nov. 1999): 36–37.

———. "Contesting Ideology in Children's Book Reviewing." *Studies in American Indian Literatures* 12, no. 1 (2000): 37–55.

———. "Native Americans in Children's Literature." In Harris, *Using Multiethnic Literature in the K–8 Classroom*, 155–62.

———. "Native American Cultures across the United States." National Endowment for the Humanities. EDSITEment. http://edsitement.neh.gov/view_lesson_plan .asp?ID=347 (16 Nov. 2006).

Reese, Debbie, and Jean Mendoza. "Native Americans: A Resource List for Teaching—To and About Native Americans." SCILS, Rutgers, The State University of New Jersey. http://www.scils.rutgers.edu/~kvander/ChildrenLit/nalist.html (16 Nov. 2006).

Reyhner, Jon. *Teaching American Indian Students.* Norman: University of Oklahoma Press, 1994.

Reyhner, Jon, and Jeanne Eder. *American Indian Education: A History.* Norman.: University of Oklahoma Press, 2004.

Richey, Donna S. "Understanding and Appreciating the Unique Needs of European Americans." In *Multicultural Aspects of School Media Programs,* edited by Kathy Howard Latrobe and Mildred Knight Laughlin, 61–67. Englewood, Colo.: Libraries Unlimited, 1992.

Riksha Magazine. 3062 S. Broad St., Chicago, Ill. 60608. http://www.riksha.com/ (16 Nov. 2006).

Rivera, José, and Luis Ramón Burrola. "Chicano Studies Programs in Higher Education: Scenarios for Further Research." *Aztlan* 15 (Fall 1984): 277–93.

Rochman, Hazel. *Against Borders: Promoting Books for a Multicultural World.* Chicago, Ill.: American Library Association, 1993.

———. "Beyond Political Correctness." In Fox and Short, *Stories Matter,* 101–15.

Rollins, Charlemae, et al. *We Build Together: A Reader's Guide to Negro Life and Literature for Elementary and High School Use.* Champaign, Ill.: National Council of Teachers of English, 1941, 1954, 1967.

Rollock, Barbara. *The Black Experience in Children's Books.* New York: New York Public Library, 1974, 1984, 1994.

Root, Maria P. P. "Issues and Experiences of Racially Mixed People." In Root and Kelley, *Multiracial Child Resource Book,* 132–34.

Root, Maria P. P., and Matt Kelley. "Books." In Root and Kelley, *Multiracial Child Resource Book,* 230–45.

———. "Web Sites." in Root and Kelley, *Multiracial Child Resource Book,* 246–49.

Root, Maria P. P., and Matt Kelley, eds. *Multiracial Child Resource Book: Living Complex Identities.* Seattle, Wash.: MAVIN Foundation, 2003.

Rosenberg, Maxine. *Living in Two Worlds: The Story of Bi-Racial Children.* New York: Lothrop, Lee, and Shepard, 1986.

Roth, Henry. *Call It Sleep.* New York: Farrar, Straus and Giroux, 1991.

Rothenberg, Paula S. *White Privilege: Essential Readings on the Other Side of Racism.* New York: Worth Publishers, 2004.

Roy, Loriene. "A Gathering of Readers." On If I Can Read, I Can Do Anything. http://www.ischool.utexas.edu/~gathread/ (16 Nov. 2006).

———. If I Can Read, I Can Do Anything. School of Information, The University of Texas at Austin, 1 University Station D 7000, Austin, Tex. 78712-0390. http://www.gslis.utexas.edu/~ifican/ (16 Nov. 2006).

Rumbaut, Rubén G., and Alejandro Portes. *Ethnicities: Children of Immigrants in America*. Berkeley: University of California Press, 2001.

Russell, George. *Native American FAQ Handbook*. Phoenix, Ariz.: Russell Publications, 2000.

Sabbagh, Sufia J. *Sex, Lies, and Stereotypes: The Image of Arabs in American Popular Fiction*. ERIC Education Resources Information Center, ED 363530.

Sainte-Marie, Buffy. The Cradleboard Teaching Project, 1191 Kuhio Highway, Kapaa, Hawaii 96746. http://www.cradleboard.org/ (16 Nov. 2006).

Salle, Ellen. "Ethnicity and Authenticity, or How Black (Hispanic, Native American, etc.) Do I Gotta Be?" *Emergency Librarian* 27, no. 2 (Nov./Dec. 1994): 22–27.

Santiago, Esmeralda. *When I Was Puerto Rican*. New York: Vintage, 1993.

Scanlon, Kevin, and Lisa Youngblood. "Living in the Salad Bowl: Serving Immigrant Teens." *Young Adult Library Services* 2, no. 1 (Fall 2003): 15.

Scherf, Walter. *The Best of the Best: Picture, Children's and Youth Books from 57 Countries or Languages*. New York: Bowker, 1971.

Schlesinger, Arthur Jr. *The Disuniting of America*. New York: Norton and Company, 1998.

Schmidt, Nancy. *Children's Books on Africa and Their Authors: An Annotated Bibliography*. New York: Africana, 1975.

———. *Supplement to Children's Books on Africa and Their Authors*. New York: Africana, 1979.

Scholastic. "Authors." http://www.scholastic.com/dearamerica/books/authors.htm (16 Nov. 2006).

Scholastic/Instructor. "How to Choose the Best Multicultural Books." http://teacher.scholastic.com/products/instructor/multicultural.htm (16 Nov. 2006).

Schon, Isabel. *Basic Collection of Children's Books in Spanish*. Metuchen, N.J.: Scarecrow, 1986.

———. *The Best of Latino Heritage 1996–2002: A Guide to the Best Juvenile Books about Latino People and Cultures*. Lanham, Md.: Scarecrow, 2003.

———. *A Bicultural Heritage: Themes for the Exploration of Mexican and Mexican-American Culture in Books for Children and Adolescents*. Metuchen, N.J.: Scarecrow, 1978.

———. *Books in Spanish for Children and Young Adults: An Annotated Guide*. Series I–VI. Metuchen, N.J.: Scarecrow, 1978–1993.

———. *Contemporary Spanish-Speaking Writers and Illustrators for Children and Young Adults*. Westport, Conn.: Greenwood, 1994.

———. *A Hispanic Heritage: A Guide to Juvenile Books about Hispanic People and Cultures*. Series I–IV. Metuchen, N.J.: Scarecrow, 1980–1991.

————. *Recommended Books in Spanish for Children and Young Adults*. Lanham, Md.: Scarecrow, 2000.

Schultz, Marylou, and Miriam Kroeger, comp. *Teaching and Learning with Native Americans: A Handbook for Non-Native American Adult Educators*. http://literacynet.org/lp/namericans/ (16 Nov. 2006).

Seto, Thelma. "Multiculturalism Is Not Halloween." *The Horn Book Magazine* 71 (March/April 1995): 169–74. Revised and updated in Fox and Short, *Stories Matter*, 93–97.

Sewall, Gilbert T. *Islam and the Textbooks: A Report of the American Textbook Council*. ERIC Education Resources Information Center, ED 475.

Shakur, Tupac. *The Rose That Grew from Concrete*. New York: Pocket Books, 1999.

Shen's Books and Supplies. 821 S. First Ave., Arcadia, Calif. 91006. http://www.shens.com/ (22 Aug. 2005).

Shipler, David K. *A Country of Strangers: Blacks and Whites in America*. New York: Knopf, 1997.

Shorris, Earl. *Latinos: A Biography of the People*. New York: Norton, 2001.

Simonson, Rick, and Scott Walker, eds. *The Graywolf Annual Five: Multicultural Literacy—Opening the American Mind*. St. Paul, Minn.: Graywolf Press, 1988.

Simpson, A., and E. S. C. Weiner, comp. *The Oxford English Dictionary*. Vol. 5. Oxford: Clarendon Press, 1989.

Sims (Bishop), Rudine. *Shadow and Substance: Afro-American Experience in Contemporary Children's Fiction*. Urbana, Ill.: National Council of Teachers of English, 1982.

Sizemore, Barbara. *An Abashing Anomaly: The High Achieving Predominantly Black Elementary School*. ERIC Education Resources Information Center, ED 236274.

Skipping Stones: A Multicultural Children's Quarterly. P.O. Box 3939, Eugene, Ore. 97403. http://www.skippingstones.org/ (16 Nov. 2006).

Slapin, Beverly, and Doris Seale. *A Broken Flute*. Lanham, Md.: Alta Mira, 2004.

————. *How to Tell the Difference: A Guide to Evaluating Children's Books for Anti-Indian Bias*. Berkeley: Oyate, 1996.

————. *Through Indian Eyes: The Native Experience in Books for Children*. Berkeley, Calif.: Oyate, 1998.

Slapin, Beverly, and Doris Seale, eds. *Books without Bias: Through Indian Eyes*. Berkeley, Calif.: Oyate, 1988.

Slippery Rock University of Pennsylvania. "Multicultural Children's Authors." http://www.sru.edu/pages/8912.asp (30 Aug. 2005).

Smiley, Tavis, ed. and comp. *How to Make Black America Better: Leading African Americans Speak Out*. New York: Doubleday, 2001.

Smith, Craig Stephen. *Whiteman's Gospel: A Native American Examines the Christian Church and Its Ministry among Native Americans*. Winnipeg, Manitoba, Canada: Indian Life Books, 1997.

Smith, Cynthia Leitich. "Children's and YA Books with Interracial Family Themes." http://www.cynthialeitichsmith.com/lit_resources/diversity/multiracial/multi_race_intro.html (16 Nov. 2006).

———. "Children's and YA Books by Native Authors and Illustrators." http://www.cynthialeitichsmith.com/lit_resources/diversity/native_am/nat_lit/nat_lit_front.html (16 Nov. 2006).

———. "A Different Drum: Native American Writing." *The Horn Book Magazine* 78, no. 3 (July/Aug. 2002): 409–12.

———. "Native American Themes in Books for Children and Teens." http://www.cynthialeitichsmith.com/lit_resources/diversity/native_am/NativeThemes_intro.html (16 Nov. 2006).

Smith, Greg Leitich. "Children's and YA Books with Asian American Themes." http://www.cynthialeitichsmith.com/lit_resources/diversity/asian_am/asian_am.html (16 Nov. 2006).

Smith, Henrietta, ed. *The Coretta Scott King Awards Books: 1970–1999*. Chicago: American Library Association, 1999.

Smith, Karen Patricia. *African American Voices in Young Adult Literature: Tradition, Transition, Transformation*. Metuchen, N.J.: Scarecrow, 1994.

———. "The Multicultural Ethic and Connections to Literature for Children and Young Adults." *Library Trends* 41, no. 3 (Winter 1993): 340–53.

Smith, Linda Tuhiwai. *Decolonizing Methodologies: Research and Indigenous People*. New York: St. Martin's Press, 1999.

Smolen, Lynn Atkinson, and Victoria Ortiz-Castro. "Dissolving Borders and Broadening Perspectives through Latino Traditional Literature." *The Reading Teacher* 53, no. 7 (Apr. 2000): 566–78.

Smolkin, Laura B., and Joseph H. Suina. "Artistic Triumph or Multicultural Failure? Multiple Perspectives on a 'Multicultural' Award-Winning Book." In Fox and Short, *Stories Matter*, 213–30.

South Asian Children's Books and Software. http://www.sawnet.org/kidsbooks/ (16 Nov. 2006).

"Speaking of History: The Words of South Carolina Librarians, Augusta Baker." College of Library and Information Science, University of South Carolina, Columbia. http://www.libsci.sc.edu/histories/oralhistory/bakerpage.htm (16 Nov. 2006).

Stampp, Kenneth. *The Peculiar Institution: Slavery in the Ante-Bellum South*. New York: Vintage, 1989.

Stavans, Ilan. *Growing Up Latino*. Boston, Mass.: Mariner Books, 1993.

Stedman, R. W. *Shadows of the Indian: Stereotypes in American Culture*. Norman: University of Oklahoma Press, 1982.

Stein, Colman Brez Jr. *Sink or Swim: The Politics of Bilingual Education*. New York: Praeger, 1986.

Stephens, Claire Gatrell. *Coretta Scott King Award Books: Using Great Literature with Children and Young Adults*. Englewood, Colo.: Libraries Unlimited, 2000.

Stokes, Theresa, and Keith Stokes. *Eyes of Glory*. http://www.eyesofglory.com/ (16 Nov. 2006).

Stritikus, Tom. *Immigrant Children and the Politics of English-Only: Views from the Classroom*. New York: LFB Scholarly Publishers, 2002.

Strom, Karen M., comp. Storytelling: Native American Authors Online. http://www
.hanksville.org/storytellers/ (16 Nov. 2006).
Studies in American Indian Literatures. University of Nebraska Press, 233 N. 8th St.,
Lincoln, Neb. 68588-0255.
Suárez-Orozco, Carola, and Marcelo M. Suarez-Orozco. *Children of Immigration:
The Developing Child.* Cambridge, Mass.: Harvard University Press, 2001.
Sumida, Stephen H. "The More Things Change: Paradigm Shifts in Asian American
Studies." *American Studies International* 38, no. 2 (June 2000): 97–114.
Suro, Roberto. *Strangers among Us: Latino Lives in a Changing America.* New York:
Vintage, 1999.
SWIRL Inc. 244 Fifth Ave., Suite J 230, New York, N.Y. 10001-7604. http://www
.swirlinc.org/ (16 Nov. 2006).
———. "SWIRL Friends" (Links). http://swirlinc.org/links.htm (16 Nov. 2006).
Takaki, Ronald. *A Different Mirror: A History of Multicultural America.* Boston:
Little, Brown, 1993.
———. *Strangers from a Different Shore: A History of Asian Americans.* New York:
Penguin, 1987.
Tan, Amy. *The Joy Luck Club.* New York: Putnam, 1989.
Tatum, Beverly Daniel. *"Why Are All the Black Kids Sitting Together in the Cafeteria?" And Other Conversations about Race.* New York: Basic Books, 1997.
Taxel, Joel. "Children's Literature at the Turn of the Century: Toward a Political
Economy of the Publishing Industry." *Research in the Teaching of English* 37, no.
2 (Nov. 2002): 145–97.
———. "Multicultural Literature and the Politics of Reaction." In Fox and Short,
Stories Matter, 154–64.
Taylor, Gail Singleton. "Pass It On: The Development of African American Children's Literature." *The Negro Educational Review* 50, no. 2 (Jan.–Apr. 1999):
11–17.
Teaching Tolerance. Southern Poverty Law Center, 400 Washington Ave., Montgomery, Ala. http://www.tolerance.org/teach/ (16 Nov. 2006).
Terkel, Studs. *Division Street: America.* New York: Pantheon, 1967.
———. *Race: How Blacks and Whites Think and Feel about the American Obsession.* New York: New Press, 2005.
Theytus Books, Ltd. Lot 45, Green Mountain Rd., RR2 Site 50, Comp. 8 Penticon,
British Columbia V2A 6J7, Canada.
Thomas, Piri. *Down These Mean Streets.* New York: Vintage, 1997.
Tokunaga, Paul. *Invitation to Lead: Guidance for Emerging Asian American Leaders.*
Downers Grove, Ill.: Intervarsity Press, 2003.
Tomlinson, Carl M., ed. *Children's Books from Other Countries.* Lanham, Md.:
Scarecrow, 1999.
Toussaint, Pamela. *Great Books for African American Children.* New York: Penguin, 1999.
Trager, Helen. "Intercultural Books for Children." *Childhood Education* 22 (November 1945): 138–45.

Tribal College Journal: The Voice and Vision of American Indian Higher Education. Tribal College, 2509 Montgomery Way, Sacramento, Calif. 95818. http://www.tribalcollegejournal.org/ (16 Nov. 2006).

Tuan, Mia. *Forever Foreigners or Honorary Whites? The Asian Ethnic Experience Today.* New Brunswick, N.J.: Rutgers University Press, 1999.

Twiss, Richard. *One Church, Many Tribes: Following Jesus the Way God Made You.* Ventura, Calif.: Regal Books, 2000.

University of California, Berkeley. Ethnic Studies Library, Native American Studies Collection, Department of Ethnic Studies, 30 Stephens Hall #2360, Berkeley, Calif. 94728-2360. http://eslibrary.berkeley.edu/ (16 Nov. 2006).

University of San Francisco. Department of International and Multicultural Education, Center for Multicultural Literature for Children and Young Adults, 2130 Fulton St., San Francisco, Calif. 94117. http://www.soe.usfca.edu/departments/ime/index.html (16 Nov. 2006).

University of South Africa. Children's Literature Research Unit. "South African Children's Literature." http://www.childlit.org.za/SAChildLit.html (30 Aug. 2005).

University of the State of New York. *A Curriculum of Inclusion: Report of the Commissioner's Task Force on Minorities: Equity and Excellence.* Albany, N.Y.: Task Force on Minorities, 1989.

von Maltitz, Frances Willard. *Living and Learning in Two Languages: Bilingual-Bicultural Education in the United States.* New York: McGraw-Hill, 1975.

Wallace, Annette. "Caribbean Children's Literature: A Select Annotated Bibliography." http://www.nalis.gov.tt/Education/BIBLIOGR.htm (16 Nov. 2006).

Wallace, Michele. "Invisibility Blues." In Simonson and Walker, *The Graywolf Annual Five,* 161–72.

Ward, Martha Eads. *Authors of Books for Young People.* Metuchen, N.J.: Scarecrow, 1990.

Warder, Rosa E. "Multicultural Children's Literature Historic Timeline." http://home.wi.rr.com/valonkent/timeline.htm (30 Aug. 2005).

Wardle, Francis. *Tomorrow's Children.* Denver, Colo.: Center for the Study of Biracial Children, 1999.

Watts, Lisa J. "A History of Tribal Museums." *Cross Paths Museum News* 9, no. 1 (Spring 2006): 4, 10–11; vol. 9, no. 2 (Summer 2006): 5, 9–10.

Weinberg, Meyer. *A Chance to Learn: The History of Race and Education in the United States.* New York: Cambridge University Press, 1977.

Weiss, Jaqueline Shachter. *Prizewinning Books for Children: Themes and Stereotypes in U.S. Prizewinning Prose Fiction for Children.* Lexington, Mass.: Lexington Books, 1983.

Wertsman, Vladimir F. "Arab Americans: A Comparative and Critical Analysis of Leading Reference Sources." *MultiCultural Review* 10, no. 2 (June 2001): 42–47.

The Western Journal of Black Studies. Washington State University Press, P.O. Box 645910, Pullman, Wash. 99164-5910.

Wicazo Sa Review: A Journal of Native American Studies. Indian Studies MS188, Eastern Washington University, Cheney, Wash. 99004. http://www.upress.umn.edu/journals/wsr/default.html (30 Aug. 2005).

Wijeyesinghe, Charmaine L., and Bailey W. Jackson III, eds. *New Perspectives on Racial Identity Development.* New York: New York University Press, 2001.

Williams, Helen E. *Books by African American Authors and Illustrators.* Chicago: American Library Association, 1991.

Williams, Lena. *It's the Little Things: Everyday Interactions That Anger, Annoy and Divide the Races.* New York: Harcourt, 2000.

Wilmore, Gayraud, and James H. Cone. *Black Theology: A Documentary History, 1966–1979.* Maryknoll, N.Y.: Orbis Books, 1979.

Wilson, Clint C. II, and Félix Gutiérrez. *Minorities and Media: Diversity and the End of Mass Communication.* London: Sage, 1985.

Winds of Change. American Indian Science and Engineering Society (AISES), 4450 Arapahoe Ave., Suite 100, Boulder, Colo. 80303. http://www.wocmag.org/ (16 Nov. 2006).

Womack, Craig S. *Red on Red: Native American Literary Separatism.* Minneapolis: University of Minnesota Press, 1999.

Wong, Jade Snow. *Fifth Chinese Daughter.* Seattle, Wash.: University of Washington Press, 1989.

Wong, Sau-ling Cynthia. *Reading Asian American Literature.* Princeton, N.J.: Princeton University Press, 1993.

Woodson, Jacqueline. "Who Can Tell My Story." *The Horn Book Magazine* 74, no. 1 (Jan/Feb. 1998): 34–38. Revised and updated in Fox and Short, *Stories Matter*, 41–45.

Woodward, C. Vann. *The Strange Career of Jim Crow.* Oxford: Oxford University Press, 2001.

Wordcraft Circle. http://www.wordcraftcircle.org/ (30 Aug.2005).

World Indigenous Nations Higher Education Consortium. http://www.win-hec.org/ (16 Nov. 2006).

Wortham, Stanton, Enrique G. Murillo Jr., and Edmund T. Hamann. *Education in the New Latino Diaspora: Policy and Politics of Identity.* Westport, Conn.: Ablex, 2002.

Wright, William D. *Black Intellectuals, Black Cognition, and a Black Aesthetic.* Westport, Conn.: Praeger, 1997.

Writers and Readers/Black Butterfly Books. Box 461, Village Station, New York, N.Y. 19914.

Wu, Frank H. *Yellow: Race in America beyond Black and White.* Boulder, Colo.: Basic Books, 2003.

Wu, Jean Yu-Wen Shen, and Min Song, eds. *Asian American Studies: A Reader.* New Brunswick, N.J.: Rutgers University Press, 2000.

Yamate, Sandra. "Asian Pacific American Children's Literature: Expanding Perceptions about Who Americans Are." In Harris, *Using Multiethnic Literature in the K–8 Classroom*, 95–128.

Yancey, George. *Beyond Racial Gridlock: Embracing Mutual Responsibility.* Downers Grove, Ill.: Intervarsity Press, 2006.

Yang, Zheng Ye. "Children's Books by Chinese American Authors: An Annotated Bibliography." http://www.white-clouds.com/cala/publications/childbks.htm (16 Nov. 2006).

Yazzie, Robert. "Navajo Justice." *Winds of Change* 15, no. 4 (August 2000): 88–91.

Yenika-Agbaw, Vivian. "Images of West Africa in Children's Books: Replacing Old Stereotypes with New Ones?" In Fox and Short, *Stories Matter*, 231–46.

YOLK: Generasian Next. http://www.yolk.com/ (16 Nov. 2006).

York, Sherry. *Children's and Young Adult Books by Latino Writers: A Guide for Librarians, Teachers, Parents, and Students.* Worthington, Ohio: Linworth Publishing, 2002.

———. *Children's and Young Adult Literature by Native Americans.* Worthington, Ohio: Linworth Publishing, 2003.

———. *Ethnic Book Awards: A Directory of Multicultural Literature for Young Readers.* Worthington, Ohio: Linworth Publishing, 2005.

———. *Picture Books by Latino Writers: A Guide for Librarians, Teachers, Parents, and Students.* Worthington, Ohio: Linworth Publishing, 2002.

Zhou, Min, and James V. Gatewood, eds. *Contemporary Asian America: A Multidisciplinary Reader.* New York: New York University Press, 2000.

Zia, Helen. *Asian American Dreams: The Emergence of an American People.* New York: Farrar, Straus and Giroux, 2001.

Zinn, Howard. *A People's History of the United States.* New York: Harper Perennial, 2003.

Zinn, Howard, and Anthony Arnove. *Voices of a People: History of the United States.* New York: Seven Stories Press, 2004.

Index

About the Author

Donna L. Gilton was born in Lynn, Massachusetts, and spent her formative years in the African American college community of Wilberforce, Ohio, where her father taught at Payne Seminary. Between kindergarten and the end of secondary school, she experienced a wide variety of cultures. Dr. Gilton attended all-black elementary schools in Ohio and in Memphis, Tennessee. She attended grades 4–8 at a public school in Lynn, Massachusetts, which was then a predominantly white but ethnically diverse community. She then integrated the Pingree School, a private preparatory school in South Hamilton, Massachusetts, which was at that time a single-sex school. Dr. Gilton earned a B.A. in elementary education and history and an M.S. in library science from Simmons College and worked at the Boston Public Library for seven years, with almost six of those years devoted to children's librarianship. Dr. Gilton then joined the Peace Corps, where she served for two years as the head librarian at the Belize Teachers' College.

While serving in Belize, Dr. Gilton became interested both in international and comparative librarianship and in the possibility of a career as an information broker. The former led her to the University of Pittsburgh, which had a research collection and a strong program on this subject. The latter led her into a career as an academic business librarian. While earning her Ph.D. at the University of Pittsburgh, Dr. Gilton served as a business reference librarian at the Western Kentucky University, Bowling Green, and Pennsylvania State University, University Park. She concluded that the two fields of children's and business librarianship were oddly similar, each with a specialized clientele, literature, publishers, and service needs. Dr. Gilton is now an associate professor of library and information studies at the University of Rhode Island, where she teaches courses on adult reference services, multiculturalism in libraries, and information literacy. This book grows out of her church and community service and brings her back, full circle, to her academic and professional roots.